D1175240

TO MY STEPSON KEVIN
1976 – 2012

You chose to give back the gift of life.
You had no further use for it but you left us too soon.

"While we have the gift of life, it seems to me the only tragedy is to allow part of us to die – whether it is our spirit, our creativity, or our glorious uniqueness."

Gilda Radner

Life Forces by Judi

NAMI of Collier County art program artist

Faced with the untimely death of her son, Deena Baxter gives a detailed personal account that walks her reader through the daily realities of the aftermath. She explores bigger questions of mental illness; genetics, family dynamics, and camouflaged elements of mental health. The book frames topics with a great deal of poise, intellect and glints of humor.

- Nydia Adames-Petty, Bilingual Family Liaison/Support Group Facilitator, Family 2 Family Instructor, NAMI of Collier County.

When an author lives a story and then writes about it, she likely leaves part of herself among her words and between the lines of her book. She becomes a part of the book as it becomes a part of her. This book is brilliantly written with all the heartache associated with suicide along with a touch of humor as the title implies. The stress, worry, helplessness, anger, sometimes denial, can take a toll on families in a profound way. Anyone who has ever had a loved one who suffered from mental illness will find this book hits close to home.

- Dottie Pacharis, author of Mind on the Run – A Bipolar Chronicle

I just finished reading *Surviving Suicide* and loved how the story touched so many of my emotions: I cried, I laughed, and I felt the intense frustration in trying to do the right thing for Kevin and his final resting place. The story was well organized; as soon as my feelings intensified, I got a break - a time-out for some artwork or a bit of levity that gave me relief and made me ready and eager to read more. Deena Baxter beautifully helps the reader see the big picture: how mental illness still carries a stigma that so often gets in the way of treatment. This personal story will validate the experiences and feelings of so many people that have experienced a family member's death by suicide.

- Kathy A. Feinstein, MS, Licensed Mental Health Counselor

Mascot Books
560 Herndon Parkway #120
Herndon, VA 20170
info@mascotbooks.com

PRTWP0614A

Library of Congress Control Number: 2014908289

ISBN-13: 9781620867686

Printed in Singapore

www.mascotbooks.com

SURVIVING
SUICIDE

SEARCHING FOR "NORMAL" WITH HEARTACHE & HUMOR

A MOSTLY TRUE STORY BY
DEENA BAXTER

Joan —
thanks for your unwaivering
support & encouragement, and
editorial input in making this
story & book a reality. thanks
for helping me
" Give mental illness a voice."
Love,

Deena
xoxo

MASCOT
BOOKS

SPECIAL ACKNOWLEDGMENT

Thanks to my generous
Anonymous Angel Benefactor, for your support.
Your significant gift gave life to The Funny Farm Project.
I am ever grateful.

TABLE OF CONTENTS

AUTHOR'S NOTE
FICTION OR NON-FICTION?
THAT IS THE QUESTION...

"Everything we hear is an opinion, not a fact. Everything we see is a perspective, not the truth."

Marcus Aurelius

Is this a work of fiction or non-fiction? I have intentionally left that ambiguous. My preference is to classify it as a *perspective*. This won't sit well with those who need to fit it into a specific category, a black-or-white constraint of literature that doesn't quite apply.

Ask me why and I will answer, "Under the best of circumstances it is impossible to fully understand what drives another's behavior. If you add mental illness and suicide to the mix, it is further complicated."

I am not and do not pretend to be a mental health expert by training or credentials. However, loving and losing a child who suffered from mental illness gives anyone who has walked that path - and survived - an informed perspective.

I have used pseudonyms for most of the people in this book, some because they requested it for privacy reasons and some to protect their identity while preserving the nuggets of actions and experiences that inform this story.

My intent is to remain true to what I experienced while honoring those

I love, including the memory of my stepson. Any errors are inadvertent and mine alone.

> "And we should consider every day lost on which we have not danced at least once. And we should call every truth false which was not accompanied by at least one laugh."

Friedrich Nietzsche

INTRODUCTION:
LIFE INTERRUPTED

"There is not much laughter in medicine but there is lots of medicine in laughter."

Anonymous

Dealing with the death of a child is a journey no parent seeks to travel. When that death is brought on by suicide, and without a final "Goodbye", it is Life Interrupted. It is a trip unlike any other – a journey through heartache, loss, and grief that cannot be delegated to others. There is no accelerated route, no shortcut to compress the distance, because the journey's final destination is undefined. From where I stand, I cannot see the end point on this map. Believe me, I have tried; when I stand at the water's edge and look ahead I see the horizon, and beyond that - eternity.

Dealing with such a sudden and absolute loss is what this book is about: the suicide of my stepson Kevin a few weeks shy of his 36th birthday. Written in two parts, using heartache and humor, the story chronicles a journey that started more than thirty years ago and shines a light on a harsher reality - how the stigma of mental illness keeps it cloaked in denial and how that can play out when the patient, the family and society collude to maintain the status quo.

What compelled me to write this story and publish it rather than keep it in a personal journal? That's a fair question; my answer is that keeping it hidden in darkness is one of the reasons mental illness can lead to suicide. This is my call to action and perhaps it stems from the era in which I came of age.

In 1964, when I was in elementary school, Mario Savio stood on the steps of Sproul Hall at UC-Berkley and delivered his famous "Bodies upon the gears" speech; inspiring students to take action:

> There's a time when the operation of the machine becomes so odious, makes you so sick at heart, that you can't take part! You can't even passively take part! And you've got to put your bodies upon the gears and upon the wheels…upon the levers, upon all the apparatus', and you've got to make it stop! And you've got to indicate to the people who run it, to the people who own it, that unless you're free, the machine will be prevented from working at all![1]

The time is again at hand to come forward and say, "The machine is broken." This story exposes the broken parts of the mental health care system by letting the mind tell the story: giving mental illness a voice. Unlike Mario Savio, I won't be hitting the streets with a megaphone, but I can play a part by saying, "The machine can't be fixed if we are embarrassed and afraid to speak up."

Kevin suffered from a mental illness - bipolar brain disorder. He exhibited all the classic signs of the illness; episodes of mania marked by out-of-control spending and enormous debts, risky and aggressive behavior, paranoia, and poor life choices; followed by episodes of deep depression and self-medication.

Our son had big dreams of being a mega-successful businessman in Brazil and moved there in 2006; however, his dreams were thwarted by realities brought on by cultural challenges that magnified his poor life choices. He left behind a grieving Brazilian wife and her family, plus his father and me and our two remaining sons – Kevin's brother and stepbrother.

Each parent's trip through grief and loss of a child is unique, with challenging twists and turns along the way. In my case, many outrageous experiences left me questioning how modern society defines mental illness and distinguishes sane from insane behavior. These played out against a background of differing customs (Brazilian and U.S.), differing religious and cultural norms and taboos surrounding death and burial, and family dynamics and tensions – all while trying to hold my family together. It left me wondering who gets to decide what's 'normal': The American Psychiatric Association, Big Pharma, Big Media, your doctor, your alcoholic mother, your ex-husband, your child, or other perfectly imperfect humans. It forced me to question conventional wisdom and re-examine my own beliefs. Perhaps it will do the same for you.

> *"The object of life is not to be on the side of the majority, but to escape finding oneself in the ranks of the insane."*
>
> *Marcus Aurelius*

In our case, 'holding our family together' meant our blended family. And like many blended families cobbled together with children from prior marriages, when a couple says, "I do," in reality it is a familial "I" that can include former spouses and extended families on both sides. In the glow of early-stage love, the eagerness to make it all work is filtered through rosy glasses, hiding the dysfunction lurking in the wings and waiting to make its debut. This often takes the form of additional stakeholders insinuating themselves into the fold, making their presence known and demanding to have a say.

Three decades after marrying Kevin's father, I read John Bradshaw's book titled *Healing the Shame That Binds You*. Bradshaw's theory of dynamic homeostasis resonated with me. Biologists define homeostasis as the ability of a system to "=maintain a constant internal environment in response to environmental changes." It is usually viewed within an organism and is a dynamic process of adaptation. Bradshaw applies the term to the family as an organism – a "system". In a healthy family, each member will change, thrive and grow – individually and as a family system. However, in a dysfunctional family where mental illness, addiction or other forms of aberrant behavior are the norm, the family becomes "frozen and static", with each member taking on "rigid roles necessitated by the family's need for balance."

This rigidity becomes embedded in the individual and family DNA and is carried forward to future generations. He believes that is why it is important to look at a person's upbringing in order to successfully help the person embrace healthy forms of guilt and shame that serve a useful purpose; protecting them, and helping them break free from self-destructive habits.[2]

This insight, among others, helped me see the lives of our family members and others through a different lens. I know for sure dysfunctional DNA is alive and well, in individuals, families and society: not just our society – it's global. It is constantly rocking the boat of life, often threatening to tip it over.

My effort to keep the Baxter Family Love Boat afloat played out like a non-stop series of Saturday Night Live routines. As irreverent as it may seem, at times the only way to cope was with humor and laughter. It was Theater of the Absurd worthy of Academy Award honors.

Welcome aboard! Warning: There are no lifejackets available on this journey.

"If it's sanity you are after, there is no recipe like laughter."

Henry Elliot

PART I

THE UNWELCOMED JOURNEY

The Journey by Diana
NAMI of Collier County art program artist

WELCOME TO THE SURREAL

"The real is always way ahead of what we can imagine."

Novelist Paul Auster

THE CALL FROM HELL

Thursday, July 5, 2012 started out like most other summer days, following on the heels of a quiet Fourth of July holiday. My husband Adam was recovering from back surgery and resting in his recliner in the family room, watching the news. I was working in my office, adjacent to the family room, trying to concentrate on a client project, but within earshot in case Adam needed me.

I'm sensitive to his preference to eat meals on time – breakfast at 6am, lunch at high noon, dinner at 6pm, whereas I am on flextime: eating when I can find time. Some people live to eat, some eat to live, and opposites attract. That keeps the gene pool balanced. Shortly after 6pm I poked my head out my office door and said, "Hun, I'm just going to finish sending this email and I'll start making dinner, okay?"

"That's fine," he said.

At 6:15pm the phone rang. It's always ringing around dinnertime in our house for one of four reasons: election robo-calls, a philanthropy seeking a donation, one of our three sons, or ones that fall in the "other" category.

This being Primary Election Season 2012, the robo-calls were coming fast and furious. You know the ones I'm talking about, the same calls you most likely get, from the mother of Candidate Smith or Jones imploring you to vote for her son because to do otherwise would invalidate her parenting skills and result in funding cuts to all your favorite causes. We don't even bother to answer those calls, we just let mom try to convince our answering machine. And last time we checked, our answering machine was not registered to vote, at least not yet, but we live in Florida where corporations are people, so nothing would surprise us.

It doesn't matter that we are on the Do Not Call Registry. That doesn't prevent certain philanthropies and non-profits from calling, and scam artists, too: and boy do they thrive on seniors in Florida! But there are also others, like the Police Benevolent Association or the Brotherhood of Firefighters. I'm always afraid of turning these guys down: if they have my phone number then they have my address and I don't want to risk being on their Do Not Respond Registry for 911 calls. No way! It's easier to just not take the call.

We have another reason for letting calls we don't recognize on Caller ID go to our answering machine. Our son Kevin has racked up years of unpaid student loans, credit card and other debts. He is thirty-five years old, lives in Brazil, and we have nothing to do with these debts. We did not co-sign or guarantee any of them and, in fact, advised him not to take them on. These debts have all been turned over to collection agencies and they use strong-arm tactics to try to locate him and recover their losses. They use the Internet to find anybody with a similar last name or association with the debtor and think nothing of calling at all hours of the day or night seeking his whereabouts or our willingness to pay. Often they are threatening and most know how to walk the fine legal line between toughness and harassment.

So those are three good reasons *not* to answer the phone. The calls we *do* take during dinner are from one of our three sons who often call us on their commute home from work. It is sometimes the only available time they have to call us and since we cherish those sacred communications, we try to accommodate them as often as possible.

When the phone rang at 6:15 on this particular night, I thought it might be Kevin calling from Brazil. I had sent an email to the family on Monday, the day of Adam's successful back surgery, and Kevin had emailed us on Tuesday, July 3rd (Great news! Love, Kevin) but he hadn't followed that up with a call. We knew he had several interviews scheduled during the week, hoping to land a new job after being unemployed for ten months. We also knew he was moving forward with what he anticipated would be a messy divorce from his Brazilian wife after procrastinating for two years. His lawyer was pushing to serve her with papers on Friday as well as have her evicted from their apartment. Kevin's ambivalence about the relationship and the speed in which his lawyer was driving the divorce was causing him additional stress and he had been calling and emailing more frequently. Due to the one-hour time difference this time of year, he frequently called shortly after 6pm (7pm Brazil time).

However, whenever he called, Caller ID would indicate "Out of Area" with no phone number. We never really know why we do something out of character or out of our Daily Normal. Caller ID didn't flash a name, only a phone number and it began with an 810 area code. I didn't know anybody from that area code (Michigan) but for some unknown reason, I took the call.

"Hello, I wish to speak to Adam Baxter," said the caller.

"May I ask what this is in reference to?" I asked, my standard response.

"It's in reference to his son Kevin."

"I'm sorry but he is unable to take the call. Are you representing a collection agency?" I asked as I was kicking myself for answering, sure at this point it was one of the numerous bill collectors on the line.

"No, I am not. I am his landlord."

Now I'm thinking it is his former landlord from Boston, where he left without paying his last month's rent, so I said, "He does not live here and doesn't live in the U.S., he lives in Brazil."

"I know," he said.

"Are you calling from Brazil?" I asked.

"Yes, I am."

I'm thinking this was his former landlord in Brazil and perhaps Kevin had put his father's name as an emergency contact. But then my stomach fell to the floor and I said, "I'm Kevin's stepmother, Deena Baxter. Is Kevin okay?"

"No, he's dead." Just like that, dispassionate and factual. I can still feel the way my body reacted to the news, as if I had the wind knocked out of me, and how my entire being switched to 'Auto Pilot'.

"Are you sure it was Kevin?" I asked stupidly, in disbelief and shock.

"Yes, I'm sure. I'm standing here in his apartment and the police are just leaving with his body."

"Is his wife Makyla there?" I asked. Kevin told us months ago she repeatedly threatened him and I was concerned he had served the divorce papers a day early and the situation had escalated out of control.

"Yes, she found him when she returned home from work and called the apartment manager who called me. I own the building." And then he filled me in on more of the details.

"Do you speak Portuguese?" I asked.

"Yes," he answered.

"Please tell Makyla my heart is broken and I send her my deepest condolences and my love. Please ask her if Kevin left a note." His wife speaks very little English and under the circumstances I knew she was in shock, as was I.

He spoke to her, came back on the line and said, "He wants to be buried in the U.S. The police took some things from the apartment and she said there was a note, maybe two, but they wouldn't give them to her. She said his family can have custody of his body, she doesn't plan to bury him here in Brazil." At least that was a relief.

I somehow found the presence of mind to ask for the landlord's complete name and contact information. We exchanged names, snail-mail addresses and email addresses. His name was Robert, he told me he was eighty-one years old, originally from the U.S. and had an international cell phone that allowed him to call the U.S. from a domestic area code. He encouraged me to call him at the 810 number without incurring overseas rates. I apologized for being a bit difficult at the beginning of the call, explained why I had done so, and told him that Adam had just had back surgery and was recuperating.

He said, a bit tersely, "I have owned apartments in Brazil for fourteen years and this is the worst thing that has ever happened to me as a landlord. I have never had someone kill themselves in one of my units. I am quite shaken." After a brief pause, he added, "I have never had to deliver this type of news and I am sorry for your loss."

"Thank you," I said. "I need to gather my senses and figure out how to deliver the news to my husband – news that will shatter his world as it has shattered mine." I hung up and just stood there, frozen in time and thinking and moving in slow motion, dreading what lay ahead and wishing I could wave a magic wand and make this nightmare end.

One thing I knew for sure, I would never again look forward to July 5th. It would now be added to those decisive moments in my life that changed me forever. Call them Days of Infamy if you will: JFK, Bobby Kennedy and MLK assassinations, the Challenger space shuttle, 9/11, and the day Kevin took his life.

THE GENESIS OF LIFE INTERRUPTED

The Old Testament includes the story of the world's creation in the first book of the Bible, The Book of Genesis. The Baxter Family's genesis story now includes the birth of *Life Interrupted*.

Months later, I still vividly remember opening the door to my office, walking into the family room, and wanting to freeze time – make it stand still. My beloved husband Adam, co-captain of The Baxter Family Love Boat, was relaxing comfortably in his recliner watching the evening news. A pillow was tucked behind him, cushioning his back incision. I envisioned the stitches weaving his wound together, the cells repairing themselves slowly but surely, knowing I was about to deliver a wound so deep it would never heal and deliver it without benefit of an anesthetic. Beyond him was the wall of glass leading out to our lanai. The late afternoon sun was casting shadows across the pool and the deer would soon be coming out of the saw palmetto preserve that borders our back yard, eager to feast on the few remaining uneaten hibiscus petals.

This peace and tranquility was real for Adam but for me, it was just an illusion. In his case, he was 'down for the count' and I was steering the ship. While he faced the stern and was enjoying the view, I was at the helm, facing the bow, watching the instrument panels flash red warning signals, the barometric pressure drop precipitously, with storm clouds rapidly approaching and right behind them, pirate ships.

I was the unwilling recipient of knowledge powerful enough to destroy another person's world. Trust me, you *do not* want to have such power. It comes with a heavy burden I never wished to possess and hope never to possess again. There was no easy way to deliver the news but I knew I had a responsibility to deliver it with more humanity and compassion than Robert had delivered it to me.

I sat on the sofa next to his chair and said, "Hun, I need to talk to you. This time I need you to be fully present. I need you to turn off the TV and listen to me." He is famous for half-listening while eyeing the TV or a magazine within eyeshot. Perhaps it was the gravity of my tone or the conviction of my words, but I was grateful he honored my request.

I took his toasty warm hand in mine, gently tracing the bruise from the IV he had been given during his surgery three days prior, and wishing I could inject a sedative by simply rubbing it. "I have some very sad news. It's about our Kevin. That was his landlord from Brazil on the phone. Hun, life just became too hard and he took his life today. He's gone."

Time briefly stood still as the news sunk in. I envisioned his brilliant brain cells that I loved so much wrapping around this information and trying to process it, but meeting resistance – The Denial Wall. In this case, it was a foot thick. Like me, Adam's first reaction was disbelief. "Are they sure he's dead?" And, like me, he was concerned that Kevin's wife Makyla had acted on her threats. I assured him that was not the case but he demanded I get the landlord back on the phone. I shared as much information as I had to give us both some time to think, not just react. Given the way Kevin ended his life, long before his wife returned from work, there was no way she was involved. I told him the landlord was a U.S. citizen and since we didn't have anyone else to rely on who spoke both English and Portuguese, we needed to keep him in our good graces. After a few more minutes passed, I called Robert back.

"Robert, this is Deena. I want to thank you for calling me. I have spoken to my husband. I know you are very upset about this, and it is understandable. Our situation is that Adam just had back surgery and neither of us is in a position to fly to Brazil to take care of the details. We know Kevin was under a lot of stress but we were trying hard to help him move forward with his life. You do not know us at all but here it is, Thursday night, and we would be eternally grateful if you would just help us through the weekend until we can get a local attorney to represent us in Brazil, and a translator."

That thawed the ice a bit. Robert offered to help us and act as our local representative, "but only for a day or two. I'm just too traumatized by this."

I took whatever he offered, grateful beyond measure, and told him so. He was still at Kevin's apartment and said, "Makyla is in very bad shape. She is having a complete breakdown. Her family is coming to the city right now and will be with her tonight. Tomorrow they will take her home to Silveiras. She can't be by herself."

I was glad to hear that and asked if he would find out for us where the police had taken Kevin's body. Adam also wanted to know if the police would be performing an autopsy. Robert and I agreed to connect by email.

Kevin's suicide brought an end to his suffering and the beginning of ours, and a level of lunacy in this place we call Planet Earth that I cannot attribute solely to the phases of the moon. All at once, a storm was upon us, and a torpedo exploded on the deck of The Baxter Family Love Boat, spewing shrapnel and body parts everywhere and threatening to take the ship down. "Mayday! Mayday!"

The Baxter Family Love Boat in Distress

But there was nobody to answer the call, this being a holiday weekend. With the Co-captain down, it fell to me to navigate our wounded ship to safe harbor.

BRIEF PAUSE
FOR A HEARTACHE

Story will resume shortly

"[A] final comfort that is small, but not cold: The heart is the only broken instrument that works."

T.E. Kalem

SHOCK AND AWE(FUL)

Missing In Action by John E.

NAMI of Collier County art program artist

"What sane person could live in this world and not be crazy?"

Ursula K. LeGuin

When the going gets tough, the tough get going…and the Crazy Gene filled with dysfunctional DNA activates Big Time. That's my totally unscientific assessment based on experience and observation but it is grounded in science: There is a fine line separating intelligence and insanity and the same gene that makes you smarter also makes you more likely to go crazy. It is prevalent in my family, my husband's family, his ex-wife's family; if the news reports are accurate indicators, I am convinced it exists to some degree in about 95 percent of every person's gene pool. This gene is responsible for bringing out the best as well as the worst in people.

I went into Program Management Mode, grabbing a pad of paper and jotting down To Do's: tending to Adam's needs, keeping in close contact with Robert in Brazil, contacting the U.S. Embassy, getting Kevin's remains repatriated, contacting immediate family, contacting Kevin's wife, and doing as much as possible with the remaining few hours of the evening. With the one-hour time difference in Brazil, it was well past close of business on Thursday but I knew I needed to get as much done as I possibly could on Friday before the weekend kicked in and businesses and government services would be closed.

Still numb and in shock, we called Brian, Adam's other son and Kevin's older brother, and delivered the news. I shared as many of the details as I knew from my conversations with Robert. Since Makyla was giving us custody of Kevin's remains, Adam wanted him cremated and his ashes returned to the U.S., and Brian was comfortable with that decision. My son Jonathan was away on vacation with his wife and children and we decided there was no need to call him until Sunday afternoon.

Adam and I agreed we would not call his ninety-two-year-old mother Dorothy, who lived in a senior center fifteen minutes from our door. Adam routinely visits her on Fridays over lunch, so we decided we would go together the next afternoon, deliver the news, and bring her home to stay with us through the weekend, possibly longer, so she would not be alone. We knew she would take the news very hard. She is a "worrier" and hoped Kevin would work through his problems but she was always concerned about him.

Time lost all significance. Our time zone shifted from Eastern Standard Time to "Before-the-Call" and "After-the-Call", separated by a thick, tall, impenetrable monolith. Think of the black monolith in the famous Stanley Kubrick film *2001: A Space Odyssey*. Kubrick's was evolutionary, ours was revolutionary – a presence that represented an instantaneous "new reality". Immediate change, however, brings with it resistance and a process of realigning the mind, body and spirit. That journey is individual, with no road map. I called AAA but they didn't offer one, even though I offered to pay double the going rate for a custom-designed TripTik.

One of the first promises I made to myself was to honor Kevin's life in a way that was respectful. We had several memorial candles given to us by the funeral home when Adam's father passed away in 2008. Each candle burns for seven days and we kept them in case of a hurricane and power outage. I took one from the pantry, cleared a space in the family room, and placed it there beside Kevin's high school portrait. Adam and I lit it together and shared some happy memories.

He went to sleep, I went back into my office. Later that night I found Adam sitting in a chair in front of the candle. In the middle of the night, unable to sleep, he had gathered every photo we had of Kevin and placed them around the candle. When I came out of my office he was there – by this shrine – with a box of tissues in his lap, sobbing. It broke my heart even more. I came up next to him and hugged him, but at a time like this nothing comforts the soul. Nothing. It is best to just wrap your arms around your loved one from behind the chair, and gently make contact – in silence.

But that was well after midnight. Earlier in the evening, before it got too late to call, I phoned our family therapist who was well aware of our challenges with Kevin over the years. She was away on vacation but made herself available over the weekend for phone support, and in the weeks thereafter, too. I phoned my dear friend Ressa, as well as Adam's brother and sister-in-law.

I called Kevin's wife Makyla but her limited English skills, marginal at best, were negated by her sorrow. All she could do was cry and say, "My Kevin, my Kevin – why?, why?, why?" I told her I loved her and left it at that.

Robert was another story altogether. We exchanged several phone calls late into the night, and several emails, too. It turns out he was a lifelong bachelor and originally from the New York City area. He was Jewish and our relationship advanced ten steps forward when I shared that Adam and I were both raised in the Jewish tradition. (I didn't mention that I was now a Unitarian Universalist and Adam was an avowed atheist.) Over the course of the next three days he bared his soul to me, sharing about his success as a businessman in Manhattan, his close ties to Brazil, his permanent move to Rio de Janeiro in the 1990s and his investments in real estate. He was very focused on himself, and a male version of a "yenta" - a busybody who loved being in the midst of such drama, despite his protests. I also sensed he was lonely.

Sleep? Are you talking to me? Forget it. Adam got some sleep that night but I couldn't think about eating or sleeping. Every time I closed my eyes an image of Kevin in his final moments flashed across my brain and try as I may I couldn't change the channel. My form of coping manifested itself in action. I was fully engaged and focused on helping my husband and family get through this intact while trying to keep our sanity. Staying busy was also a way to postpone having to deal with my own Life Interrupted.

Knowing time was of the essence I called our senators and congressional representative, spoke to their answering services, and left messages requesting guidance on how to repatriate remains of an American citizen. Only one of the three called me back over the next week – most likely because I wasn't a seven-figure contributor to their 2012 re-election campaigns. The fact that it was the middle of the night on a Thursday didn't help since nothing was open, but thanks to Google I was able to find just what I needed: The U.S. Department of State website. I cannot say enough about the resources, almost too much of a good thing; but with patience and persistence, I was able to locate the contact information for the American Citizen Service Unit (ACSU) in Rio de Janeiro, Brazil.

Thanks to their online resources I took a self-guided overnight immersion course in overseas treaties, rules, laws, and most critical of all, regulations and legal statutes related to Death of U.S. Citizens Abroad by Non-Natural Causes. Can't say I ever wanted expertise in these areas but it is better to be informed going into the unknown. Also available was their business calendar and I realized, much to my horror, that Monday was a holiday and their offices would be closed for a three-day weekend – only in Rio. Just my luck (or lack thereof.) This made it even more critical to connect with them first thing Friday morning.

And that's just what I did. Since sleep wasn't on my agenda that night, at 6:30am I called the embassy in Rio de Janeiro. It was 7:30am their time, and although the ACSU didn't officially open until 8:30am I was hopeful I could connect with someone – anyone – who could help us. I am ever grateful to the embassy receptionist; after giving him a brief summary of our situation he sensed the urgency and put me through – to an angel without wings, Natalie Martin, Chief, American Citizen Services Unit. She had just arrived, hadn't even taken off her coat (it's winter in July in Brazil) or reached her desk but she took my call. For the next thirteen hours she worked non-stop to help us.

COFFEE BREAK
The story will resume shortly

"That is the truest sign of insanity--insane people are always sure they are fine. It is only the sane people that are willing to admit that they are crazy."

Nora Ephron

STOP THE WORLD
WE WANT TO GET OFF

"Beam me up, Scotty. There's no intelligent life on this planet."

Adapted from Star Trek quote
that was never actually spoken.

Our life was interrupted but that's not what happened for the rest of humanity. Looking back on it, our journey through loss and grief played out against the hubbub of the Olympic Games in London and the U.S. 2012 election cycle. It continued without commercial interruption through the fall, well after the late October memorial service we held to honor Kevin's spirit (no body) in Massachusetts.

For weeks, as these two major events blanketed the news 7x24, I often found it incredulous that the world was moving forward at the same hectic pace as before July 5th. How could that be when our world as we knew it was blown to smithereens? Why wasn't the nation in mourning and flags flown at half-mast? Why were people smiling and laughing? Why were newspapers, mail, and delivery services still arriving as scheduled? Why were previously scheduled meetings being held and my clients' priorities not deferred? I even found myself annoyed with toddlers having meltdowns at the grocery store. I was more annoyed than usual by The Florida Geezer Factor: elderly citizens with major hearing loss who refuse to wear hearing aids and as a result end up shouting in their "outside voices", and senior drivers whose licenses should never have been renewed. Even more annoying were those younger folks DWT&T - Driving While Texting and Tweeting. (This was before Miley Cyrus blessed civilization with a whole new fad and a term to go with it – "twerking": otherwise that would have also annoyed me, and been added to the list.)

My tolerance was especially low for politics, normally a subject of primary importance to me especially during national, state and local election cycles. I didn't have the stomach for the cable news shows, especially when egomaniacs like Donald Trump were featured. Everyone with half a brain was enjoying their Fifteen Minutes of Fame, some getting more than their fair share. It seemed to be a race to the bottom with candidates rushing to the lowest end of the spectrum for intelligence and civil discourse. What passed for serious debates were little more than staged theater productions with little substance and infinite post-debate dissection. They would have done well to embrace Michael Dell's philosophy:

"If you're the smartest person in the room, find another room."

Tweet by Michael Dell (Oct. 4, 2013)

Perhaps all reasonably intelligent candidates were sitting on the sidelines, respectfully mourning our loss? Maybe so but whatever the reason, the national, state and local primaries had me feeling embarrassed to be an American. Adam continued to write letters to the editor but I just didn't have the energy or the stomach to do so. Although we committed to host a fundraiser for our candidates of choice, we bowed out. What I found most incredible was why the elections weren't put on hold for six months.

Keeping up with international and business news was difficult: with my mind distracted and wandering aimlessly, I read and re-read important articles and updates and retained nothing. In fact, the only thing I *was* retaining was water.

As for the Olympics in London, from the opening ceremonies on July 27th to the closing ceremonies on August 12th, they held little interest for me. I felt so disloyal to all those dedicated athletes for not being able to watch the time-delayed prime time broadcasts and root for the USA. The only events I watched were the women's gymnastics finals and any swimming relays where the U.S. was favored to win. For all other events I just went on the Web and read the spoilers listing the event outcomes. How could that be? All that fanfare, all that pomp and circumstance seemed out of place, disrespectful, downright vulgar in its excess with the faux Queen Elizabeth II and James Bond parachuting into the park to open the games as well as the extravagant closing ceremonies. Inquiring minds wanted to know: Why weren't the Olympics cancelled? Well okay, maybe it was only *my* inquiring mind.

Sadly, our journey also played out against the backdrop of four other tragedies that happened in quick succession within the next six months. Most all of these rocked not only The Baxter Family Love Boat but the Humanity Love Boat, too.

On Friday, July 20, 2012, just two weeks after Kevin's death, a mass shooting occurred inside of a Century movie theater in Aurora, Colorado, during a midnight screening of the film The Dark Knight Rises. The gunman, James Eagan Holmes, dressed in tactical military fatigues, created mayhem by setting off tear gas grenades and shooting into the audience with multiple firearms, including an AR-15 assault weapon, killing twelve innocent people and injuring fifty-eight others. His legal defense team was planning a 'not guilty by reason of insanity' plea.

On September 18th, my son and his wife lost Little Baby Ladybug, their third daughter, at the end of the fifth month of the pregnancy. The loss was compounded by a life-threatening complication suffered by his wife ten days later.

Early on October 29th, Hurricane Sandy zigzagged its way up the coast, wreaking devastation to the Mid-Atlantic and Northeastern United States, including Atlantic City and greater New York City. The aftermath continued months later, with record numbers of people still displaced, dealing with physical and emotional stress, and unable to rebuild their lives due to stalled disaster relief funding in Congress.

Our year from hell ended with the December 14, 2012 Sandy Hook Elementary School shooting in Newtown, Connecticut. Adam Lanza first shot his mother, Nancy Lanza, at their Newtown home then drove to the school and fatally shot twenty children and six adult staff members. As first re-sponders arrived, Lanza committed suicide by shooting himself in the head. He was heavily armed with automatic weapons and high capacity magazine clips. Lanza was reported to have suffered from mental illness.

Our journey included a cast of characters exhibiting Darwin's evolution-ary principals of natural selection in all its many varieties – the good, the challenging, and the crazy. These traits were often mutually inclusive and, unlike a weekly TV series, we didn't have the luxury of holding auditions or following a predetermined script. In our series it was a total reversal: non-Darwinian random selection of characters, unscripted scenes in no set order, and the director and production crew reacting to the actors and recording on the fly.

"I'm the one that's got to die when it's time for me to die, so let me live my life the way I want to."

Jimi Hendrix, Axis: Bold as Love

Jimi Hendrix's flame of life burned bright and hot, fueled by genius, an-ger, and on-the-edge living. Like Kevin's life, Jimi's was extinguished all too soon.

Kevin came into my life when I met Adam. He was an adorable, curly-haired four-year-old boy and I loved him early on. He lived with his mother but visited us on alternate weekends and vacations. His paternal grandfather suffered from depression. His mother suffered from severe depression and her brother committed suicide when Kevin was a teenager. By that time, Kevin was starting to exhibit all the classic signs of bi-polar brain disorder. He lived on the edge from the time he was a child: an adventurous dreamer, fearless and daring, loyal to a fault, an impulsive risk-taker in mind, body, and spirit, gifted in math, smart to the point of arrogance but lacking in common sense, good judgment and social skills.

Like many in his generation, he felt a sense of entitlement to The Good Life. As a result, he was High Maintenance: as a child, through his teen years, and well into adulthood right up to the time he died. His erratic behavior made it hard to love him, despite his wish to be deeply loved and understood. His highs included reckless spending and questionable decision making, and frequent Ready-Fire-Aim cycles that left him mired in debt, unemployed, unemployable, and surrounded by drama in intimate relationships from which he was unable to extricate himself.

He lived in the manner to which he aspired and traveled the world seeking adventures everywhere he went. To his credit, he wanted to experience it all, and he wanted to experience it now. Unfortunately, he refused to live within his means, which was especially troubling considering his credentials (MBA, University of Chicago) and career aspirations - international high finance (private equity, venture capital) and resort development in Brazil. He often told us he had years of grueling work ahead of him and since he would be successful, wealthy and retired in his forties he had no concern about taking on debt now. Adam and I tried to give him love and support, tough love when needed, and tools and guidance to help him through his frequent lows. He is the main character in this story but sadly he exited stage left long before the curtain fell.

The first year of his two-year MBA program at the University of Chicago, in 2002, Kevin met Marcelina, a beautiful undergraduate exchange student from Italy with whom he was involved during this time. Similar to the relationship with his former girlfriend, Maia, this relationship also had its ups and downs. Kevin was one to always keep his options open when it came to women – a polite way to say he had a "wandering eye." Although he longed to find the 'perfect' partner, he didn't always appreciate the hard work required for any successful and harmonious male-female relationships. By his second MBA year, his Italian girlfriend was back at her university in Italy. Although Kevin had spent six weeks visiting her in Italy during the summer, the challenges of a long-distance relationship were taking a toll.

Kevin's first trip to Brazil was in 2003, when one of his University of Chicago MBA classmates invited him to attend the wedding of a friend. It was a last minute decision but that was the norm for Kevin. Carpe diem! Since the wedding was during their December break and it was summer in Brazil, he was soon on his way and it would prove to be a life-changing event. Kevin became enchanted with the festive culture and the beauty of the islands off the coast of Bahia, where the wedding was held. Bahia is one of the twenty six states of Brazil, located in the northeastern part of the country on the Atlantic coast. He delayed his return to school by two months, came back long enough to check in with his professors mid-semester, get his books, request an extension on taking his mid-terms, and promptly turned around and flew back to Brazil for Spring Break – an extended one that lasted six weeks.

The ambience in Bahia and Rio - wine, women, and song - was intoxicating and this is where his dream of developing an exclusive resort community along the remote coastal area of Bahia took root. He had grand plans for a way of financing this dream – with seed money earned from a start-up company he would launch: arranging hedonistic college spring break destination vacations in Brazil and providing round-trip air travel from the United States and hotel accommodations at a beach resort. The dream fed his dysfunctional DNA on many levels.

Several times during his trips to Brazil we received urgent phone calls with requests for money, a habit of Kevin's that started when he was in this teens and continued throughout the rest of his life. Lack of funds rarely slowed him down: he was often able to find other relatives and friends to loan him money when we instituted Tough Love and cut off The Bank of Us.

During his extended Spring Break trip I received an urgent call from

Kevin at 6am. He was in a panic, highly agitated that the manager at The Ritz had called the police. This was because Kevin had run up a $1500 phone bill and upon checkout, was refusing to pay. In prior phone calls he bragged about it costing only USD $60 a day to stay there but he was making many international calls to the U.S., letting everybody know he was having the time of his life. In one call to me he bragged, "I'm a chick-magnet, like Tom Cruise, and have to go now because I have twenty dates tonight."

When he called at 6am, I asked him if he made all the calls listed on his tab and he said he had but he didn't know they put an additional surcharge of two-dollar-per-minute on each call made from the room. Kevin said the hotel manager "hit me and I'm in the right and will tell that to the police."

I told him it was well known by me and anybody else who traveled internationally that calls from the hotel room phone are prohibitively expensive, and hotels are required by law to post their rates right by the phone. You always use an international calling card when you travel abroad. (The year before, in the spring of 2002, he quit his job and traveled around the world for six months before starting his MBA, so we assumed he knew this.) I calmed him down enough to tell him he simply couldn't mess with the Brazilian police, that they would side with the hotel manager and to keep his mouth shut and get out of there immediately. I had him put me on the phone with the hotel manager and I settled his bill, adding the amount to a long list of outstanding 'loans'. When Adam came home from golf, I told him what happened and how worried I was that Kevin was out of control and not reachable. I was unsettled throughout the day and tossed and turned all night, worried about his safety and wellbeing.

The next afternoon the phone rang and to my relief it was Kevin. Concerned, I asked him if he was okay and told him how worried I had been. He totally ignored this and said, "I'm with a beautiful girl and we were just swimming with the dolphins off the coast of Brazil." That woman was Makyla, a Brazilian woman a year younger than him. She had quit school in tenth grade and had a ten-year-old daughter who was being raised by her mother. The child's father was absent. Where did she and Kevin meet? On Ipanema Beach in Rio de Janeiro, where many lovely Brazilian woman wearing little more than string bikinis waited for "The Rich Americans." For her, that was Kevin, and for Kevin, she was his Girl From Ipanema.

This relationship, like his prior relationships, was also tumultuous but three months later, he flew her up to attend his MBA graduation in June 2004. He was somehow able to graduate but instead of landing a great job like his classmates, he borrowed money from a relative and planned to spend the next year traveling so he could "show her this great country called America" before launching a successful career. He had already squandered his mother's modest inheritance on his world travels and taken out student loans to finance his MBA, but that was not a major concern for him. In his grand plan, he would someday be making oodles of money. He refused to listen to our concerns about his increasing debt load.

TIME FOR AN ICE CREAM BREAK

"YOU CAN'T BUY HAPPINESS, BUT YOU CAN BUY ICE CREAM. AND THAT'S KIND OF THE SAME THING."

The story will resume shortly

"They say revenge is a dish best served cold. They also say revenge is sweet. This means, basically revenge is ice cream."

Anonymous

We all do stupid things – and not just when we're kids or teens. I was talking to my friend Keith recently. He and I are probably the only two people in town who revere plain vanilla Dairy Queen and Carvel soft serve and are truly puzzled by all the hype surrounding the more popular gourmet ice cream boutiques. If you read the ingredients in these creamy delights, the first 5-10 ingredients are pure chemicals – a delectable convergence of Better Living Through Chemistry and Latin 101. I don't care – it is the texture I love, the softer the better. I confessed to Keith that I would sometimes hold my cone out the window while driving and in SW Florida it took a nanosecond to soften to the perfect consistency. But one hot July evening, coming home from work, I misjudged the outside temperature, held it out there for too long and it splattered back through the open window and onto my glasses. Not exactly safe, I never tried that again.

Keith's response: "Driving under the influence of vanilla? That's no crime in my book, though perhaps it was a bit too up close and personal with one of our favorites."

"Age does not diminish the extreme disappointment of having a scoop of ice cream fall from the cone."

Jim Fiebig

Others have their doubts but I never doubted how much Makyla loved him. She may have equally loved his dreams and promises of a future filled with wealth, international travel, U.S. citizenship, and a way to a perfect life, but given her circumstances it was logical she would be enticed by that vision.

They were married on November 29, 2007 in Brazil. We received the news of his marriage the same way we had received the news of his engagement one-month prior – in an email blast sent to everybody in his e-address book. They had a rocky start and volatile marriage that was compounded by the cultural, language, religious and socio-economic differences, in addition to mental illness – possibly on both sides of the partnership. They were under additional stress from ongoing economic insecurity and during their four-and-a-half year marriage Kevin was employed for only fifteen months. His student debt, credit card, and other debts weighed heavily on him and cast a dark shadow over their relationship.

Makyla resisted getting a job or learning English, but to his credit, Kevin insisted she earn her GED and guided her through the application process for college. She failed the majority of her courses the first year and had to repeat several courses but he continued to encourage her education. She attended school at night, Monday through Thursday, and that's when Kevin usually called us to confide what was going on at home and with his career (or lack thereof).

When he visited us in December 2010 he told me he only married her so he could stay in the country and that the marriage was over about one hour after the ceremony. He blamed Adam and me for not giving him $1500 for a work visa, which was typical behavior for him. He often blamed me or his father or others for his failings. He also said she was bipolar but it made me sad how he continuously obsessed over her mental health while neglecting his own.

We had flown the two of them to Florida for a visit with us in July 2011 and that is when we met Makyla for the first time. We welcomed her with open arms and made an effort to make her feel right at home. I bonded with her early on and though her English was poor, Adam and I enjoyed our time with her and found her to be pleasant and loving towards Kevin. What we weren't prepared for was Kevin's daily trips to Miami, 250 miles round trip from our home in Southwest Florida…to purchase marijuana. When we found out, we terminated their visit early, midway through the planned eight-day visit, and sent them on their way. Four days later they headed to Boston for two weeks to visit family and friends. Those visits were equally challenging for his brother Brian and other friends and family.

Upon his return to Brazil he was let go from his job under unfavorable circumstances that left him without a solid job reference. It was not all his fault but he had a history of alienating work colleagues with his arrogant and defiant style. He liked to highlight (and flaunt) his University of Chicago MBA and felt he was better educated than his bosses and many of the Brazilian executives. We cautioned him repeatedly about these patterns in his life but he refused to accept his part in any given situation: a case of "Winning the battle, losing the war." He remained unemployed for the next 10+ months and this contributed to his stress and depression. The debts continued to pile up. Although Makyla and I had been connecting by email for a few weeks after their return home to Brazil that soon came to an end and by October, when I spoke to Kevin about this, he asked me not to contact her. I honored that request.

Kevin's calls and emails came almost daily, sometimes more often, during these ten months. We spent hours on the phone, on email, and I changed my schedule when he called even if I was heading out for a meeting. It was disruptive. Starting in October 2011, he told us Makyla was threatening him, they were fighting all the time, and he claimed on more than one occasion she assaulted him. In one instance, he went to the police to file a domestic abuse report.

Although we limited our financial support to birthday and holiday checks with amounts equal to what we sent our other sons and their wives, we did let him know at the end of October that we would help cover his legal fees and encouraged him to explore the process for getting a divorce and remaining in Brazil. He was reluctant to do this. Over time, I realized it was because he really did have feelings for her after all, and he also shared with me his fear of being alone and being lonely. She was also afraid of being alone. That co-dependency didn't make for a strong marriage and it made me sad that their home life was not providing a safe harbor for either one of them. I often reminded family members when they defended Kevin and pointed fingers at Makyla that we were only hearing one side of the story.

Makyla had started her first real job, a paid internship, on July 2nd, and came home on July 5th to find his lifeless body. My feeling is that nobody deserves that. Those of us who love our children and lose them so tragically and in the full bloom of adulthood may be inclined to defend and hold them blameless but I still maintain that nobody deserves to come home from work and find their spouse so horrifically.

Given her shock and grief, Makyla had a total breakdown. When Robert was there with her at the apartment the night he called, I wasn't surprised that this was the case; the surprises for me would come in a different form.

My conversation with Makyla later that night was, as I mentioned, brief and sorrowful. All she could say in her broken English was, "My Kevin, my

Kevin – why? Why? Why?" I told her I would call her the next morning to see how she was doing but I don't know if she understood. I told her I loved her – this she understood. I was unable, and will never be able, to answer her question.

TIME OUT FOR A HEART BREAK
Story will resume shortly

Broken by John E.
NAMI art program artist

"A broken heart bleeds tears."

Steve Maraboli: Life, the Truth, and Being Free

TGIF (THANK GOD IT'S FRIDAY) OOPS – HOLD THAT THOUGHT!

"If only you could kill time without injuring eternity."

Adapted from quote by Henry David Thoreau

Friday's early morning call to the Embassy in Brazil pretty much set the agenda for the entire day…and night…and then some.

By phone and email I provided Natalie Martin, Chief, American Citizen Services Unit, all the information we had for Kevin including his address, ID information, Makyla's and Robert's contact information, and any and all details Robert had been able to provide. Late Thursday night he was able to talk with the precinct police chief to get the name and address of the government medical center where Kevin's remains were located, and I gave Natalie that information as well.

"Did he leave a Will?" she asked.

"No, but according to Robert he left one or two notes. Unfortunately the police took them before showing them to Makyla or Robert. The deputy was kind enough to tell Robert that one note said Kevin wanted to be buried in the U.S.," I said.

Since Makyla had given us permission to have total custody of Kevin's remains, on Friday we worked with Natalie at the Embassy from 6:30am to 4pm ET on that assumption, with Robert, bless his soul, acting as our representative.

Sometime during Thursday night, I mentioned to Adam that most likely

Kevin would have wanted to be buried next to his mother in Worcester, Massachusetts. Adam wanted to honor Kevin's last wishes, if only we could find out what those were. Absent any details, he preferred to have Kevin cremated in Florida and at a later date we would have a memorial service in Boston and toss half his ashes at the Boston Marathon finish line and the remainder at Tuckerman's Ravine on Mount Washington in New Hampshire, where Kevin did daredevil skiing in his teens. Adam ran this by Brian in an email and asked for his feedback: he responded with several phone calls. At least these interactions helped us begin the process of determining whether Kevin's remains would be returned to a funeral home in Massachusetts or to a funeral home and crematorium in Southwest Florida. Brian agreed with Adam so we had our baseline. It would be Florida.

This came in helpful and enabled Natalie, Robert, Adam and me to work as a team, moving forward at lightning speed to get as much done before Friday ended and the long holiday weekend began. We quickly took care of the legalities, appointing Robert as our local representative, having Adam appointed as the custodian for repatriating Kevin's remains to the U.S., and getting all supporting paperwork in place.

Natalie was trying to get from the police, copies of the notes Kevin left, and she also let us know it could take up to 8-10 weeks to have Kevin's remains returned to the U.S. "The process will require extensive paperwork and there are significant fees."

The fees weren't a concern, the timeframe was. It would require him being embalmed, not a common practice in Brazil, and then there was an extended process to have his physical remains processed through customs. Would it make a difference if he was cremated in Brazil and his ashes sent to us? Natalie said yes, that would make it much more timely and the red tape and fees would be less. It would also make it easier to get U.S. Customs clearance as well. She was working to get us the names of some local funeral homes in Rio de Janeiro with whom we could work. The Embassy had a short list of businesses with whom they partnered and who knew the required procedures. We spoke with Brian about all this and the three of us agreed to have him cremated in Brazil and his ashes sent to us in Florida.

The next important priority was to have Makyla meet with Robert. I called her and thankfully, she answered.

"Makyla my love, it is important for you to be at Robert's apartment at 10am," I said. Using Google Translator, I repeated it in Portuguese as best I could. I would not have won a prize for correct pronunciation, of that I was sure, but my message somehow got through the grief that fogged her mind.

She was there when we called Robert at the appointed hour, which was 9am our time. Her sister accompanied her and I was relieved to know that her family had arrived and she was not alone. After a brief discussion, the plan was for Makyla and her sister to return in ninety minutes with her photo ID, their marriage license, Kevin's passport and his visa. At that time, Robert's assistant would accompany them to Robert's lawyer to have the legal papers put in place so we could repatriate Kevin's remains. Makyla did let us know that Kevin wanted to be buried next to his mother, so that was helpful. We would bury his ashes there.

At 2 that afternoon, we drove to my mother-in-law's senior living center to deliver the news, which we knew would devastate her. A 'worrier' by nature, she often expressed concerns about Kevin and her hope that he would be able to turn his life around and be successful. Although she was resistant, we encouraged her to come home with us for several days so she would not be alone in her grief, and she reluctantly complied.

Back home, when we walked in the door at 3:30pm there were three urgent messages on voicemail from Natalie at the Embassy and one from Robert. While Adam got his mother Dorothy settled in the guestroom, I called Natalie.

"Deena, I have some bad news. Makyla changed her mind about Kevin's remains. Her family arrived and is with her and they are pooling their resources and will bury him in Brazil."

Say whaaaa?! "Natalie, oh my goodness, what happened? We had everything set up with Robert and his assistant to work with her to get everything put in place."

"Seems that has changed. And with that change I need you to know that Makyla, as his wife, is Kevin's legal next-of-kin. Without a Will stating otherwise, his family has no rights to act on Kevin's behalf, even if his wishes were written in a note, unless the note was signed and notarized. U.S. and Brazilian laws are the same in this regard. Therefore, with the situation as it is right now, we are required to work with her and represent her interests. I am so sorry, but our hands are tied."

Since it was close to 4pm Brazil time and they closed in fifteen minutes, I told her I would get right back to her after talking with Robert.

"Yes, it's true," Robert said. "She and her sister never returned to my apartment. Her family told her not to release his remains to Kevin's family so they never showed up. "

"Do you know why?" I asked.

"Well, I told her you were planning to have him cremated here and his ashes returned to you but she's Catholic and she doesn't want him cooked." Yes, that's what he said, "…cooked".

I couldn't believe he shared the details with her, but it was too late now. This was yet another example of dysfunctional DNA paying it forward and bringing additional instability to the damaged Baxter Family Love Boat. I swear if Robert had been within reach I would have performed surgery on his private parts sans anesthesia. Conspiracy theorists will be comforted knowing we, too, were not immune. This set in motion what I called "The Conspiracy of The Will (or lack thereof), The Willing and The Willful," with Kevin, Robert, Makyla, Brazilian law and the universe as co-conspirators. Dastardly doings were happening on every level, from my perspective - at the helm of The Baxter Family Love Boat.

"I think she is being really cruel to do this, knowing he wanted to be buried in the U.S.," Robert said. That wasn't helping matters – not one bit. I turned down his offer to contact her and try to reason with her on our behalf and told him I would get back to him. I wanted to keep him in our good graces through the long weekend in case things changed, but I had just learned the hard way that it was best to limit the details we shared with him. We were between a rock and a hard place.

I called Natalie back and asked if, before closing, they could contact Makyla to see if it would make a difference to her if we did not cremate him.

"Please let her know we didn't realize she had strong feelings about this but now that we know, we would, of course, honor them."

After a sequence of phone calls Makyla still would not give us custody. Natalie continued to work this on our behalf, and before she left the office, at 8pm her time, she let us know she just spoke with the police chief and he confirmed that Kevin's note said he wanted to be buried in the U.S. She also told us due to the circumstances of Kevin's death, an autopsy would be required and most likely that would not be completed until early the following week. We were banking on that – having the long weekend to at least give Makyla time to reconsider Kevin's last wishes, especially since he had left a note stating that in writing.

I tried calling Makyla that evening and on the third try I finally got through. She was heavily sedated and mumbled in Pidgin English, "I love my Kevin. My family they love my Kevin. He is in a very bad place, I move my Kevin tomorrow to a better place." I assumed she meant she was moving him to a different state medical center so the autopsy could be performed.

"Makyla, my love, I'll email you tomorrow," I said. Email was a better way to communicate since I always included a Portuguese translation with my messages. She was crying, I told her I sent her my love and that I was so very sorry for all her pain.

I soon learned that when the going gets tough, the tough get going and the critics make their views known each and every step of the way. There is also veracity in the saying "Blood is thicker than water," and family loyalties kick in regardless of the circumstances.

The rest of the evening, as I tried to get a late dinner on the table, I had to deal with my mother-in-law Dorothy's anger at Makyla. "How could she disregard his last wishes?" That was the part I could print, the rest I'll leave to your imagination.

Adam's anger was directed at both Makyla and Kevin: he blamed Makyla for creating a hostile home environment (based solely on conversations with Kevin) and he blamed Kevin: "He made it just as hard as he possibly could to make his last wishes possible."

We were able to call Brian on his way up to the family's summer camp in

Maine. Cell phone reception is a problem up there so we were glad we could update him. He was upset, too, and said he would find a way to call us on Saturday morning so we could keep in contact. We told him we planned to send Makyla an email asking her to reconsider, and Brian said he wanted to contribute to that letter and would send us his two-cents on Saturday. We planned to send the email on Sunday.

Adam's brother Steven was also upset and the volume on the Anger Dial was amplified when my mother-in-law got on the phone and shared her frustration, adding "She's just doing this to spite us." Kevin was being elevated to sainthood and Makyla was being crucified.

I tried to lower the volume by saying, "Look, this is out of our hands. As his wife, she has every right to bury him in Brazil. Whether we like it or not, they loved each other in their own dysfunctional way. Her family loved him, too. If we cannot be granted custody of his remains and he is buried in Brazil, we can be comforted knowing Kevin will be buried in the country where he sought his dreams. We will honor his spirit with a memorial service in Worcester, at his mother's graveside."

Later that evening I was able to reach Brian's wife Sari at the campsite and though the connection was poor, I was able to share my thoughts about accepting and seeing the positive side of Kevin being laid to rest in Brazil. She also saw both sides of the situation and I was grateful for her support.

My beloved husband Adam, ending his third day of recuperation from back surgery, was supposed to be 'resting and taking it easy' per doctor's orders. That's not exactly what the past 24+ hours had been by any means, sapping him physically and emotionally. He was a real trouper, but I still had to 'steer the ship', doing the navigating in order to give him time to recover and also time to deal with the enormity of losing Kevin. I was playing to my strengths; we often work like this as a team, me defining the plan, with his input, and then implementing. I'm an organizer and events/program manager by profession – are you surprised? PS – Don't worry, I am *not* a community organizer, at least not yet…but hold that thought.

Friday night, while Adam and Dorothy slept, I was in my office exchanging emails with Robert and trying unsuccessfully to unwind, but adrenalin was rushing through my veins, blocking all feelings and, sadly, the flood of tears I longed to have wash over me.

I found solace in starting to write Kevin's obituary, and then the "Ah-ha!" moment came to me: We would email the obituary to family and friends and attach a tribute to Kevin's life – a photo portfolio that shined a light on the good that he brought to the world. The family always chided me for having a camera in their face and keeping mementos – large and small – of family vacations, report cards, awards, graduation programs, artwork, greeting cards, etc. I spent the night pouring through the 20+ family scrapbooks and found many treasures long hidden but waiting to be found.

Never in my wildest dream did I think I would use these archives for this purpose, but that's how the forces determining our existence played out and one thing is for sure, we can't always know or control the timing.

As I poured through the scrapbooks, I selected special photos and milestones in Kevin's life and scanned and pasted them into the e-portfolio. Around 3am I came across a poem that Kevin wrote and submitted to a contest in his hometown. Its power and prescience overwhelmed me. The poem had won Honorable Mention and it had been published, along with the other poem receiving recognition, in the town newspaper.

SPRING POETRY CONTEST
HONORABLE MENTION

SPRING

Kevin Baxter, Age 11, April 1988

Every hour, a beautiful flower comes to life.
It's as if someone had planted it,
maybe Adam, maybe Eve.
Anyway a flower it is,
born to bring beauty to people's lives.
A dream is like a leaf,
sometimes dead,
sometimes alive.
If you wish it away,
it might stay.
If you dream it away,
all the way,
it will go to a far off place,
Maybe to sulk, maybe not.
In time a new leaf will sprout,
with it a new dream will shout.
All you need to do is follow a dream –
like a leaf blowing in the wind.

THE WEEKEND
THAT WOULD NOT END

"Weekends are a bit like rainbows; they look good from a distance but disappear when you get up close to them."

John Shirley

"Only Robinson Crusoe had everything done by Friday."

Anonymous

Adam is an early riser and under normal conditions I am the polar opposite. Bright and early Saturday morning, Adam was surprised to find me in my office at 4:30. Picture this – fifteen scrapbooks scattered around every available surface on my desk and half of the floor, and more stacked by my computer, with Post-It notes marking various pages in each book. I showed Adam the work-in-progress tribute photo portfolio for Kevin and he not only loved it, he spent the better part of the day with me selecting photos and memorabilia that I scanned and included.

It was so poignant and meaningful to do this together, reliving our wedding day, weekend visits with the boys, family vacations, holidays, other weddings and special occasions, and milestones like graduations and report cards. The days and hours spent collecting and cataloging these icons of our life together were instantly validated. After all those years of being chided by the family for keeping mementos and sticking a camera in their faces, I was finally vindicated.

News clippings from Kevin's first Boston Marathon race, at age twelve, were there. He entered the race unofficially, not qualified by the committee or given an official number and with a start time in the order of his qualifying run time. But he did receive an unofficial number and he was the youngest person to complete the course since it began in 1897. This was a testament to his athletic abilities and determination. He just went out for a run, sort of like Forest Gump, intending to take a short stroll that ended in a 26.2-mile run.

A reporter interviewed him at the finish line and asked, "What training did you do?"

"None, I just thought it would be cool to run the race and see if I could finish."

"Well, what were you thinking after you finished running up and down Heartbreak Hill?" That's the last of the four world-famous "Newton Hills" starting at mile-16 and ending after mile-21 of the 26.2-mile course, and notorious for breaking the spirit of seasoned marathon runners.

"Ah, nothing much, really. I was thinking about having Chinese food for dinner."

What's even more amazing is that he ran that race in a pair of old sneakers. And yes, we did take him out for Chinese food to celebrate.

Two years later, at the age of fourteen, he ran it again but under far different circumstances. He was on the high school freshman cross-country team and his coach told him if he ran the marathon he would be off the team. He explained that stressing his body to that degree would compromise his performance longer-term and adversely impact the team for the rest of the spring season. True to form, Kevin became defiant and ran the race. It was 90 degrees and humid, he completed the race but was seriously dehydrated, suffering from hyperthermia, and was rushed to the Red Cross tent for an IV. They also wrapped him in a foil blanket to control his body temperature. He was lucky it wasn't more serious. That ended his marathon competition – and his coach kicked him off the team.

I was so glad I had recorded his completion times for both races and we included those in the tribute photo portfolio as well, focusing only on positive accomplishments, nothing negative.

 # REACHING BACK IN TIME
Story will resume shortly

"No man is sane who does not know how to be insane on proper occasions."

Henry Ward Beecher

This wasn't the first or last time Kevin would run against the tide. But haven't we all? When I was seven years old I ran away from home. I felt my mother was being unfair and mean so I took my little ballet suitcase and emptied its contents – just dumped my leotard, tights, and ballet shoes on the floor, and filled it with six peanut butter and jelly sandwiches and an orange. Down the block I went, past the neighbors' homes, to the intersection where our street met the main road. And that's where they found me, sitting on my suitcase, crying. Under penalty of death, my parents had told us kids we were forbidden to cross the busy main drag without an adult. Now, if Kevin had been with me, he would have simply defied that order. We would have crossed the street and been half way across town by dinnertime, enjoying our PB&J sandwiches on a park bench.

The tribute photo portfolio was taking shape. I tried to find a poem to include but nothing quite fit so I took a few lines from one that I liked and wrote new lines that worked for us:

When we think about your life we won't dwell upon its close;
We'll remember all the good times and forget about the lows.
We'll remember all the happiness, the joy and not the tears;
The assurance and the confidence, the hopes and not the fears.
Our lives were touched so deeply by your passion and your spirit;
And our hearts will ache forever with the empty space now in it.

Love, Dad and Deena

One of the knotholes we got through was Adam's insistence on adding his own message. I thought that was a great idea until I read his first draft. It was filled with love but a lot of anger too, and I told Adam it wasn't the place to vent his frustration and disappointment.

"It's very healthy for you to have written this but I simply can't allow it to be included in our tribute to Kevin's life. We want to honor The Best of Kevin. Please hear me out – to include this would reflect poorly on you and in hindsight you will come to regret it."

To his credit, he went back to his study and edited it. And when he emailed it to me, I went to his office and gave him a hug. He was crying at his desk and he said, "Thanks. You were right; it wasn't the place to include it."

What we included was poignant and lovely:

Dear Kevin,

I loved you from the first second you popped out (I was there watching it happen) and will continue to do so until the moment my brain stops working. My love is unconditional; it has been and always will be so. This is not to say that from time to time I didn't become frustrated with some of your behavior, as I am sure all parents do. However this did not affect my love for you one bit. I always had high hopes for you, as I know you had for yourself. My hopes were that you would be happy in your life as in the end that is all that matters. I love you more than words can express and always will and I wish I had said this more to you when you were alive.

Love, Dad

We waited patiently to receive Brian's draft letter to Makyla and as we worked together on the tribute portfolio, Adam and I also talked about what we wanted to include in the letter to her, too. We were cautiously optimistic she would come to her senses in a few days and realize letting us bring him home was the right thing to do.

I continued to work on the tribute for Kevin as well as the obituary, and Adam disappeared into his study. It turns out he was writing what he planned to say at Kevin's funeral, since we were still hoping that would happen. What he wrote would eventually morph into the beautiful speech he read at Kevin's memorial service months later.

I dashed out in the early afternoon to pick up some groceries and called Adam from the produce section.

"Hun, we should think about including one or two charities in the obituary, something that would have meaning to Kevin, perhaps related to athletics, the Boston Marathon, or even the National Alliance on Mental Illness."

By the time I got home, Adam had the perfect suggestion: we would establish a math award or scholarship in his name at Fenton College in Connecticut, where Kevin had excelled academically, achieved highest honors and two math awards as an undergraduate, one in his junior year and the second one at graduation.

Saturday night, just forty-eight hours after The Call From Hell from Robert, I was making dinner for Adam and my mother-in-law. The three of us were tired and drained…and the phone rang. It was Adam's cousin Peter. I took the call.

"We are sorry for your loss. I loved Kevin. Elaine, Franny and I are shocked."

"Thanks, Peter. How did you hear the news?" I asked. Turns out Adam's brother had called him.

Adam signaled to me that he didn't wish to talk to him. Peter means well and has a good heart but he frequently misreads the important unspoken messages – social cues the rest of us tune into. He didn't disappoint me.

"How awful – suicide. Since there are only three ways to do this, do you wish to share how he did it?" he asked.

"Peter, no we don't. We wish to be respectful of Kevin and will not be sharing the details of his death. We wish to honor Kevin by encouraging everybody to remember his strengths and the happy times." End of discussion and yet another example of dysfunctional DNA being activated.

After Peter hung up, Adam, my beloved international tax attorney and consummate analytic, opined, "I can't believe it. I can think of a lot more than three ways to commit suicide," and he proceeded to list them.

Just what we needed – dinner with a side order of the macabre.

At 10pm that same evening, Adam's cousin Candy called us. Although she doesn't share the same bloodline as Cousin Peter, she, too, is kind-hearted but lacks emotional intelligence.

"Deena, that's just awful about Kevin. I'll send Brian a card." Then without missing a beat she launched into the real reason for her call. "Carl (her adult son) is at a conference in Chicago and I told him to go visit the street where Dorothy was born in 1919. I need you to get me the name of the street because he's in Chicago right now and will be leaving tomorrow." Hello?

I put my mother-in-law on the phone but I could tell by her curt tone that she was annoyed. She told Candy "How should I know, and besides, I'm sure the street no longer exists." Meanwhile, I tried to bring an end to the conversation by getting the family history book I created for my husband's family back in 2008. I knew it contained Dorothy's birth certificate, and it did list a street address. I got back on the phone and gave her the information.

"Oh, thanks. Here's Carl's email address, you can just email it to him," she said. At which point I did insist that she get up off her tuffet, grab a pen and paper, write it down and get it to Carl herself.

In closing, she added, "When's the funeral service in Massachusetts? Carl, Hannah and Ruth (her son, daughter and niece) all want to come but we need to know if it will be within the next two weeks because Gary (her husband) and I are going on a cruise."

My thoughts boiled down to one word: Clueless. That was magnified later that night and Sunday when she sent me a total of three long, rambling emails asking where to send a contribution (name, address, account routing number so she could do it electronically) followed by their various schedules and the weekends that would be doable for them to come to Massachusetts. She also included details about her grandchildren and details of the trips she and Gary were planning for the summer and fall. It was like reading the Fielding Travel Guide with a detailed description of each destination.

I was totally overwhelmed by the quantity and content of her messages and by her insensitivity and finally sent her the following email, "Candy, I must ask that you respect our family's privacy at this time while we sort out the details of Kevin's death and how we will be honoring him. We will be sending out an announcement to family and friends sometime next week and you will be copied on that. Love, Deena"

PS – She did receive the announcement with all the information and sent us periodic emails over the course of the summer that had nothing to do with Kevin's death. We never received a card or any other form of sympathy from her or her children. She did call and ask if we could drive over to Miami with my mother-in-law to visit, just before they boarded the ship for their two-week cruise: "We're too tired to drive over to your place," she said. As for us, we couldn't quite fit that in - we had a few other priorities that were higher up in the queue.

Robert and I exchanged several emails and brief phone calls throughout the weekend. He was unsuccessful reaching Makyla by phone or email and so was I. It was unsettling when he started sharing details of Kevin and Makyla's behavior as tenants. It seems on several occasions, their fights escalated to shouting matches that disrupted the neighbors. On several occasions the president of their resident association sent them written warnings about disturbing the peace, and efforts were underway to evict them.

According to Robert, since Kevin's death, and before her family took her back to their home town, Makyla was telling the apartment concierge and several other residents stories of Kevin's enormous debts and that his family had money but wouldn't give him any. That was really nobody's business and it wasn't totally true but I was getting annoyed that he felt the need to share this. I could understand Makyla being angry to a certain degree, and yes, Kevin had mentioned their fights. But I felt this was airing information between a couple and not something that would be helpful to anybody at this point, especially us. Still, I tolerated it because Robert was helping us in many other ways, and it helped me better understand that his initial reluctance to get involved in helping us was due to the problems Kevin and Makyla created for other residents. He had no way of knowing what type of people we were, but thankfully the relationship we were quickly establishing dispelled his concerns.

During our phone calls, Robert told me his assistant, Lorenzo, was in his forties and was a man he trusted with his life. He put Lorenzo in charge of all his personal affairs and when he died everything was in place for his remains to be returned to the U.S. for interment. Lorenzo would inherit everything and I was happy for him that he treated his assistant like his son.

He dependably included during each phone call variations on the same theme, delivered in a quivering voice and close to tears: "This is just the worst thing that has ever happened to me, having a tenant kill himself in one of my apartments. I don't know how I will ever get over this." That made two of us! All I could do was listen and try to comfort him. After all, he didn't ask to be put in this position and he was doing the best he could.

Adam and his mother can sleep through anything but not me. I was running on fumes and adrenalin, glad to have something constructive to work on, and unable to really cry the way a human should cry after sustaining such a huge loss. The inability to cry was my own insanity – permanently turning off my tears in 2002 after my brother died. I honestly thought my tear ducts were dry but that was not the case. I just stopped crying but I do know that is not healthy. I long for the cathartic relief that tears can bring and envy my husband's ability to cry watching sad movies or deeply moved by something, like Brian's wedding or Kevin's death. Peeling an onion works, but that's external. Tear gas would work, but that's a bit extreme. I'm open to suggestions…

At 8am on Sunday, I made the call I had been dreading since Thursday night. I left a voice-mail for my son Jonathan to call me that afternoon on the way home from Maine. He and his wife and two daughters had spent the long Fourth of July weekend with his father. I was glad he didn't answer - I just wanted him to call me later in the day, at the end of their holiday. Much to my dismay, he returned my call immediately.

Jon took the news very hard, and we talked for a while. He was pretty much estranged from Kevin since 2007 and I knew he would have a tough time dealing with that. I handed the phone to Adam and the two of them cried together and shared their thoughts. I was to learn later that Jon and his wife Jacqueline walked down to the beach after our talk with him to give him time to collect his thoughts before their two girls woke up. I was glad Jacqueline was there and his father, my ex-husband, too.

 # A SHOWER BREAK
Story will resume shortly

"Through humor, you can soften some of the worst blows that life delivers. And once you find laughter, no matter how painful your situation might be, you can survive it."

Bill Cosby

Sunday morning was the first day Adam was able to take a shower. Early Sunday morning I had to remove the large, bulky bandages on his back and gently wash the incisions and sutures and was glad they were out of his view – he gets queasy from the sight of blood and never aspired to be a doctor, which was a wise decision. His mother told me he passed out when having a splinter removed when he was five years old. Pursuing accounting and inter- national tax law was a better career choice.

I had no problem playing Florence Nightingale, and was more than happy to apply the ointment and fresh dressings. He felt much better after being able to get cleaned up, and the discomfort was mostly when he sat or reclined in a certain position. I must qualify that these visible wounds would heal, the permanent wound to his heart caused by the loss of Kevin would never heal.

Adam stopped taking pain medication after the first night, and had eighty-eight potent tablets of OxyContin left. I didn't want them in the house. Our area is well known for illegal drug-traffic since Miami and the Florida Keys are entry points from South America. The newspaper often runs articles about Pill Mill doctors being arrested.

Since I try to find viable solutions to problem, I tossed this out for consideration: "How about if I go out to the intersection with a big sign. I could sell these in about four minutes, maybe less." Adam assured me this wasn't necessary: the stock market was improving and so were our investments. But if we have a repeat of the Great Recession, at least I have a "Plan B".

By 10am we still hadn't received an email from Brian but Adam was getting antsy about sending something to Makyla. He didn't want to wait so he drafted an email to her and forwarded it to me. I made some edits, added a Portuguese translation, and sent it to Makyla with a copy to Robert and Brian. I followed that up with a phone call to Makyla, without success. And then I called Robert, who said he would try to reach her and read it to her in Portuguese. He reiterated his hope that she would grant us custody of Kevin's remains so he could be buried according to his wishes. We felt the same way, and it was kind of him to say this.

Date: July 8, 2012 11:37:57 AM EDT
From: Deena
To: Makyla
Subject: To: Our beloved Makyla. Honoring Kevin's final request

Dearest Makyla,

We wanted you to know our hearts and thoughts are with you. We can only imagine how horrible it was for you to come home from work and find your beloved Kevin had taken his life. We are glad your mother, sister, and brother came to be with you so quickly, and hopefully Rosa (her daughter) is there with you, too. We know Kevin had big dreams about his life in Brazil: marrying you and launching a successful and exciting career in a dynamic, vibrant culture. We know he wanted the best for you, and for himself. We are sad that those dreams did not come true. And we know it caused such disappointment and heartache for you, for him, and for us, too, because we wanted that for both of you.

Since you are Kevin's wife, you are his legal representative and we respect your right to make the final decision regarding how and where he will be buried. We understand it would be comforting for you to have him buried in Silveiras, Brazil, to be near you. We also know his final wish was to be buried in the U.S., and be laid to rest next to his mother, whom he loved very much. The police confirmed he left behind a note stating he wished to be returned to the U.S. And we know you found it difficult to think we might have his remains cremated, but once we knew about his final request and your wish we would never do that. Is there anything we can say or do that would make it possible for us to honor his last request? If so, please let us know.

We send you our deepest condolences and our love,
Deena and Adam

Mid-afternoon on Sunday I was working on the obituary for Kevin when the phone rang. It was another relative, Brigit. She hardly ever calls so it was kind of her to reach out and offer her condolences. After her brief chats with Adam and Dorothy, I got on the phone.

The conversation started off fine. For the first twenty minutes I talked about Kevin and what we had been doing to help him, especially the past nine months. But soon the call shifted into *The Twilight Zone* and for the next 75+ minutes, Brigit proceeded to tell me she knew exactly what we were going through because she lost her stepsister to suicide. She went into excruciating detail about her life and death – a young woman she hardly knew and with whom she had very little contact. Brigit longed to be an actress and she has achieved that quite successfully in the role as the family Drama Queen. French Renaissance scholar Michel de Montaigne's self-assessment could apply to Brigit…

> *"[Her] life has been filled with terrible misfortune; most of which never happened."*

> *Adapted from original by Michel de Montaigne*

Adam gently interrupted me three times during her long monologue, pointing to his watch, and I waived him off, pointed to the phone, and shrugged. I put her on mute and told him what was happening and he told me to just hang up, but I just let 'er roll on. I made good use of the time folding two loads of laundry, doing the ironing, cleaning my mother-in-law's bathroom and packing her suitcase because she wanted to go back to her apartment after dinner. She is most comfortable in her own space, and our space was getting a bit loony with these phone calls and trying to resolve the details of Kevin's remains. I was seriously tempted to crawl into the suitcase and go home with her…

I was so unsettled and depressed after listening to Brigit that when I went back into my office to continue working on Kevin's obituary, I included my son's middle name…and omitted his first name. It was an error that none of us noticed until the obituary ran in the newspaper and my cousin called me. Ugh! Apologies to my beloved son Jonathan.

On the way home from Maine, Brian called and I answered the phone as I usually do. I told him to check his email when he got home because we copied him on our letter to Makyla. I also told him we were working on the obituary we planned to submit to three local newspapers in the Boston and Worcester area and would be sending it to him and Sari for review.

Brian went ballistic. He said he absolutely did not want an obituary to go out until he was ready. He wasn't ready for people to be asking about Kevin's death or talking about it. Sari was adding her two cents in the background. He was also upset that we had sent the letter to Makyla without his input. I wasn't expecting this reaction, but soon it became evident what was happening.

Brian had been put in an untenable position frequently throughout his life, dealing with his mother's mental and physical illnesses, including her emphysema, brain aneurysm and untimely death in 2002, her brother's suicide, and his maternal grandmother's elder care. It did not occur to him that Kevin's death was our responsibility, not his. He fully intended to manage all the details on behalf of his brother. He and Sari struggled over the weekend how to break the news to their two sons, Frank and Caleb. And unlike us, he had not been immersed in all the details as we had been for three-and-a-half days non-stop.

Oh my goodness, I had a heart-to-heart chat with him and it really broke my heart to think he felt that burden. It was bad enough to have had to deal with Kevin's erratic behavior over the years much less his suicide. Now that I knew what was happening, I apologized for what must have been received as taking away from him responsibilities he felt were his.

"Brian, it was quite the opposite. Dad and I do not want this falling on your shoulders. We want your input and to keep you in the loop as we – the three of us – move forward together. But we want you to be able to concentrate on getting through this and helping Sari and the boys get through it. You have enough to deal with, this is our responsibility."

I told him Adam didn't want to wait any longer to contact Makyla, and I filled him in on the tribute portfolio that we planned to include as an attachment with the obituary when we sent it out to family and friends. We would send him and Sari a draft of that for their review shortly, and we would wait until he felt comfortable with us sending it out.

Adam overheard part of the conversation and was as shocked as I was that Brian had felt such a burden. I lost the connection with Brian – he had been calling on his cell phone on the way home from Maine. Adam called him immediately and reinforced what I had said, and more, in more forceful terms. He added, "You said you would send us an email Saturday morning and you didn't. I couldn't wait any longer. If Makyla grants us custody of Kevin's remains, I will be appointed the executor of his estate, not you, since legally I am his next-of-kin."

After dinner and taking my mother-in-law home, I finished the draft of the obituary and sent it to Brian and Sari along with the work-in-progress tribute portfolio.

Then I went on the Fenton College website and found the contact information for the director of development and alumni relations. After discussing it with Adam, we called and I left a voice-mail regarding the purpose of our call and our desire to honor Kevin in some way. I included our phone number. We are well familiar with how alumni development works, and we knew we would be receiving a call on Monday, which turned out to be the case.

Before it got too late, I tried to call Makyla one last time, without any luck. Robert let me know in an email that he hadn't made contact with her all weekend. That left us hanging, not knowing whether she was reading email or not.

Later that night, Brian copied us on the email he sent to Makyla and he tried to call her as well, without success.

Date: July 8, 2012 8:43:29 PM EDT
From: Brian
To: Makyla
Subject: Honoring Kevin's final request

Dear Makyla,

I am very sorry for your loss as well as my loss. He was my only brother. I know how hard this is for you. I can't begin to understand why he did this. Sari, Frank, Caleb and I are so sad. I know Kevin wanted to be buried with our mother in Worcester, Massachusetts. Please consider this. We will pay for all of it. I would really like to be able to visit my only brother and mother and be able to bring Frank and Caleb to see him as well. It is a Jewish cemetery and he was proud to be Jewish and wanted to be buried with his family. I hope you find peace and happiness someday. I hope Kevin is resting in peace now.

Love, Brian

Perhaps Brian's email coupled with our email would work? Only the divine knew the answer, but one thing I did know was that it was out of our hands. Meanwhile, on the home front, the priority was to keep The Baxter Family Love Boat afloat with glue, tape, and staples.

I spent the rest of the evening on yet another challenge. Sadly, Kevin had few remaining friends at the time of his death. I knew of three: two ex-girlfriends, Maia and Marcelina, and a friend from high school. (Kevin seemed to fall in love with women whose names started with 'M'. His three long-term relationships where with Maia, Marcelina and Makyla.) I felt I owed it to Kevin to try to track them down. Brian wasn't able to help but this is where LinkedIn, Facebook, www.whitepages.com, and other Internet and social media resources really help if you are persistent. Oh, did I mention 'persistence' is my middle name? I can't remember.

I started keeping an online file of these three people and over time, others as well. It was slow going, with stops and starts. His high school friend Tanner had a last name with an unusual spelling, his ex-girlfriend Maia had married and changed her last name, and as for Marcelina, I only knew her first name…and nobody seemed to remember her last name. Kevin's old emails didn't provide me with any helpful clues. But I was determined and took the "Spray and Pray" approach – get the message out and pray something will hit the bulls-eye.

"The difference between perseverance and obstinacy is that one often comes from a strong will, and the other from a strong won't.

Henry Ward Beecher

"MONDAY, MONDAY CAN'T TRUST THAT DAY. MONDAY, MONDAY SOMETIMES IT JUST TURNS OUT THAT WAY."

Lyrics by John Phillips, The Mamas and Papas[3]

At 9am on Monday, we received a call from Petra Conners, Director of Development at Fenton College. I took the call, had Adam pick up an extension phone, walked into his study and high-fived him. I served for twelve years on the alumni board of my alma mater and knew this type of situation was considered Manna From Heaven for development offices. Petra was incredibly responsive, as we anticipated, but in her case she went the extra mile by providing us with some highlights of various ways we might honor Kevin, with a huge heaping of compassion included.

Adam said, "I've been doing some reading about this type of situation and it's wise not to make hasty decisions when emotions are so raw. We expect to make a final decision over the next six months but would like to definitely include Fenton in Kevin's obituary as the place we wish people to send contributions in his memory, should they wish to do so."

We gave Petra our email addresses and she agreed to follow-up by the end of the day with the wording for the obituary as well as more specifics on options for named math awards and other ways to honor Kevin. She also confirmed that Fenton would set up an account earmarked specifically for Kevin and once we made a final decision on how we would honor him, the money in that account would be applied. Later in the afternoon we received her email, including specifics for a math award, named scholarship, named faculty chair, etc. The faculty chair was out of our range and the named scholarship was more than her original estimate but at least we had the information for future consideration. Since we were favoring a math scholarship we included that in the obituary, along with the Fenton address and account information.

Shortly before noon, the crap hit the fan:

(Translated from Brazilian Portuguese and edited for clarity):

Date: Monday, July 9, 11am
Email From: Makyla

To: Brian

Brian I appreciate your letter. But the burial has been performed. The burial could not be delayed due to the condition of the body. If you want his body transferred to the U.S. the procedure can be performed; however, you would need a court order granted by the laws of Brazil and need to hire a lawyer to complete this transfer. The burial took place on Saturday, two days after he died. I am not able to be resolving this situation as I am not doing well and cannot be involved. You will need to come to Brazil to take care of all the details. Please contact Martina, number (11) xxxxxxxx at the consulate. She is aware of Cemiterio Jardin da Angels and the funeral home in Silveiras and can be reached at xx-yy-zz. Your brother was dealing with deep depression about being unemployed and desperate that he was not successfully getting interviews. He discovered that his former employer was giving bad references about his work.

Makyla

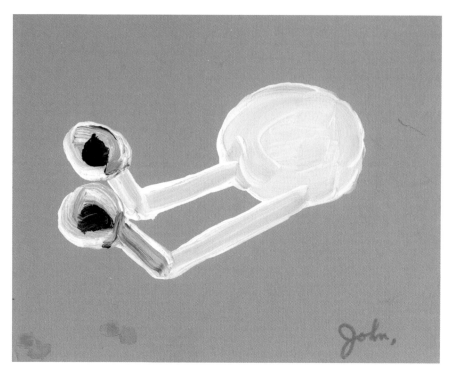

Strikeforce by John E.

NAMI of Collier County art program artist

Did you ever feel like you've been punched in your gut and every bit of air has been sucked out of you – twice within four days? How about the entire universe? Similar to Robert's Call From Hell, that's how this news hit us. It felt like running headlong into a brick wall – without a helmet. Now I understood what Makyla meant when I spoke with her on Friday night and she said she was 'moving Kevin to a better place' – a cemetery not a different medical center. All our efforts to contact her over the weekend were for naught. Once again, our hearts were broken.

We spent time on the phone with Brian and agreed I would contact Natalie Martin at the Embassy ACSU office first thing on Tuesday, after the long holiday weekend in Brazil. Brian sent me Makyla's original email in Portuguese so I could forward it to Natalie in advance of my call.

Adam was getting some rest and I spent the afternoon trying to locate Kevin's two ex-girlfriends, Maia and Marcelina, and his high school friend

Tanner. I couldn't find the correct spelling of Tanner's last name and Brian, Sari and Adam had no other information. When time permitted, I also went back over emails from Kevin to find those that might include references to, and in some cases emails from, people he worked or socialized with in Brazil. At some point I hoped to send all of them the email with Kevin's death notice and tribute.

One glimmer of success was that just before Kevin moved to Brazil in 2007, he was collecting unemployment in Massachusetts. He asked his ex-girlfriend Maia, who lived in the state, if he could have his last check forwarded to her so she could forward it to us, which she did. I had saved the envelope and a copy of the check before Adam deposited it and wired the money to Kevin. Her return address was a company in Waltham, MA. This was before she was married, so she was still using her maiden name, and I wasn't sure if the company was still around. As luck would have it, yes it was, and I was able to find their website online. Nobody was listed with her maiden name but there was a person named Maia who worked there! Whitepages.com was very helpful – I was able to find a listing for her with both last names and what I assumed was her husband's name, too, with two different addresses. I called the company, asked to speak to her, and was put through to her voicemail.

"Maia, this is Deena Baxter. I hope I have the right person – I am looking for Maia Rosen who dated my stepson Kevin. If I have the right person, please call me at telephone number xxx-yyy-zzzz. I would like to give you an important update."

That was all I could do for now with Kevin's friends so I concentrated on contacting our immediate family and close friends, as we didn't want them receiving the news of Kevin's death by email later in the week when we hoped to send out the obituary and tribute.

One of the most helpful conversations was with a long-time friend, Nina, who lived in New Hampshire and had lost her husband to melanoma. I knew Nina had close ties to Worcester, Massachusetts, where there was a large Jewish community. In fact, her ancestors had purchased a large family plot with thirty gravesites at Rosewood Memorial Park, the same cemetery where Kevin and Brian's mother had been buried next to her brother and close to her father. I asked her if it was possible to have a bronze marker put on Kevin's mother's grave in memory of Kevin, or next to her headstone.

Nina said, "I don't know what they allow or what is possible, but what I do know is that they don't allow headstones at all. There are no protruding vertical grave markers of any kind; they only allow bronze footstones that rest horizontally on the grave."

At dinner that night, I had an idea that I ran by Adam. I told him about my conversation with Nina and suggested we needed to give Brian a place to bring his wife and sons to remember and honor Kevin. Maybe we could have a bronze marker put on or next to his mother's grave.

"How is that going to do anything for him?" he asked. "There won't be a body there."

Did I mention Adam is an atheist?

"That may be so but his spirit will be there and it would be a respectful way to honor Kevin," I responded.

In return, I got the 'rolling eyeballs skyward' look that my beloved always sends my way when I talked about anything having to do with intangible forces. As an international tax attorney he has an intellectual capacity I greatly admire and an ability to absorb and apply two-inch thick tax journals published quarterly with updates on the latest IRS regulations. This also made him view the world in absolutes - everything is a debit or a credit, black or white. I worked in the grey zone, and of late it seemed I was working in the oohhh-zone.

There are times to listen to your heart and honor what it is telling you, and for me this was one of those times. "I think we should at least run this by Brian. We really need to be thinking about Brian, Hun. Sari was raised Catholic, the boys are being raised Catholic, and we need to help them through this, too. It's not just about us."

As we talked it through, I understood this was more than just Adam being an atheist; it would be difficult to move forward with a marker for his son that would be on or near his ex-wife's grave. That was understandable; their fourteen year marriage had been rocky and their divorce adversarial and destructive to the boys. That dark cloud also hung over every aspect of our relationship – dating, engagement, and marriage - and it lasted for twenty years, up to her untimely death.

With gentle persistence on my part, Adam reluctantly supported suggesting this option to Brian but he told me to do it, he wasn't interested. He was tired and drained, and given he was still recuperating and had stitches in his back, I understood.

I called Brian and presented the grave marker suggestion and told him I would be happy to contact Rosewood Memorial Park and find out what was doable. He told me to go ahead and get more information.

I ended the long day sending two emails.

The first one was to Natalie at the Embassy in Rio with several critical updates and requests:

1) Could she please confirm whether Makyla's email was correct: that Kevin was buried in Silveiras on Saturday; that we would need to hire an attorney, come to Brazil and petition the court to bring him home. I attached the two emails we sent to Makyla over the weekend plus her response to Brian.

2) If he was, in fact, buried at Cemiterio Jardin da Angels, could she provide the address and phone number, plus any plot information, so if our family wanted to visit his grave we would know where to go and whom to contact.

3) Could she please fax or email us a copy of the note(s) Kevin left behind.

4) Adam and I want to make sure Makyla knows about two of Kevin's assets in case decides to move back to Silveiras to be with her daughter, and her family. She will need to let them know of her new address. She deserves to have this money:

a) His bonus from his former employer of 17,000 reals. She can contact the company and get the bank routing information if she doesn't have it already.

b) Kevin was expecting a tax refund from the Brazil government in June but it hadn't arrived when we last spoke with him. He thought perhaps it was delayed until September. He didn't let us know the amount.

The second email was to Rosewood Memorial Park explaining that our son passed away unexpectedly on Thursday in Brazil and didn't leave a Will and we were awaiting confirmation from the U.S. Embassy on whether his Brazilian wife may have already buried him. I said his mother was buried at Rosewood and asked if it was possible to have a small graveside service and a marker in his memory placed near her grave, and if so, to please provide me with all the necessary information to make this happen.

A MONDAY BLUES BREAK

Story will resume shortly

"If each day is a gift I'd like to know where I can return Mondays."

Anonymous

TUESDAY HEARTBREAK

"I wanna be with you when the nighttime comes, I wanna stay with you till the morning runs."

Stevie Wonder

First thing Tuesday morning I called Natalie at the Embassy ACSU office. She checked her email and saw what I sent late Monday night. Since Makyla didn't speak English, Natalie's colleague Martina, a native Brazilian, had been assigned to work with her. That made sense. What didn't make sense is the timeframe: How could Kevin's body have been released by the police and the medical center on Saturday, after little more than a day and over a holiday weekend? It was our understanding there would be an autopsy and other details to work out and that would take a significant amount of time. After talking to Martina, Natalie called us back with an update.

"The police did their investigation at the scene on Thursday night and the circumstances of Kevin's death were not questioned by Makyla, who is legal next-of-kin. Since she is a Brazilian citizen, different rules apply even though Kevin was a U.S. citizen. They do not embalm and do not keep remains any longer than necessary for uncontested deaths. I forwarded your email to Martina and she will contact the funeral home and try to confirm if the burial did, in fact, take place or is planned for some time this week. Makyla may not have been given all the correct details. He may not have been buried yet so don't give up hope. In Brazil, the family doesn't customarily attend the burial.''

"Natalie, thanks. We're in shock. I was a bit confused in her email to Brian: that she would tell him he could request a transfer of Kevin's remains to the U.S. as long as he took care of all the paperwork. We don't understand why she would go to the trouble and expense of burying him when all she had to do was grant Adam custody on Friday, per the original plan.''

"I think she just said that to Brian because she can't deal with anything right now,'' she said. "Her family took care of all the details of the funeral. Makyla is not able to take care of herself right now and is heavily sedated.''

"Well, under the circumstances it would be cruel for us to move forward with any plan to transfer his remains. We wouldn't have Brian do this anyway, but neither Adam nor I can travel right now – he still has stitches in his back and is recuperating. But if there is still a chance for us to prevent this we would like to know what would be involved and what you recommend.''

"Well, I want to warn you in advance that if we confirm that Kevin has been buried in Silveiras, you should definitely not come down here. What Makyla most likely doesn't know is that once a body has been interred in Brazil, it can't be exhumed under any circumstances for three years. No exceptions can be made. Whatever you decide to do you need to add three years on the front end starting from the date of internment.''

"So we're looking at July 7, 2015? Even if we get a court order?''

"It is highly unlikely that would be granted. They would give preference to Makyla as the wife and as a Brazilian citizen.''

I thanked her for the information, hung up the phone and updated Adam. We called Brian with the news and all three of us were beyond frustrated, forced into a holding pattern and waiting for confirmation one way or the other from Natalie and Martina. Meanwhile precious minutes were ticking away. Tick-tock goes the clock and in our case it resembled a German cuckoo clock. Would we or would we not be able to bring our son's remains home? Two steps forward, three steps back, and now inertia. In real life, Superman is never there when you *really* need him. That goes double for Batman, Wonder Woman and Zorro.

INTERMISSION
Story will resume shortly

"Doing nothing requires effort. Over time, that effort is greater than the effort necessary to improve, or move somewhere better. The trick is to redirect energy."

Max McKeown, Adaptability:
The Art of Winning In An Age of Uncertainty

We interrupt this saga for a brief intermission – a tutorial on how I deal with inertia. Here's a clue: on the best of days, patience is *not* my strong suit. As Will Rogers said, "Even if you are on the right track, you'll get run over if you just sit there." And here I was sitting, feeling totally impotent and powerless.

I am an action-oriented person by nature, genetically predisposed to forward motion. This was instilled in me from a very young age. My friends got to 'sleep in' on the weekends, but that was considered a Cardinal Sin on our home – and we weren't even Catholic! If we weren't up-and-at-'em by 7 on Saturday or Sunday morning, my mother would decide that was a fine hour to vacuum outside my bedroom door. There were weeds to be pulled from the garden, a list of inside chores to be done, babysitting my younger siblings, or other demands. On hot summer afternoons, if caught in a reclining position on the porch doing needlepoint or knitting with my cousin at our grandparent's beach house, my mother would come out and say, "Well, well, Girlie, if it isn't Theda Bara!" Who the heck was she? No, not Girlie - that was me - I mean this gal named Theda? I had no idea but one thing was for sure - she must have lounged around a lot and if she decided to do an overnight at our casa she would also get 'The Vacuum Treatment at 7am.

I was learning first hand that author Max McKeown's words rang true – doing nothing really does require effort, a great deal of effort, and I did as he suggested; I redirected my energy.

Shortly before noon I received a response from a woman named Deborah at Rosewood Memorial Park.

Date: Tuesday, July 10, 2012 11:34:04 AM EDT
From: Deborah
To: Deena
Subject: Re. Request for info a.s.a.p.

We are very sorry for your loss. In order to have a bronze marker placed here in Rosewood you would need to own a burial space. Even if you do not use that space for a burial, we would then call the bronze marker a cenotaph. (No one interred but a marker on the lot.) We would also need to know Kevin's mother's name and then one of our Family Service Counselors could talk to you about the cost to purchase a single space for the bronze cenotaph to be installed on, which would be as close to her as possible.

I immediately called Rosewood Memorial Park and asked to speak with a Family Services Counselor and was put through to a gentleman named Joshua Becker. We spent a good deal of time on the phone. I gave him Kevin's mother's name and he was able to locate her grave and confirmed that her brother, Kevin's uncle, was buried in the adjacent grave. Their parents had two spaces that were in the next row, one where her father, Kevin's maternal grandfather, was interred and one next to him where his wife, Kevin's grandmother, would be buried. She was ailing and in a nursing home close to Brian and his family (and by the end of the summer she would end her life's journey at ninety-four and would be there, too).

"Joshua, we don't yet know if we will be granted custody of Kevin's remains and, if so, how long it would be before we got through the bureaucracy of getting him back to Boston. We hope to know more information today and are waiting to hear from the Embassy. If he has already been buried in Brazil we would get a cenotaph plaque. I'm not totally surprised that you don't allow a second marker to be placed on an existing grave but I am surprised that we would need to buy a whole plot. I thought perhaps you had a section for cenotaph plaques," I said.

"No, that doesn't exist," he said.

"Well, at least he will be next to his mother in spirit."

Not so fast, girlfriend! Joshua soon dispelled that thought by clarifying, "Well, not right next to her. Other families have bought plots surrounding them, some are used some are not yet used but those are not available for sale. I only have two plots remotely close to hers: one is eight graves away in the next row and the other one is about fifteen graves away in the same row."

"How many feet away from her would those be?" I asked.

"The first one is about ten feet, the second one about twenty feet," he said.

Yes, I was drained and tired but not that tired to know this couldn't be right. I knew going in that this whole thing was going to be a tough sell for my husband, but it was getting tougher by the nanosecond.

"How big are the gravesites? A casket is at least three feet wide, isn't it?"

He suspected where I was going and said, "Well, maybe it is more like thirty-feet away and fifty-five-feet away."

"That makes more sense," I said, and couldn't resist adding, "I was wondering if your gravesites are only for very short Jews, or that maybe you bury people standing upright like they do in Israel." I was quickly learning that death and burial come with their own brand of humor and even Joshua laughed at that comment.

Joshua gave me the cost information and I knew right away that this was going to be much more of a hard sell for Adam. At my request Joshua immediately faxed to me a cemetery plot diagram for that section, with marks indicating the location of the four existing graves and the two that were available for purchase. He agreed to hold the two available gravesites until I had a chance to discuss it with Adam and Brian.

I assumed the price quoted included the cenotaph plaque – silly me.

A FISCAL
REALITY BREAK

Story will resume shortly

"That man is the richest whose pleasures are the cheapest."

Henry David Thoreau

This is a good time to clue you in on an important bit of information. One of the things that attracted me to my husband is that he's frugal, and so am I. Another way to say this is I'm cheap and he's cheaper, and sometimes those roles are reversed. My crazies stem from being raised by a frugal father whose wife was clueless about money and couldn't balance a checkbook, coupled with my first husband whose favorite bottom line was "in the red". Adam's crazies come from his parents who were at odds over their limited financial assets, each using it as a weapon. This was yet another example of dysfunctional DNA paying it forward and finding a compatible host on The Baxter Family Love Boat. Adam and I have always lived below our means and never wished to be a burden – financial or otherwise – to our children.

There are many positives in being kindred spirits on financial matters since this is often a source of conflict in relationships. Our shared frugality has worked in our favor. Drilling down a bit further, Adam and I both have finance and business background, though mine is more general, and we are both very comfortable talking about money. So our World View is filtered through lenses that tend to follow "The Money Trail". We look for the business model and the return on investment (ROI) in just about everything – politics, economics, healthcare, financial investments, estate planning, and religion. Who is benefitting, who is being served, whose pockets might be getting lined and who might be getting taken advantage of (i.e., screwed). Even in a haze of grief, our Frugal Genes were alive and well, and we were mindful of yet another truth: capitalism thrives even in death. There is an entire industry surrounding death and dying…Buyer Beware.

And then there are times when doing the right thing must take precedent over the costs involved. For me, it turned out to be a challenge balancing the needs and wants of my beloved husband and doing what I felt was right for Kevin and his brother Brian. I loved them all. Who ever said life was fair or easy? As the song says, "It ain't necessarily so…"

As soon as I received Joshua's fax I went into Adam's office to discuss everything. Ironically, he was relieved that the two available gravesites were a short distance from Kevin's mother's grave. This would make it easier for him to go there for Kevin's funeral.

A little after 2pm another disappointment came our way.

Date: Tuesday, July 10, 2012 2:16:01 PM EDT

From: Natalie

To: Deena

CC: Adam and Brian

Subject: Follow-up to this morning's phone call

> *Deena, Adam and Brian,*
>
> *We were just able to speak to the cemetery and confirmed that Kevin was buried on Saturday 7/7/2012. He was buried at:*
>
> *Cemetery name: Cemiterio Jardin da Angels*
> *Address: Rua Grande Mercado s/n,*
> *Parque da Santo, Silveiras, state of Sao Paulo, Brazil.*
> *The telephone number is: 55-12-xxxx-yy-zz.*
> *The specific location within the cemetery is:*
> *Placa 20652,Quadra CLI, Lote 215*
>
> *We are still working with the police to get a scanned copy of the note and we are also still trying to reach his wife by phone. Once we have accomplished either of these things I will let you know.*
>
> > *Again, I am so very sorry for your loss.*
> > *Natalie*

Brian was as devastated as we were. We would be unable to make Kevin's last wish come true: to be laid to rest by his mother. None of us could stomach the thought of having Kevin's body exhumed three years down the road.

When we spoke with Brian on his way home from work, we shared our sadness and also updated him on the information about the cenotaph plaque and the available gravesites close to his mother. There was no reason to discuss the cost since this would be our responsibility. Brian was disappointed that the closest gravesite wasn't right next to his mother but there was obviously nothing we could do about that. Given the emotions that were flowing it was evident he was in no position to make a "Go/No-Go" decision and there was no reason to push.

"How about if we ask Joshua to put a hold on the two gravesites until Friday?" Adam suggested. "He's only holding them till tomorrow. That will give you and Sari more time to think about it."

Brian appreciated the Time Out: he needed time to absorb all that had happened.

With the burial in Brazil now officially confirmed, I said I would update the obituary accordingly. Given this latest development Brian was comfortable having me send it out to family and friends, along with the photo tribute. He planned to forward it to his own contact list.

He also gave two thumbs up to proceed with submitting the obituary to the three local newspapers in the greater Boston area. Adam and I had no desire to have it run in our local paper in Florida - all our close friends would receive the news by email and we would send hard copies via snail-mail to those who didn't have e-addresses.

Before it got too late I called Joshua back at Rosewood Memorial Park – their office closed at 4pm. Adam was in on the call as well. We updated him on the latest developments and he said he would put a "hold" on one of the gravesites, the one that was closest to Kevin's mother. I asked him if he could fax me a contract agreement.

"No, it is a multi-part form and must be signed and dated with a check enclosed in order for it to be valid."

"Can we pay by credit card?" Adam asked. I know how he thinks – at least we'd get mileage reward points. Joshua said he'd look into this as normally they only accept a check. We told him we would be paying in full. We knew he would not walk away from a bird-in-the-hand (well, in this case, a bird-in-the-trees-but-within-reach). And that turned out to be the case. In anticipation of Brian wishing to move forward with this, I asked Joshua to mail it to us and I would get back to him before close of business on Friday.

Adam had an appointment with his back surgeon late Tuesday afternoon and then we stopped at the printer to place the order for sympathy acknowledgement cards. We decided to design our own, including Kevin's photo on the front and the last two lines of his poem: "All you need to do is follow a dream – like a leaf blowing in the wind." The printer is one I use for my consulting work and he is terrific. Ironically, he was also working on a major job for us, printing and binding keepsake books of 6+ years of family photo portfolios, and in addition to placing the order for Kevin's cards, I brought him the front and back cover designs for the book. We agreed to make a last minute addition, ending the book with Kevin's photo tribute, and I agreed to email that to him along with a few other minor changes. We stopped for dinner at our favorite Chinese restaurant, trying to find a sense of normalcy, but it all seemed out-of-body.

When we got home, Adam was tired and settled in front of the TV and I went back into my office and considered calling Robert, Kevin's landlord in Brazil, but just didn't have it in me. Instead, I did the final edits on the obituary and sent Robert an email.

Date: Tuesday, July 10, 2012 8:55:53 PM EDT
From: Deena
To: Robert
Subject: Update and tribute to Kevin Baxter (1976-2012)

Robert - I promised to keep you updated and I also wanted to send you what I am sending out by email tonight to family and friends regarding Kevin. I hope it will give you a bit of the positives of his life. Regrettably, Makyla buried Kevin in her hometown of

Silveiras on Saturday, before we'd sent her the email. She let us know we can petition the court if we want to challenge this but Natalie at the Embassy told us today that now that he is buried, Brazilian law does not allow a body to be exhumed for three years. Our family isn't interested in pursuing this further with Makyla - she is having a very tough time, is on mega-tranquilizers, and she's been through enough. We hope to honor Kevin here in the U.S. with a marker near his mother's grave. Thanks for trying to help in every way that you could. I wish you good health, continued success, and happiness. I will always think of you by the stove making gourmet soup every day for lunch. Bon appétit.

In deep appreciation for all you did on our behalf,
Deena Baxter

About fifteen minutes after pressing 'send' Robert called me. He was very upset and I tried, once again, to comfort him.

"Well, thank you. This has been a nightmare for me. I still can't believe how someone could do this in one of my apartments!" This script was getting old. Then he vented for another ten minutes, switching from anger to tidbits of information about the rent having been paid through July 31th and wanting Makyla to vacate as soon as possible.

I thought that was unfair. "In defense of Makyla, she is unable to function right now and is in the care of her family. Kevin paid the rent through the end of the month. Please give her the remaining three weeks to regain a bit of her equilibrium and come back into the city to move her belongings."

He reluctantly agreed. I spent the rest of the night sending out an email blast to 150+ family and friends, and then checked the three websites for the local newspapers in Greater Boston. They make it easy to transact everything online for posting an obituary – well, easy on paper, that is. In reality it turned out to have some twists and turns and yes, surprises, too.

SNOOZE BREAK (SORT OF)
Story will resume shortly

"Sleep is when all the unsorted stuff comes flying out as from a dustbin upset in a high wind"

Sir William G. Golding

Confession time: It wasn't just the stress of losing Kevin that kept me from sleeping. I suffer from insomnia. It's an inherited trait, passed down from my father, to me. Adam can drink a cup of high-test, megatron-caffeinated coffee at 11pm and be sound asleep fifteen minutes later. I, on the other hand, could drink a cup of de-café at 7am and be wired at midnight.

On the 6th night of *Life Without Kevin*, I turned out the light at 2am but kept playing reruns of our two weeks of daily communication – by phone and/or email – leading up to his death. What could I have said differently? What could I have done differently? Tears were elusive and yet I longed for them to come and wash over my grief.

According to Kevin, everybody was out to screw him. Adam often tried to dispel that view but Kevin seemed too caught up in his story to listen. He was more interested in venting his anger, placing blame on his ex-boss, his wife, the landlord, etc. Kevin asked both of us for help and guidance with his job search and his divorce, but was unwilling to implement it. Every suggestion was met with resistance.

Adam started tuning out months before. He had just so much tolerance for the non-stop chaos of Kevin's life, but he tried in his own way to help. I hung in there, staying actively engaged, still trying to give him coaching and career tools and suggestions for working effectively with a divorce lawyer. He really appreciated that but when it came to taking action he kept asking me to do the hard work. He seemed incapable of focusing on the actual effort involved, much of which focused on writing things down and getting his thoughts organized. He had a tendency to lose his audience with long, rambling responses to questions during interviews, sharing way too much information that raised red flags and left a bad impression. Follow-up interviews never seemed to materialize and he couldn't understand why. Our frequent coaching sessions involved shoring up his confidence, helping him develop a short "Two minute elevator speech" showcasing his strengths and value, and ways to project a positive and self-confident image. I gently and persistently encouraged him to see a therapist, but it was like walking through a minefield: never certain when it would ignite Kevin's explosive temper. With him thousands of miles away, I didn't want to risk losing complete contact.

Ten days before he took his life I was experiencing total burnout. I was spending hours each day emailing or talking to or worrying about Kevin. At the end of June we were heading to Boston for five days for family visits with our other two sons, and we were busy coordinating the delivery of new beds we ordered and getting them set up before Adam's back surgery on July 2nd. I was also wrapping up some consulting priorities. Exhausted, I finally walked into Adam's study and said, "Hun, I don't think Kevin has either the capability or the capacity to move forward with any of my suggestions."

We agreed Adam would send him an email letting him know that in the future he needed to email his questions to us in advance and during follow-up phone calls he needed to have a pen and paper ready to take notes. He could no longer rely on us to be doing all the heavy lifting. He should start using the tools I sent to him, start filling in the blanks and stop asking us for advice and then ignoring or challenging us. Yes, we loved him and would be there for him, but he needed to start taking charge of his life.

Guilt? You betcha! When my head hit the pillow each night I kept replaying those tapes. Should we have delayed our trip to Boston? Did he feel abandoned? Did I push too far? Why couldn't I have hung in there longer?

Adam was dealing with his own guilt. He ran out to get the mail as soon as it arrived; sure that Kevin had sent him a final letter – a final goodbye. But he had done that on Friday, June 1st, when Adam was visiting his mother over lunch. Kevin sent Adam a very distressing email stating he was at the breaking point; unable to cope with his wife, the escalating level of emotional and physical abuse, and his inability to land a new job. It was the first time he accepted responsibility for most of his bad decisions. He thanked both of us for our love and support and wanted to be remembered for what he accomplished, not his failings. However, an hour later he sent a follow-up email, telling his father he had been in a really bad place but was now okay. He apologized for scaring him with the prior email and said he was going to a Jewish service that evening and would call us over the weekend.

Adam didn't see either email until he arrived home later that afternoon; he read the second one before reading the first one and came into my office to talk about the situation. I hadn't received Kevin's two emails but ironically, I had sent him an "I love you" email in between his first and second messages, letting him know I hoped his job interviews had gone well, sending him my best wishes and lots of love. I showed it to Adam.

We were both very concerned and agreed on a possible solution: bring him back to the U.S. and get him stabilized and re-grounded in a safer environment. Adam sent him a loving, supportive email, expressing our concern about his state of mind, that all his challenges were fixable and not to despair. He offered him a one-way ticket back to the U.S. and promised him he wouldn't be homeless unless he chose not to help himself. We tried all afternoon to reach Kevin by phone, without success. I tried to get some client work done but it was difficult to focus on anything other than successfully reaching Kevin. We felt totally impotent. At 5 we left for a dinner date with friends but Kevin's presence-by-his-absence hovered like a rain-filled cloud over our heads.

Kevin didn't call us for four days. After attending the Friday night service at the Jewish synagogue, he and Makyla went camping for a long weekend and he didn't call us until Tuesday. For him, it was like nothing had happened and he said they had a good time camping in the mountains. He blew off Friday's distressing email without a second thought. The volatility was unset-tling. Adam repeated his offer to send him a one-way ticket back to the U.S. and said we would help him get settled in Miami and be able to look for a job stateside, but Kevin said there were no opportunities here, even in New York, since the finance industry was still suffering badly from The Great Recession. He insisted there were far more opportunities for him to get a great job in Brazil where the economy was booming. It was tough to argue with this since there were so many unemployed finance types who were more credentialed and had stronger resumes and credit scores than Kevin.

We will never know if Adam's offer or my continued coaching and cheer-leading helped him regain his footing, if only for another five weeks, or if we were just experiencing the eye of the hurricane; the calm before the storm surge that leaves death, destruction and heartache in its wake. What we do know is that the first email Kevin sent that Friday morning, five weeks be-fore his death, was, in hindsight, his goodbye.

This was reinforced two more times. When Adam spoke to our family therapist and brought copies of Kevin's emails, she confirmed that the first one was his final statement. The second was when Adam spoke with his close friend Ray, who was a psychiatrist. He wondered whether Kevin meant to take his life or if it was just a cry for help so he asked Adam what happened. This wasn't information we were sharing with others, but because Ray was a psy-chiatrist and Adam's close friend, he shared some of the details. Ray's response was, "No, that wasn't a cry for help. He wanted to end his life. There are differ-ent ways people choose to exit if they are ambivalent about ending their life, but there are other ways they choose if they are sure. Kevin was sure."

This just added to the guilt. As much as we knew this line of thinking would drive us crazy, it was tough to shake. It's analogous to what astrono-mers call a "black hole" - an infinitely dense force field that collapses under its own gravity, trapping light and making it invisible. That's what happens - your life feels like it is being sucked out of you, into this black space where you are trying to breathe but there is no oxygen, no light, and nobody can see you. If you let it, it will consume you - but you fight back, seeking the light. At such times, I would reach over and hold Adam's hand, and sometimes he would wake up and we would have Pillow Talk Time and share our heartache. This post-suicide stinkin' thinkin' disorder – maybe it's yet another form of insanity. I'll need to check that out.

"O Sleep, O Gentle Sleep, Natures Soft Nurse, How Have I Frightened Thee, That Thou No More Wilt Weigh my Eye-Lids Down And Steep My Senses In Forgetfulness?"

William Shakespeare

YA GOTTA HAVE FRIENDS, FRENEMIES, WINGNUTS...AND LEST WE NOT FORGET...THE CLUELESS

"I was told to keep my friends close and my enemies closer, but nowadays I can't tell the difference between the two."

Anonymous

Things that Matter by Yvonne

NAMI of Collier County Anything Goes: Art-From-The-Heart Project

Isn't Wednesday supposed to be, "Over the Hump" Day? Our humps seemed to be major speed bumps, the type that rip your transmission to shreds. My heart was already shredded and the rest of my body was following right behind with so little sleep and so much stress. From this point forward, the days started to blend together and clock time was suspended.

According to Webster's Dictionary, a friend (noun) is "a person whom one knows and with whom one has a bond of mutual affection, a person who is not an enemy or who is on the same side." These folks possess an abundance of functional DNA, enrich our lives, and are welcome visitors who bring stability to The Baxter Family Love Boat. I am blessed to have many good friends. And as the renowned psychologist and advice columnist Dr. Joyce Brothers said, some friendships last for a lifetime and some come and go, like the seasons – they have a beginning and an end. In our case some came and went in a flash – like lightening.

There are also frenemies and according to Deena's Dictionary, a frenemy (noun) is "a person with whom one is friendly despite the fact that they live in Bizzaro World." These folks possess a 50/50 ratio of functional versus dysfunctional DNA, complicate our lives, but are sometimes invited for a visit on The Baxter Family Love Boat to do maintenance and root canals. To build on a quote by Alanis Morissette, "[You] love them but they could surely benefit from a couple more showers".

The wingnuts and the clueless were in their own category and don't need a description. These folks possess a 35/65 ratio (wingnuts) or 20/80 ratio (clueless) of functional versus dysfunctional DNA, and those ratios are only estimates. Some fall below those and some aren't even starting out with a sum total of 100, which makes exact computation impossible. It doesn't need to be precisely measured - you know it when you see it. The wingnuts and the clueless threatened the stability - and sometimes the very existence - of The Baxter Family Love Boat. They seemed to find us when we are most vulnerable. Like pirates, they appeared at the most inopportune time, circling our boat and sometimes gaining a foothold in the dark of night. We tried our best to fire warning shots to keep them at bay but it didn't always work.

We experienced some of each in rapid succession, fine examples of dynamic, static and atrophied homeostasis invading our 'family system', most of it playing out in a series of emails and phone calls, as I tried mightily to keep the ship afloat and on course. That was a bit of a challenge with the map and all the navigation equipment long since having fallen overboard and the destination unclear.

THE UU CARING COMMITTEE

I am a member of the local Unitarian Universalist (UU) Congregation. Adam is not a member and although many of the couples we socialize with are UU members, there are many others at the UU who know me but who do not know Adam. As the news spread among our friends and my friends, I realized the UU Caring Committee would be graciously rallying their Casserole Brigade. It is just one of the many outreach activities they do for members and their families.

I know my husband all too well: he is a loner by nature and covets his privacy and his personal space. He does not like talking on the phone (and that includes talking to me), and he struggles with small talk and idle chitchat. We are polar opposites. As he likes to say, "If I have something important to say, I'll say it. Otherwise, I don't have a need to talk or hear my own voice."

When he is recovering from any medical procedure, he does *not* want company. That coupled with the loss of Kevin, would make him even less inclined to be comforted with sympathy visits from well-meaning friends from my congregation.

Additionally, he was on the Dr. Gott Diet – no sugar, no flour of any kind, and the last thing he wanted were rich pastries he would find hard to resist. He also is very particular about the foods he likes: Adam never met a casserole he liked, not even mine. He doesn't eat ham, hates mayonnaise and cold salads like shrimp salad, egg salad and pasta salad, and won't eat them just to be polite.

I have so many food allergies, I bring my own food to dinner parties and my friends no longer get offended – it is just easier for the host and healthier for me. It kills me to throw food away, and I didn't want to accept dishes and toss them down the garbage disposal. So this was one of those times I needed to respect and protect his space. I called the head of the Caring Committee, who happens to be a good friend who lost her daughter to suicide, and she understood.

There was one couple, Kati and Dave, who I knew Adam would be comfortable being with and when Kati reached out, we made plans to meet for dinner. It was an emotional evening but helpful for Adam to talk to Dave while I found solace talking to Kati. And I kept in contact with many more UU and other friends by email or by phone but wasn't always in a mood to talk. Often we let phone calls go straight to the answering machine.

AND THEN THERE WAS ROBERT THE LANDLORD

Date: Wednesday, July 11, 2012 5:14:46 PM EDT
From: Robert
To: Deena
Subject: May I add you to my e-mail list?

Deena,

I have enjoyed our communications, even under these sad circumstances. You told me that I seemed like a very nice person, and you do too.

Our building is like one big family, where everyone knows everything that is happening all of the time. Should you agree, I would like to add you to my e-mail list of recipients. I enjoy exchanging interesting things that my friends and I find on the internet.

If you don't mind my repeating the gory details that you might not know about, I'll do so.

Robert

I warned you in advance he was a busybody, didn't I? When I started reading his email, I honestly thought he was joking about "repeating the gory details". What followed was a mixture of gossip, mean-spirited and hurtful speculation, and first hand details of the last day of Kevin's life, reconstructed by Sherlock Holmes Robert. I was incredulous that he would assume I would want such detailed information, especially given the past several days being on an emotional rollercoaster. How insensitive could a person be? These were details I knew I would never share with anybody, especially Adam and Brian. Oh, did I mention I did not reply and I am not on his email list?

"If you are what you eat, then clearly you've had 2 heaping bowls of annoying today."

Anonymous

OUR GUARDIAN ANGEL NATALIE FROM THE EMBASSY

Natalie Martin, Chief, ACS Unit, U.S. Embassy in Brazil: There aren't enough words of praise for Natalie. She was a constant source of information and support.

Date: Thursday, 7/12/2012 3:48 PM
From: Natalie
To: Deena, Adam, and Brian
Subject: Kevin's notes

I have attached a photograph of the notes that Kevin left. Although they don't offer much detail, hopefully this provides you with a little bit more closure. On the paper that says Adam, "pai" means father and there was nothing more written except for the phone number. There was also a note written in Portuguese that I didn't include that stated he was leaving a little money there for Makyla and wanted to be buried in the U.S.

Sincerely,
Natalie

Date: Thursday, July 12, 2012 3:50:52 PM EDT

From: Brian

To: Deena and Dad

Subject: Kevin's notes

I know she means well, but how is that closure? He didn't get what he wanted.

Date: Thursday, July 12, 2012 4:05:49 PM EDT

To: Brian and Sari

From: Deena

Subject: Kevin's notes

Brian and Sari - Natalie's email was tough for us, too. It didn't offer us any new information, but we were hopeful perhaps there would be a bit more. Under the circumstances, and considering we have no other option in Brazil for at least three years, it seems we're left to find closure together, defining it as best we can. If you and Sari have any thoughts on how we can do that, other than what we proposed at Rosewood Memorial Park or perhaps building on that idea, we would be open to that.

All our love,
Deena and Dad
xoxoxoxoxoxoxo

And on Friday the 13th, Brian let me know…

Date: Friday, July 13, 2012 10:25:59 AM EDT

To: Deena and Adam

From: Brian

Subject: Obituary and…

Hi, How's it going? We're doing "OK". Did you put Kevin's obituary in the papers? I haven't seen it yet? Do you know when it will run?

I have thought about Kevin's memorial and would like to have
a place to go with my family to visit and think about him. Let's move
forward with Rosewood Memorial Park in Worcester. Let me know
about what we're able to put on the plaque.

Thanks, Brian

MORE LEARNING ON THE FLY WITH JOSHUA

I immediately called Joshua Becker, our Family Services Counselor at Rosewood Memorial Park, and let him know we planned to proceed.

"Joshua, it turns out Kevin's wife did bury him in Brazil. We got confirmation from the U.S. Embassy in Brazil on Tuesday. We haven't yet received the contract or other information from you in the mail but we want to move forward with the cenotaph plaque."

He assured me he mailed it earlier in the week and it would arrive shortly. He also confirmed they would be closed on Saturday, the Jewish Sabbath, but he would be in the office on Sunday. That was good news.

"If we sign the contract on Sunday, how soon would we be able to hold a small memorial service at Rosewood Memorial Park?" I asked.

"We don't have a place to host a memorial service," was his response.

"Well, then we'd like to have a graveside service with the unveiling of the bronze cenotaph," I said.

"Oh, that wouldn't happen for 10-12 weeks from the time you sign the agreement. You can't place the order for the plaque before you sign the agreement for the gravesite. The plaque requires a separate agreement."

"A separate agreement? Isn't that packaged in with the gravesite?" I asked.

"Oh, no. The agreement is for the space and the perpetual care. Internment and a plaque are handled separately."

Like I said, silly me. Adam was in my office listening to the call on speakerphone and I could see the steam rising from his ears. It was evident we were dealing with an a la carte menu and unfortunately that wasn't made clear to us in advance. This was turning into a learn-as-you-go initiative and a clear case of "What you don't know can hurt you."

"Well, how much is a bronze marker?" I asked.

"It depends on the type, style and size, and whether you want it mounted on a stone or granite base."

"Could you give us a range? We would want a contemporary, simple bronze plaque and most likely a granite base."

After much delay we got him to give me a ballpark figure and it was clear the marker would be more than the gravesite. At this point, concerned about my husband's health and emotional wellbeing, I encouraged him to go watch TV; I'd handle the details.

I'm glad I did because Joshua then added, "Oh, I happen to represent the company that designs and manufactures the bronze plaques, so I can handle all those details, too." No surprise there!

I knew I could work with a local company in Florida but it turns out Joshua was a manufacturers rep for the only two companies whose plaques were allowed at Rosewood Memorial Park.

"Did you include all the info about the cenotaphs in the package you mailed on Tuesday?"

"No."

"Joshua, please send me another package – I need to understand everything that would be required for a gravesite, bronze plaque, base, installation, graveside memorial service, etc. I really need to know all the individual pieces, no surprises."

He assured me he would send the additional items. I knew Brian wasn't going to be happy with more delays and we weren't either. We wanted to get all of this behind us, not drag it out for 3-4 months. Adam hated traveling to Boston when it was cold: his no-travel blackout period was October 15th – March 15th. Every time I pushed this a bit, it proved to be a disaster. The prior October we visited the kids and grandkids over Halloween weekend and there was a first time ever on record snow-and-ice storm on October 29th with power outages and delayed and cancelled flights. It wasn't just Adam I had to consider, this time we would be flying with my ninety-two-year-old mother-in-law and that would be challenging in the cold since she uses a walker.

I hung up the phone and found Adam in his study. My update from Joshua did not make him a happy camper (understatement!).

Date: Friday, July 13, 2012 2:54:28 PM EDT
From: Deena
To: Brian and Sari
Subject: Confirming obituary info, Rosewood Memorial Park plans

Brian – I'm glad we talked this morning. I promised to follow up with an email so you would have it in writing, and it will be helpful for Sari and Adam, too.

- - - - - - - - - - - - - - - - -

Obituaries: Since you asked for a bit more time to absorb what had happened I thought it made sense to wait and run the obituaries next weekend. All three obituaries will be the full two-column write-up similar to what we had in the email to Family & Friends, and each will include Kevin's high school graduation picture.

- - - - - - - - - - - - - - - -

Rosewood Memorial Park: We are glad you and Sari decided to move forward with this. And on a personal level, I think you are doing the right thing for Kevin, for your family, and for what it's worth, this helps me, too. Since this is the plot closest to your mother, this is what Adam and I would have purchased if we had been given legal custody of Kevin's remains.

- - - - - -

Plot and Plaque Contract: When we receive it, we will review it and I can scan and email it to you for review. It makes sense to have the contract in Brian's name and we will take care of the costs. We have no desire to remain in contact with Makyla and petition the Brazil court in three years to exhume his remains and move him to Rosewood Memorial. However, by having Brian as the owner of Kevin's plot at Rosewood Memorial, it allows you to do this should you decide to pursue it in the future.

- - - - - -

Bronze Cenotaph (Plaque): According to Rosewood, when no one is interred but a marker is put on the lot, the bronze marker is called a "cenotaph". We need to sign a separate contract for that and I won't have the information on it until I receive it in the mail. It will be sent today. It will take 10-12 weeks from time of purchasing the plaque to get it manufactured and installed on the grave. Joshua said they have a specific layout for the information that is put on the cenotaph and I can send you a mock-up of that once we work the details with Joshua. We want to include the last two lines of Kevin's poem on the plaque. Joshua said that was doable.

- - - - - -

Small Unveiling/Memorial Service: This is something to think about for the future and there is plenty of time to discuss what works best for you. We could have an unveiling and graveside service in the mid-October timeframe, if that works for you.

- - - - - -

Love,
Deena

When we spoke late Friday afternoon, Brian was happy with the progress we were making but not a happy camper about the memorial service being delayed to October. Like father, like son, like stepmother. But we had no choice. This was the best I could do for our Kevin, and that's what mattered most of all.

OOPS!
A CORRECTIVE
ACTION BREAK
Story will resume shortly

"A life spent making mistakes is not only more honorable but more useful than a life spent doing nothing."

George Bernard Shaw

Here's what $1000 got us for one of the major papers that ran Kevin's obituary. After transacting everything online, including uploading the complete text and a photo, they ran it online and in print with his last name spelled wrong. I couldn't believe it – the only thing they needed to type was the name that appeared at the top, and that did not make it through the proofreaders. Mind you, the obituaries are also run in a teeny tiny font size so the only thing that screams out is the bolded name of the deceased – Kevin Baker. I was not amused and I certainly wasn't in the mood to let this go. I tried calling the newspaper but the main office was closed for the weekend so I sent an email about the error and how I was *not* a 'Happy Camper'.

Reaching them on Monday, the fellow who took my call said, "Okay, we will correct it online so it reads Kevin Baxter."

"That's not good enough for our son or for us. This was totally your fault. A corrected version also needs to run in the paper and it needs to run tomorrow and again next Sunday, since I paid a premium for it to run on the weekend," I insisted.

When he resisted, I immediately demanded to speak to his supervisor, and he reluctantly put me through. When the woman came on the line, I explained what had happened and what the corrective action needed to be. Her attitude and tone were totally different. She apologized profusely for the error and followed through on my request.

It took two more calls and three days for the online version to be corrected.

"Some of the worst mistakes of my life have been haircuts."

Jim Morrison

JEREMY – A BRIGHT RAY OF SUNSHINE

Our Friday was somewhat lightened by my beloved nephew Jeremy. Often I tell him he is my favorite nephew. He always reminds me he's my only nephew and my response is always "Don't sweat the small stuff." Jeremy runs an exclusive summer camp in New Hampshire, and July is beyond busy, especially around the July 4th holiday, which is the first week of camp. His wife and two young sons spend the summer there, too, and it is mostly a 7x24x7-weeks Black Out period for anything but camp priorities. That's why I was startled to receive a phone call late Sunday night, July 8th, with his name flashing on caller ID.

We spent close to an hour on the phone consoling each other. Jeremy grew up in the same town as Kevin, and when Adam and I got married, he periodically joined us for some weekend visits when Kevin and Brian came. Jeremy was the same age as Kevin and although they traveled in different circles, the weekends spent with us were mostly harmonious, fun-filled family times. Brian stopped coming regularly when he turned fourteen, two years after we were married, but Kevin was seven years younger and he loved coming and spending time with us and Jonathan, who was four years older, until Jon left for prep school when he was fifteen.

As Jeremy and I were reminiscing, he told me a poignant adventure he remembered from one of those weekend visits, and he made a point of asking me to retell it to Adam. It touched me on many levels and I felt I would not do it justice in retelling it: the story would have far more impact coming from the source. There were so many mixed emotions we were all dealing with, from wanting to remember good times but then having to deal with so much chaos, I knew Adam needed some positives sent his way. And yet I was very reluctant to ask Jeremy to take time out of his busy life to send Adam an email. As a tribute to our life-long affection of each other, he said he understood my dilemma and would definitely find time to do so. And he did, five days later.

Date: Friday, July 13, 2012 10:57:12 AM EDT
From: Jeremy
To: Adam
Cc: Deena
Subject: A Letter from Jeremy

Dear Adam,

I cannot imagine the sadness and loss that you and Deena are feeling right now. I do know how profoundly I have been impacted by Kevin's passing. In these circumstances friends and family often pull away, and can feel conflicted about how to best remember the lost loved one. Please know that I do not intend to do that at all. Like you two, I want to remember my cousin for all of his strengths and charm and amazing attributes. I also feel like I need to share with you some information about Kevin that you may not know. If these stories bring you more pain, then I apologize: my hope is that they demonstrate how much I loved Kevin, and articulate how much he meant to me.

Kevin was my protector when we were kids. Middle School was the most wretched time of my life. I was awkward and nerdy and un-athletic and really lost. My cousin Kevin was this popular kid with good grades who ran marathons and played soccer on an elite level. Many kids in Kevin's situation would have either ignored me, or resented that we were related. Some might have even made me a target. Not him. He invited me to social events that I would never have even known about. He asked me to be in his project group for the Latin class taught by the infamous Mr. Woliver. He stood up for me in the hallway when other kids decided to torment me. He stuck his neck out for me when there was no foreseeable reward. On occasion, he took me aside and constructively said to me "you know, you don't have to be such a dork". There was zero malice in his comment. He was trying to help. It wounded my pride, but I also knew he was right. When I went off to boarding school those conversations stuck in my head as I began to rethink who I was and who I wanted to be.

Going back further, I keep thinking about the first time that I stayed at your house. Kevin wanted to go exploring in the woods. We were maybe five or six years old at the time. Having been utterly sheltered up to that point, the notion of walking through an unfamiliar forest without a parent terrified me. I know that I whined much of the way, and I'm pretty sure at one point I broke down in tears when I realized that he wasn't quite sure where we were. I recall him saying to me, "Listen – we're in a town. We'll find our way at some point. We're fine." Minutes later we were standing on the fairway of the golf course, and he was proven correct. Throughout our childhood he was always trying to encourage me to take healthy risks and explore the world beyond my comfort zone. That has always stuck with me.

The other strongest memories I have had of Kevin this week have been about the great times that we spent together in the years after college: Boston Marathon parties at his place in town, or meeting for dinners at that dive of a chicken joint he loved in the Back Bay, or at bars with each of our ever-changing roster of girlfriends as well as Phish and Dave Matthews concerts. Golfing and doing stupid things together at my bachelor party. Our weekend together on the Vineyard during Jon's wedding, where we barely left each other's side.

I love my cousin and I miss him. And I will continue to miss him. I will continue to smile when I recall our three decades of moments that we shared together, and all of the memories of him that will stay with me. I am sorry that I cannot be in Florida with you and Deena during this time, but I will see you soon. And when we see each other I look forward to us remembering him together. Please know that I love you and am just so sorry for your/our/his loss.

With love, your nephew,
Jeremy

Adam was so moved by it he cried. And when he regained his composure he sent Jeremy a thank-you email. What Jeremy didn't know was just how much we all needed that email. He gave me permission to forward it to Brian and Sari, my son Jon and his wife Jacqueline, and Adam's brother and niece. It's hard to imagine I could love Jeremy any more than I do but this was one of those times I knew that yes, it was possible. Functional DNA at its finest.

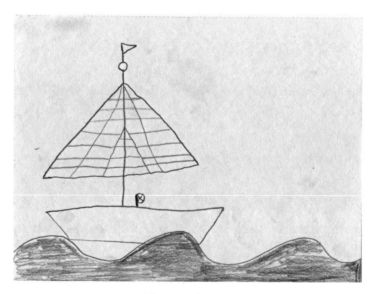

Navigation by Ana

NAMI Anything Goes: Art-From-The-Heart Project

The group had a conversation about how navigation is a word that is so relevant to getting around and getting through life. The compass is pointing north.

(Author's note: I sure could have used that compass to guide me on this journey.)

A BRIEF TIME OUT TO MEET THE OUTLAWS

Story will resume shortly

"Accidents will occur in the best regulated families."

Charles Dickens

Blended families have family trees with extensions and air-roots, and some with hidden roots that rarely, if ever surface. The Baxter Family had an abundance of them all – In-Laws and Out-Laws. One of those hidden roots suddenly made its way to the surface and enriched our lives.

Kevin and Brian's mother had two brothers: David committed suicide in middle-age and Bernie left the area and made a life for himself in California as a successful businessman. I had never crossed paths with Bernie, given the distance between us – literally and figuratively. Despite my many serious attempts at détente, Adam's ex-wife wasn't interested in peaceful engagement on any level. So for 20+ years we lived in parallel universes, with in-laws, nothing-in-laws, and out-laws coming and going.

The phone rang late on Friday night – after 9 Eastern Time. It was Kevin's Uncle Bernie calling from California. Adam had gone to bed (he's an early-to-bed early-to-rise kind of guy) and I was busy working in my office.

It was an incredible reunion of sorts. After thirty years of marriage I finally had a warm and civil discussion with a very caring, loving man who was broken-hearted at losing his nephew under such painful circumstances.

We talked at length about Kevin's highs and lows, his triumphs and his struggles. Bernie had many questions about Kevin's journey and I filled in as many of the blank spaces as I could. He was moved to tears when he learned about the love and support we had given Kevin through the years and especially the final months and days leading up to his death.

It turns out Brian had given him our phone number. I was so glad he did and that Bernie reached out with a phone call. We talked about his sister, Kevin's mother. I shared my sadness at being unable to reach a level of peaceful coexistence with her for the benefit of Kevin and Brian. We both understood her own demons prevented that from happening, since she suffered from lifelong depression.

We exchanged contact information and the next day I followed up by emailing him Kevin's obituary and tribute.

I closed my email with the following message: "I meant it when I said *please* feel free to contact us at any time. I let Adam know we had spoken and he feels exactly the same way. From my perspective, our talk last evening is one of the few positives to come from our shared heartache in losing Kevin all too soon."

In the weeks and months that followed I kept him updated on other details and I had the pleasure of meeting him when he flew in from California for Kevin's memorial service.

Bernie is the only surviving member of Brian's mother's immediate family. He is a warm and caring human being. It is a great comfort knowing Kevin had such a loving uncle and I am glad Brian and his family have Bernie in their life.

ADVENTURES WITH MAIA - THE EX-GIRLFRIEND

Maia met and dated Kevin from 1999 – 2002, off and on. She loved him very much and although he cared for her, the chemistry wasn't there for him. He broke it off permanently when he met Marcelina, the beautiful Italian exchange student, during his first year of graduate school at the University of Chicago, when he was studying for his MBA. However, he continued to keep in contact with her, unable to let her go and keeping her "in the wings"…

just in case. Kevin put a very high priority on physical appearance; he liked his women trim and sexy and the chemistry just wasn't there for him given Maia's curvaceous body. I felt it was unfair to Maia the way he kept her dangling from a string, but I kept those thoughts to myself.

Kevin came to visit us by himself in December 2010 and he told me Maia met and married a man in the mid-2000s and had given birth to twin boys who were now three months old. He said she wasn't happy in her marriage. I liked her very much and was sad the relationship with Kevin didn't last. My hope was that she was at least fulfilled being a mother since I knew she longed to have children. My efforts to find her were successful and although it saddened me beyond measure to deliver the news about Kevin's death, and by phone no less, she seemed very fulfilled with motherhood and emailed me photos of her twin boys. I let her know how happy I was, and I meant it.

The joy of reconnecting with Maia lasted exactly seven days, and then her Crazy Gene activated and spun our world off its axis.

> *Date: Tue, 17 Jul 2012 11:36:33 AM*
> *From: Maia*
> *To: Adam, cc: Deena*
> *Subject: Kevin's burial*
>
> *Hi Adam - I don't know if you have the wherewithal to fight this but I thought you should know that Kevin was buried in a mass grave with three other people and no marker whatsoever. A friend of his in Brazil went to his plot over the weekend and let me know. I'm horrified to think that he will remain there. Is there any way to fight this - perhaps you can go to Brazil and bring him back? I hope I'm not overstepping my bounds in telling you this but I thought you should know. All the best, Maia*

When Adam received this he shouted for me to come into his study. He was very upset, mostly by receiving this message in an email and its insensitivity given his medical condition and everything we had been through the past twelve days.

"I sure as hell hope she hasn't sent this to Brian," he said.

I offered to call her to head that off, but I was too late. When I got her on the phone she had already posted the same message to Brian's Facebook page. I explained that she was intervening in a situation for which she did not have all the facts, and that it was very upsetting for Adam and would be equally so for Brian. I had already told her Adam had back surgery just before Kevin's death and reminded her, once again, that neither he nor I were in a position to fly to Brazil.

She became angry and emotional, crying uncontrollably and shouting, "Kevin was thrown in a mass grave with three other people with dirt tossed over him. How can you not get on a plane and fly down there and bring him home?" I told her that although I knew she was trying to help, she needed to back off and respect our privacy.

I got off the phone and updated Adam and he became unglued. I have rarely seen him so emotional. While he fumed on the couch, I called Natalie at the Embassy ACSU office in Brazil and asked her to confirm if Kevin had, in fact, been 'thrown into a mass grave with three other people'. She told me she would follow-up with the cemetery and get back to us.

When Adam had regained his equilibrium, he drafted a response to Maia. He asked me to review it, and sent it.

Date: Tues., July 17, 2012 2:03:08 PM
From: Adam
To: Maia, bc: Deena
Subject: Kevin's burial

Maia, unfortunately there is nothing we can do. We tried to get his wife to give us control of the body, at first she agreed on the day of his death but then she changed her mind. Deena called her on Friday and Saturday. Both Brian and we sent her email requests and Brian called her on Sunday (as it turns out the day after he was buried). This was after we had the consulate person talk to her in Portuguese on Friday to prevent any misunderstandings and ask her again to give us control of his remains so that he could be buried next to his mother. It was actually Makyla who told us the day before of Kevin's desire to be buried in U.S., next to his mother. Kevin had never brought it up before with any of us, but that's not unusual for someone in his or her mid-30s. However, he never legally put this in writing. The consulate women said that Makyla had changed her mind after consulting her family. There is nothing we can do at this time. Adam

Date: Tue, 17 Jul 2012 3:05:57 PM
From: Maia
To: Adam
Subject: Kevin's burial

Adam, I'm very sorry to hear this and even more sorry if I've made this worse by telling you this information. I felt that were I in your shoes I'd want to know. I find it hard to believe that it wouldn't be possible for you to at least contribute towards his burial down there (I was told it was due to lack of funds). I will stay out of this I just wanted to do right by him. Maia

Date: Tue, 17 Jul 2012 6:29:19 PM
From: Deena
To: Maia
Subject: Maia - I ask for your understanding, please

Maia – Adam forwarded to me your second email and he is too upset to respond. Please understand not only has this been a nightmare for our entire family, but also as I told you a number of times, Adam had back surgery two days before Kevin's death. Your second email made him even more upset than he already was when I called you, and this is undermining his health.

You have no idea what our family has done to try to honor Kevin's last request. What we are able to do and plan to do – in the U.S. and in Brazil – is a family affair. We have complex legal, language, and international constraints to deal with, and since he left no Will, Kevin's wife has the right to do whatever she wants, same as if they lived in the U.S. Since he didn't leave a Will, Kevin did not make it possible for us to do any more than we are doing. You are not privy to the details of what has been transpiring with his wife, our family, and our U.S. State Department contact in Brazil; and your two emails with thoughts about what we should do are not helping us during this very difficult time. Please allow us the space to do what is feasible - again, this is a family matter. It is best if you do as you said you would: "...stay out of this." Deena

Date: Wednesday, July 18, 2012 9:06:46 AM
From: Maia
To: Deena

Hi Deena - You have to know that I've been contacted by one of Kevin's friends in Brazil and he wants to help you. He's trying to see what he can do to have Kevin honored properly. I can put you in touch with him if you'd like. I'm sorry if it's made things worse but I could never just sit idly by and let Kevin lie in a grave with three other people because his wife had no money to bury him and none was sent to her for this. Let me know if you'd like to pursue this, otherwise I won't say another word about it. Maia

Date: Wednesday, July 18, 2012 12:31:31 PM
From: Deena
To: Maia

Since you brought it up, have Kevin's friend contact me directly if he is trying to help us. It is making it difficult for you and for us to put you in the middle. I have been working this on Kevin's behalf since I first took the call that shattered our life. But in many respects, our hands are tied by international and legal constraints.

You and Kevin's friend are assuming we wouldn't send money. His wife didn't want money. On behalf of my family, I am and have been on top of this and working everything through our proper legal channels. Trust me, I know you are trying to help but it is doing just the opposite - especially involving Adam in his current state, and Brian.

Thanks for dropping this. Deena

She just didn't get it. Adam was beyond upset and his biggest concern was that if she didn't feel she was making headway with us, she would involve Brian, who didn't need this added stress. In addition to Kevin's death he was also dealing with his maternal grandmother's deteriorating health and with his Uncle Bernie living in California, Brian was her sole caregiver. Adam called Brian and advised him to delete any and all communications from Maia, which he did.

Date: Wednesday, July 18, 2012 12:49:36 PM
From: Maia
To: Deena

I'm in touch with him on Facebook so I don't have his email address but I've messaged him and asked that he contact you directly. His name is Theo Antoni and he visited the grave over the weekend to put flowers there from him and me. Perhaps traveling to Brazil would enable you to have more of an effect on getting things done the way the family would have wanted? Maia

Date: Wednesday, July 18, 2012 1:08:50 PM
From: Deena
To: Maia

Thanks. You can now drop this. Deena

She didn't. I never did receive an email from Theo but Maia sent me his email and I had plans to contact him.

WE PAUSE FOR A 'TEACHING MOMENT'

Story will resume shortly

"Why does life keep teaching me lessons I have no desire to learn?"

Anonymous

Sleep was even more elusive with nightmares resulting from the details included in Robert's email and visions of Kevin lying in a mass grave in a remote village in Brazil. And then my angel came to the rescue.

Two days after Maia's last series of emails, I received an urgent email from Natalie at the Embassy requesting that I call her a.s.a.p. Since it was mid-afternoon on Friday and Brazil was an hour ahead, I dropped what I was doing and immediately contacted her. Thankfully she answered the phone.

"We have contacted the cemetery and I have information about Kevin's burial." But then she paused and I wasn't sure what was coming. "Would it help if I explained about local burial customs? I'm not sure you want all that information after all you've been through."

I didn't have to stop and think, I said, "Absolutely, I would welcome that."

Her brief tutorial on funeral and burial customs was invaluable. It provided the context for how Kevin was laid to rest. Since bodies are not customarily embalmed, burials take place immediately. There are private cemeteries where a family can purchase an individual plot but for the general public, including Makyla and her family, it is common to bury a loved one in a public cemetery. She assured me that public cemeteries and the funeral industry in general are highly regulated in Brazil. Yes, Kevin was buried with three other people but he was not "thrown in a mass grave with dirt tossed over him" as we were led to believe, it was quite the contrary. The deceased are laid to rest in an underground mausoleum, a crypt where each person is in their own casket and in a stack but each with their own space. The crypt is sealed in cement and covered with dirt.

"Makyla plans to have a marker put on Kevin's grave in the future", she said. "There is dirt there right now because it was freshly dug and over time it will have grass there."

"Could he be moved to a private plot at that cemetery if Makyla agreed?" I asked, adding, "We would cover all the costs."

"You would have to wait three years to do that but yes, that would be a possibility."

Natalie went on to say that unlike in the U.S., it is not customary for the family to be present during internment. She added, "In fact, it isn't allowed at all at the public cemetery where Kevin was buried as it is considered inappropriate for the family to be there. Unlike in the U.S., graves are close together here, and families are very big and to have four large families at the internment at one time would be impossible."

That made sense, since we knew Makyla had ten siblings.

In closing she added, "Most of all, I want to assure you that Kevin was buried respectfully and in accordance with Brazil's strict laws."

Angels really can be human. When I told Adam he wept and we just hugged each other – hugs of relief and gratitude that Natalie was in our life. Her legal obligations to us ended the minute Makyla retained Kevin's remains the day after his death. And yet here it was, fourteen days later, and she was there for us – once again.

As soon as I hung up with Natalie, I knew what I had to do on behalf of Adam, Brian, myself, and most of all, Kevin.

Date: Friday, July 20, 2012 3:59:19 PM EDT
From: Deena
To: Maia and Theo
Subject: Update re Kevin Baxter's burial

Maia and Theo,

As I told Maia, I have been working closely with the U.S. Embassy in Brazil on Kevin's behalf. They confirmed with the cemetery that Kevin was buried respectfully in his own casket and his own space in a crypt with three other people, in a public cemetery, compliant with the customs and regulations in Brazil. Makyla plans to have a marker placed there in the future.

Maia - I know you were trying to be helpful but you ended up introducing a level of pain needlessly into our lives at a time we were already hurting so badly. So Adam and I just wanted our final communication to inform you that Kevin has been laid to rest respectfully in the country where he sought his dreams, and we are comforted by that.

Deena

Date: Friday, Jul 20, 2012, at 4:21 PM
From: Maia
To: Deena

I wasn't trying to "help", Deena, I was trying to ensure that one of my best friends was buried respectfully. When Theo told me about Kevin's grave I was inconsolable - I knew that telling Adam and Brian would make them hurt but I felt it was more important that they knew. You know full well how sensitive and kind a person I am so to unnecessarily keep jabbing at me just says everything doesn't it? I'm very sorry that I made the hurting worse for Adam and Brian, but I made it clear that from the information that I was given by Theo (having actually been to the gravesite, unlike you) the grave was nothing more than an earthen burial with random people thrown in. You certainly didn't give me any information and when Theo had *told me what he found after offering to bring flowers from me to Kevin's grave, I was absolutely horrified that this was to be his final resting place. Isn't it bad enough that he's dead and never to be seen again? To be dishonored that way was not something I could sit idly by and leave alone. Sometimes life is hard and hurtful and it kills me that I'll never see or speak to him again - I loved him more than most people and had promised his mother that I'd take care of him and wasn't able to. So I did the best I could and I'll be ok with that.*

Well it's done and finished with and you never have to speak with me again. Maia

Date: Friday, July 20, 2012 7:50:12 PM
From: Deena
To: Maia

I received the information from the Embassy late this afternoon, just before I sent it on to you and Theo.

So that was the end of our kumbaya time with Maia. Kevin had told me many times that Maia never stopped loving him. It was with sadness I realized this was the backstory playing out throughout the past four days. Adam was adamant he wanted no further contact with Maia and did not want her at any memorial service we planned for Kevin, so I respected that request. I wish for Maia peace and closure. This was one of the sad legacies Kevin left behind. Dysfunctional DNA can manifest itself in relationships between genetically unrelated people: yet another way it pays forward. This one added serious wounds to The Baxter Family Love Boat.

ALL ABOUT TANNER

Tanner was Kevin's friend from high school whom I had hoped to find. When Kevin was younger and visited us on his alternate weekend schedule, sometimes Tanner would come, too, similar to Jeremy. He was a delightful boy and we got to know his parents, who ran a successful health food store in town. They were vegetarians and one of the few families who stayed true to the ideals of the Hippy Generation. I was always fond of Tanner and his entire family.

During Kevin's solo visit with us over the holidays in December 2010, Tanner called but Kevin was out for dinner with his grandmother, Dorothy. Tanner was driving to a conference a couple of hours away and that gave us plenty of time to chat as I was cooking dinner. He told me about his college years, law school, his job, and how he met his wife. He asked how Kevin was doing. It wasn't my place to share any details. I simply said he was doing fine and that Kevin would fill him in when they connected. I did let him know Kevin was planning to head up to Boston for two weeks after leaving our house and encouraged him to try to connect with Kevin when he was visiting Brian. He also updated me on his parents and his brother. I was hoping Kevin would come home before we ended our phone call but that didn't happen. It never crossed my mind to ask Tanner for his contact information.

When Kevin came home after his dinner with Dorothy, he was disappointed at having missed Tanner's call. Although he tried calling Tanner's number he wasn't successful connecting so I brought him up to date on the news that Tanner shared with me.

"When was the last time you saw Tanner?" I asked.

"It was at his wedding," Kevin responded.

"Was that the wedding where you brought Marcelina, your former Italian girlfriend?"

"Yes. She had returned to Italy to finish her undergraduate degree and we parted ways. She had a lot of hang-ups. But she came back to the U.S. to attend law school at the University of Michigan and at the time of Tanner's wedding I was back in the U.S. and I was hoping that we could at least try to see each other again. So I invited her to come as my date."

"Weren't you dating Makyla in Brazil at that time?" I asked.

"From my perspective, Makyla and I had broken up but she didn't see it that way. She was so jealous of Marcelina, and she still is."

"Oh, so I guess you don't ever plan to take Makyla to visit Tanner and his family and view their wedding album…?" I asked rhetorically.

Tanner and Kevin's lives went in very different directions and they were not in regular contact with each other. Tanner had been an attorney with a firm in Boston but when they started a family, he and his wife moved to up-state New York to be near her parents.

Before the relationship with Maia went south she did give me the correct spelling of Tanner's last name but she didn't have any contact information for him. Knowing the correct spelling of his last name allowed me to search for him on Google and on whitepages.com and as luck would have it, I was able to find his current law firm. I called and left him a voice-mail.

He returned my call just as we were about to meet with the printer to place the order for Kevin's sympathy acknowledgement cards. When I shared the news with Tanner I heard him close the door to his office and break down. Oh how I wished I could have been there to soften the blow. When he was able to regain his composure, I suggested we continue talking later, after work and to give him some time to regain his bearings.

"I wasn't a good friend. I should have reached out to him more than I did" he said, between sobs.

He was being so hard on himself. He went on to share that it had gotten so difficult dealing with Kevin's continual crises that it had just worn him down. He was shouldering too much regret and I told him I would call him that evening. By then he had talked with his wife and we were able to talk in detail about our shared grief. He was so glad I had tracked him down, and Adam and I felt the same way.

Tanner's reaction was not unlike many others. This is what is so difficult about dealing with people who suffer from mental illness. Left untreated, and sometimes even when treated, it can simply wear out friends and family. The estrangement that results is the polar opposite of what the person with mental illness needs. Then come the feelings of regret and guilt at having walked away simply because you are human. Tanner was one more member joining us on the trail of heartache.

It was a gift to Kevin and to all of us that Tanner attended Kevin's memorial service and reception. It was a ten-hour round trip for him and he refused our offer to cover his hotel. Tanner is the epitome of a true friend. Brian and my son Jon were as comforted by his presence as we were.

AN "I FEEL YOUR PAIN" BREAK

Story will resume shortly

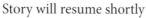

"The brilliance of your mind is completely destroyed by the ignorance of your mouth."

Nishan Panwar

In addition to those mentioned previously, we had other well-meaning relatives and friends who could use a short course in how to comfort people who have just suffered the death of a loved one. The night Kevin died, I called another close relative who started talking about 'the need for closure and grieving' followed by questions about our plans for the funeral service – a mere three hours after the initial call from Robert informing us of Kevin's suicide. I seriously considered telling him where to park his 'closure' but thankfully had the presence of mind to bite my tongue. Thankfully even his wife counseled, "Kevin's still in Brazil. For goodness sake, give them some time!" I appreciated her support.

And then there were others, like my relative Brigit, who called and soon after expressing their deepest sympathy insisted on reliving their own stories of loss, with us ending up comforting them at a time we were so vulnerable.

At times like these, it is helpful to get some constructive advice for all of us imperfect but well-intended humans, from that wise sage of etiquette - Dear Abby[4].

DEAR ABBY: I lost my mom last year. It was unexpected, and my father and I are still hurting. Mom had a friend who never fails to tell me how the loss of her mother and her husband was much more painful for her than my loss. Every time I have the unfortunate luck of answering the phone when she calls, she'll ask how I'm doing, then launch into how hard it was on her and I don't know the true pain that she has.

I am sick of people telling me they understand how I feel and what I'm going through. No one knows the depth of what I'm experiencing, except maybe my sibling. I moved back home to take care of my wonderful mother. She was my best friend. I could tell her anything and she was never judgmental. I love her and I hurt from her loss.

Please tell people when offering condolences to just listen and be there. That's what anyone who suffers a loss needs more than anything. Do not compare your pain to theirs.

And Abby, please know how sorry I am for the loss of your own dear mother, and thank you for letting me vent. - Hole in My Heart in Ocean Springs, Miss.

DEAR HOLE IN YOUR HEART: I'm sorry for your loss, too, and you're welcome. Please know that no rule of etiquette says you have to listen to that woman's insensitive prattle. The next time she starts, it is perfectly acceptable to stop her cold and tell her that when she compares her pain to yours she is being insensitive, and that if she does it one more time, you will hang up. Clearly, she is not calling to see how you're doing; she is calling to dump. There are times when you must protect yourself, and this is one of them.

And for those photo buffs who come to funerals with a camera in hand, here's more wise advice…

DEAR ABBY: What is proper etiquette for someone who takes pictures at a funeral?

I am a recent widow who received a package from an out-of-town relative. In it were several envelopes for my family. One of them was for my sister, who lives 40 miles away. I gave my sister a call and told her it looked like it contained a stack of pictures. She said I should go ahead and open it.

Inside were photos taken at my husband's funeral -- pictures of the funeral home, inside the church, the casket, and some of me and my daughter sitting at the gravesite. Abby, it was like going to the funeral all over again! The latter were particularly disturbing.

To me, it felt like voyeurism. Why would someone take pictures of such a sad event? I hope you print this and tell me and others what your opinion is so they may heed your advice -- particularly my in-laws. – Grieving Widow in Indiana

DEAR GRIEVING: Please accept my sympathy for the loss of your husband. I can only imagine the shock you experienced when you saw the photos. No one should take pictures at funerals without first having received permission from the immediate survivors such as the widow, widower or children.

That said, the practice is not as uncommon as you might think. After a period of time, family members have been known to find comfort in having them. Short of asking your permission, your trauma could have been avoided had the relative who sent the pictures thought to label the envelopes or include a note explaining what was inside them. That way, you wouldn't have had to view them until you were ready -- if ever -- and were prepared emotionally.

"History, despite its wrenching pain, cannot be unlived, but if faced with courage, need not be lived again."

Maya Angelou

LOST AND NOT FOUND
(OOPS – I SPOKE TOO SOON...)

As for Kevin's ex-girlfriend, Marcelina from Italy, the best I could do was send an email to the alumni office at the University of Michigan law school, asking them to contact her and have her call me. It didn't bode well for a positive outcome since nobody knew her last name. When Kevin last spoke about her he said she was working in a law firm in California but that wasn't enough information to build on. I certainly wasn't about to ask Makyla since the mere mention of Marcelina's name would have brought her even more pain. I did the best I could and then…

NEWS FLASH!
LOST AND FOUND
Story will resume shortly

"Sanity is madness put to good uses."

George Santayana

Late breaking news: as I was writing this section, I tried one last time to find a lawyer named Marcelina in California with connections to Italy and the University of Michigan Law School. Luck was on my side - I struck gold. (Thanks, Google and Linked-In!)

It was not lost on me – the irony of being happy about connecting with a person in order to deliver such sad news. In this Life-After-Kevin mode, successes were measured by a very different standard. I was slowing getting used to this New Normal. Perhaps 'happy' isn't the right descriptive – it was more like relieved.

The law firm where she worked included her profile, contact information, and a photo. Kevin had mentioned she was a model when she was in her teens and it was evident from her profile and photo that she had matured into a beautiful, successful lawyer. I sent her an email and within ten minutes the phone rang – on a Sunday afternoon! We spent forty-five minutes talking about Kevin. Thankfully, I wasn't delivering the news for the first time. She told me she had sent him an email three days before his death letting him know she would be visiting Rio de Janeiro on business. They planned to meet for lunch.

"I wasn't overly concerned," she said. "Kevin told me his wife Makyla was very jealous and didn't trust him. I told him to bring her along so she could see there was nothing to be jealous about – I am engaged and my fiancé and I have been together for five years."

But after a number of failed attempts to connect with Kevin, she Googled him and his obituary showed up.

"I was completely shocked. But this was in December, six months after his death, and I didn't feel comfortable posting a message on the newspaper's website. I also felt uncomfortable contacting the family since I didn't know you. I apologize."

"There is no need to apologize," I said. "I'm just glad I was able to find you. I just wanted to thank you for being an important part of Kevin's life and I wish we could have connected with each other last summer. We wanted to invite you to his memorial service."

We shared our memories of Kevin – poignant and painful. After I hung up, I emailed her the photo tribute we had sent out in July.

Date: Sunday, February 24, 2013 5:20:27 PM EST
From: Marcelina
To: Deena
Subject: News re Kevin Baxter (1976 - 2012)

Deena,

Thanks for reaching out - It was a pleasure speaking with you and please let me know if there is anything I can do. Meeting Kevin was a blessing and I will truly miss him. I have pictures in Italy you might like to have. I will send you copies next time I go home (probably in the summer).

All my love to you and Adam,
Marcelina

Finally, after many failed attempts, I felt a sense of closure on Kevin's behalf, being able to connect with his two ex-girlfriends, Maia and Marcelina, and his high school friend Tanner. Was this obsession healthy? The jury is out on that one, but I felt I owed it to Kevin and perhaps it was yet another way I tried to make sense of his sudden and total absence from our life.

FRIENDS IN NEED

"The truth is, everyone is going to hurt you. You just got to find the ones worth suffering for."

Bob Marley

Fractured, But Not Broken by John C.
How mental illness speaks to him – an awesome insight!
NAMI Anything Goes: Art-From-The-Heart Project

There were several instances where Adam and I experienced friends needing support from us. They deserved that support since they were living their own nightmares and were in need of compassion.

Carrie was the matron of honor at our wedding and she lives in Oregon. We have kept in contact periodically over the years, mostly by email, and traveled many roads together in 'parallel universes', separated by 3000+ miles. She was one of our friends I called in advance of blasting out the email with Kevin's obituary.

After telling her what happened, there was complete silence. And then…

"I have dreaded receiving a phone call like you got from Kevin's landlord, but it is only a matter of time," she said, her voice filled with such emotion and sadness I could feel it through the phone.

What followed was a long monologue of her attempts to help her oldest daughter get free of her addiction to cocaine. For more than ten years, her daughter's struggle with this addiction turned Carrie's life upside down, and she had never shared it with me.

I knew her daughter Lyndsey had two little girls, a toddler and a four-year-old, and although they lived together she refused to marry the father. It turns out both Lyndsey and her boyfriend were active addicts and Family Services had recently removed the girls from the home. This happened when the boyfriend was taking care of the girls and passed out from intoxication. In his case it was booze and pills – a lethal combination.

Carrie's youngest daughter Laura was in her early twenties and was granted legal guardianship of the girls while the family put Lyndsey in a residential rehab center – the umpteenth attempt to get her body detoxed and her life back on solid ground. After many failed attempts, the family wasn't sure Lyndsey would ever be able to get free from the clutches of her addiction. I could hear the fatigue and sense of resignation in Carrie's voice.

She cried intermittently as she shared details long locked inside. It explained why she rarely returned my phone calls. I knew all about her work life and the achievements of her husband Barry, their son Graham and daughter Laura. But I was shocked and saddened that for more than ten years she had been living this hell-on-Earth-that-would-not-end.

For close to two hours she poured her heart out.

"Why didn't you share this with me through all these years?" I asked. "You knew we were struggling with Kevin's ups and downs."

"I know. But I was just too ashamed. Lyndsey has been a challenge since she was fourteen. It has been such a nightmare. All those times you reached out to me, and I just couldn't tell you. It's been all-consuming and I don't have your strength or energy. Now my youngest daughter Laura – at twenty-one years old – has to give up her own dreams to be caretaker for her nieces. Barry and I couldn't take this on. Our main responsibility is to try to help Lyndsey recover so she can regain custody of her children. But of course we help Laura out with the girls all the time."

I ended the call with a heavy heart. I knew Carrie's husband had problems with substance abuse and lived on the edge, and perhaps this was yet another instance of the family's DNA paying it forward. The sad reality is that when a loved one choses to deal with their emotional and mental challenges by self-medicating, it creates chaos for the entire family. As cruel as it may sound to those looking in from the outside, the chaos can become so all-consuming and intense that you pray for it to end – in recovery or…a Call-From-Hell.

MEMBERSHIP ROLL-CALL BREAK
Story will resume shortly

"Families aren't easy to join. They're like an exclusive country club where membership makes impossible demands and the dues for an outsider are exorbitant."

Erma Bombeck

There were many other times when friends shared stories of family members with mental illness and/or substance abuse addictions. Our friend Logan, an attorney in Boston, told Adam about his stepson who was addicted to heroin and had a recent near-death episode in the ER.

I have an uncle who committed suicide; there were stories about my maternal grandmother's bouts with depression; one of my parents is an alcoholic and one of my siblings, too, and the rest of us have struggled with our own dysfunctional behavior. Adam's father dealt with severe depression and his brother got into drugs during the counter-culture years but is now addicted to AA and proud of it (and rightfully so!).

It amazed me how many families have been directly or indirectly affected by suicide, mental illness, and brain disorders; many managed with substance abuse. It seems it touches just about everybody – but it's often hidden in dark places. We found ourselves mutually commiserating with members of a club in which none of us sought to be a card-carrying member.

> *"Please accept my resignation. I don't want to belong to any club that will accept me as a member."*
>
> Julius *"Groucho"* Marx

THE BRAZIL CONNECTION

Reaching out to Kevin's circle of friends and colleagues was challenging enough without adding the additional dimensions of language barriers and distance.

One of the notes that Kevin left behind was the name and phone number of his friend Carlos. I didn't have his email but I at least had his mobile phone number and was able to reach him about two weeks after Kevin's death. Seems the police had contacted him immediately after they confiscated the notes so that is how he heard the news. Carlos was struggling to contain his emotions on the phone. I thanked him for his friendship with

Kevin and he expressed his deepest condolences. His English was halting but good enough that I came to understand they met at work and became good friends. I then understood who he was: Kevin had mentioned his friendship with a colleague who worked in Rio de Janeiro during the week and returned home to his wife and family in the south of Brazil on the weekends. Carlos was that friend.

He knew the history of Kevin's employment problems, the four-year gap between jobs, and the challenges he was having at this new company. He was in a difficult position because he was still working for the company and Kevin had been fired. He also knew the company was not providing a good job reference for him with prospective employers and he knew about the tensions Kevin was dealing with at home with Makyla. As he spoke he became so distraught I told him we didn't need to continue but I stayed on long enough for him to give me his email address. I sent him the obituary and tribute as well as our contact information and his response was very moving and personal.

There were several other people whose names and emails I was able to decipher from emails Kevin had sent to me. Most of these were from times I was helping him expand his network during his long job searches and he was seeking my advice. He was in a holding pattern with many of them, waiting to receive follow-up interviews with them or others in their organization and/or requests for him to contact them in the near future. There were also some headhunters with whom he was working. I sent them an email with the news and heard from almost all of them. They appreciated knowing and were saddened by the news.

Neither Adam nor I knew the divorce lawyer with whom Kevin was working and were unable to let her know. Perhaps Kevin had sent her an email on the last day of his life? We will never know for sure but I hadn't received an update from Robert about her showing up on Friday to deliver the divorce papers to Makyla, and I was sure he would have let me know – in intimate detail and with the appropriate histrionics. Additionally, we hadn't been contacted about any outstanding bill for the work she had done, but she may have demanded a retainer up-front.

Several of his networking connections through the University of Chicago alumni office and other avenues resulted in meetings with U.S. ex-pats who had long and successful careers in Brazil. This led to Kevin being connected to the large and well-connected Jewish business and religious community in Rio de Janeiro. For months he kept us updated on these relationships and we were quite surprised when he befriended some people who were active in the Chabad.

According to Wikipedia, "Chabad-Lubavitch is a Hasidic movement in Orthodox Judaism. One of the world's larger and best-known Hasidic movements, its official headquarters is in the Crown Heights section of Brooklyn, New York. The organization is the largest Jewish organization in the world today, and a powerful force within Judaism. Chabad maintains institutions in over 1000 cities around the world. By 2010, there were an estimated 3,600 Chabad Institutions worldwide, in seventy countries, providing outreach and educational activities for Jews through Jewish community centers, synagogues, schools and camps. 1,350 institutions were listed in the Chabad directory as of 2007. The movement has over 200,000 adherents, and up to one million Jews attend Chabad services at least once a year. Chabad's adherents follow Chabad traditions and prayer services based on Lurianic kabbalah."[5]

For us "Chabad-nicks" were a cult-like sect but we also realized Kevin needed a sense of community to help him stay grounded. I kidded him in a playful way, "Hey, kiddo, your father is a bit concerned you're going from one extreme to the other. It would be a good idea if you keep me in the loop should you decide to adopt their traditional 1800s garb. I want to prepare your father for your arrival should you be wearing a long black tunic, beard, top hat and pais (long side curls)." He assured me he would keep me posted.

I was able to find two names and email addresses for his Chabad contacts – Nate and Richard; three weeks after Kevin's death I sent them a personal note introducing myself and including Kevin's obituary.

Date: Friday, July 27, 2012 12:38 PM
From: Deena
To: Nate and Richard
Subject: Update re Kevin Baxter

Dear Nate and Richard,

My stepson, Kevin Baxter, let me know how helpful you were when he contacted you several months ago. I wanted you to know what had happened to Kevin and am sad to send this in an email, but I wanted to thank you for the help you extended to him.

Kind regards,
Deena Baxter

At 2:30pm the phone rang and I found myself listening to a painful wail on the other end of the phone. It was Richard and he was sobbing uncontrollably. I had barely identified myself when he poured out his anguish.

"She killed him didn't she? His wife – she killed him." And a slew of vindictive profanities followed.

I didn't know whether to hang up or not but I simply couldn't let that line of thinking go unaddressed. I assured him that was not the case, that Kevin took his life when Makyla was at work. At first he challenged me but when I finally got him calmed down, he put his hand over the phone and was talking to someone. Again, I heard yet another wrenching wail, this one from his wife Sonya.

I encouraged her to pick up an extension and updated both of them. They felt personally responsible for Kevin's death. They recognized his loneliness and welcomed him into their home and their life with open arms. He spent time with them and Richard used to invite Kevin on afternoon walks with his dog as they toured some of the galleries and shops in the Chabad neighborhood. In-between sobs, they shared their heartache. Since it was Friday, they were leaving soon for shul (Friday evening service welcoming the Sabbath) and Richard promised to send me the name and contact information of the rabbi at the Chabad, who knew Kevin. The rabbi was from Brooklyn, NY, and as it turned out, Richard was, too.

They ended the call with Sonya saying, "Richard, it is time for you to rest and take your medicine. You must get off the phone." It was like she was talking to a child.

A week later, Richard sent me the contact information for the rabbi and also called again. This time he told me about his life, a sad tale of a person who suffered from severe depression and epilepsy and moved to Brazil in the 1990s. He had been divorced and was now remarried to Sonya, who nursed him lovingly and mothered him like a child. I was happy he had found such a wonderful caregiver and life partner. But flashes of anger continued to spew from him and I felt it was in his best interest (and mine) to end our communication since it brought him so much pain – and me, too. By this time, I also had been receiving other information about Kevin's home life that gave me a more balanced view of his relationship with Makyla, and Richard only had heard Kevin's version. Perhaps you have heard the expression "No sense in beating a dead horse." Here was one instance where that applied.

He called once more but I didn't take the call. He did send me a lovely photo of Kevin and himself with his dog, and a young man who owned the gallery they were visiting. I responded by thanking him and encouraging him to hold those memories near to his heart.

CALMS IN THE STORM

"Friends are relatives you make for yourself."

Eustache Deschamps

Stress Less by Ana
"Relaxation--take all the stress out. That's how the ocean makes me feel."
NAMI Anything Goes: Art-From-The-Heart Project

I have two friends, Karen and Marla, who are successful local business-women and special people in my life. They also happen to be sisters who have been working together most of their adult lives. I know and admire them, their families, and their parents, too. Sitting by my computer as I type this is a photo of the three of us plus another of their friends at Karen's 50th birthday celebration with the goofy blinking headband and pink boa I gave her. The four of us are smiling ear-to-ear. They sent a bountiful fruit-and-goodies basket – more like a hamper – filled with so many treats it was like finding a treasure chest on your doorstep. I knew they had lost their brother twenty years ago in a tragic accident in Brazil, and it was comforting to be able to talk to them. We met twice for coffee within three weeks of Kevin's death – I stopped to pick them up at their fabulous accessories boutique, and it's impossible to stay in a funk long-term when you walk into the store. The positive, energetic and colorful ambience brightens even the gloomiest of spirits. They shared valuable insights about the legal obstacles and bureaucracy in Brazil, and the ten-year effort to repatriate their brother's remains, assets and accompanying paperwork.

My niece Jessica is another ray of sunshine in my life. She was home over the summer, having completed her freshman year at college and about to start her sophomore year as a transfer student at Emerson College in Boston. I was thrilled she applied and was accepted, and we had two long, meaningful chats over the summer. She is wise beyond her years, and has been through family challenges of her own. This seems to have made her stronger and given her insights not often found in a person not yet twenty years old. I loved our chats about her career plans, college experiences, summer jobs, and more. When I flew to Boston to take care of my granddaughters over Columbus Day weekend, she stopped in for a long visit, staying for the afternoon and early evening. We had so much fun together.

And speaking of my granddaughters, they are gifts from my beloved son Jon and his lovely wife Jacqueline - seven-year-old Jesslyn and five-year-old Janelle. To them, I am "Nonie" (pronounced NO-knee) and they are two precious gems in my life that fill my heart and soul with smiles. Thank heavens for SKYPE and the wonders of modern technology!

MEDITATION
BREAK

Story will resume shortly

"You are not your mind. Compulsive thinking is the greatest obstacle. It is not necessary to think all the time. Whenever you step out of the noise of thinking, that is meditation, and a different state of consciousness arises."

Eckhart Tolle, "The Power of Now"[6]

On my personal journey to repair my own dysfunctional DNA over the years, I flunked Meditation 101 and Yoga 101 three times - along with bridge and tennis. In early September I saw an announcement in the UU congregation newsletter about a bi-weekly Eckhart Tolle meditation study group. I wasn't familiar with his teachings but I contacted the coordinator and signed up. It was held on Saturday afternoons at the congregation's social room. We watched one of Tolle's workshops on DVD followed by a ten-minute meditation session. It was the first time a spiritual master really spoke to me in a language I could understand. Unlike so many others who present themselves as a prophet coming down from the mountaintop with The Word, he didn't put himself on a pedestal. His self-effacing humor and realism appealed to me and opened me to a whole new world view – a way of thinking about the elements of time, pain and suffering that I found profoundly healing.

I didn't want to wait another two weeks to hear more of his teachings, so I went on the website of our local library and found many of Tolle's books, CD sets and DVDs. Ever since, I have been taking out a different CD series and each night listen to 20-30 minutes of his various programs. I put on my headset and listen to his soothing voice and intermittent chuckles and get my daily dose of "ET". It is helping me live for the present moment. Am I there yet? Heck no – that's like saying you have traveled to the end of the Information Superhighway – the World Wide Web.

I was reminded of how far I have to go when I contrasted Eckhart Tolle's concept of "the present moment – the *now*" being timeless, formless, and worth sitting still to fully enjoy and embrace with Mike Libecki's *"now"*. As he and his buddy restlessly waited for the right moment to scale a treacherous steep pillar of rock in Antarctica, surrounded by icy winds blowing at high velocity, daredevil Libecki announced: "You know, my grandmother told me the time is now. I got that from her. We used to ask, 'Grandma Bertha, what time is it?' And she'd say, 'The time is now, goddamn it!'" Nike said it, too: "Just Do It!" Come to think of it, so did Kevin Baxter!

Yes, I have a long way to go, but I am working hard at it and it's not like checking off a task on a To Do List. You should worry if you find me perched in a meditative pose on a mountaintop in Tibet (or on a treacherous peak in Antarctica). That's a signal that I have totally lost all sense of reality and need you to rescue me - real fast. I'll cover your airfare and the cost of the Sherpa guides who will bring you to the mountaintop. I will be waiting…

> *"The statistics on sanity are that one out of every four Americans is suffering from some form of mental illness. Think of your three best friends. If they're okay, then it's you."*

Rita Mae Brown

WELCOME TO BRAZIL

"Culture clash is terrific drama."

Ken Follett

I experienced the wonders of Brazil long before Kevin fell in love with the culture and the country. Beginning in the mid-1990s I was program manager for an international research program at the Massachusetts Institute of Technology, until 2005. In 1995 and 1996, I visited Brazil to plan and manage one of our sponsor and researcher meetings as well as a one-day workshop for the Brazil manufacturers and suppliers.

During these two trips, each lasting two weeks, I was inspired by the positive energy of this emerging economy and the hard working men and women who were determined to succeed and very proud of their work-in-progress.

The multi-national company that hosted our banquet rolled out the Red Carpet and brought in the mulatas. These gorgeous, scantily-clad, Amazon size dancers were adorned in their magnificent costumes from Mardi Gras in Rio, where dance contests are high-stakes competitions. These dancers invest a major part of their free time and treasure in dance lessons and costumes. With enough wine, coaxing, and encouragement from the dancers who invited our international group of executives and academics to join them, we spent the evening enjoying the music and new dance steps.

I also got a taste of the corruption – the bills left unpaid by the Brazilian companies who were supposed to be underwriting the meeting, the revenue-sharing for the one day workshop that never materialized, and major visa problems selectively targeting our wealthier U.S. sponsors. Back in the mid-1990s Brazil was considered an emerging country but at the time, there were political tensions between the U.S. and Brazil that manifested themselves in tough visa requirements. I sent all our sponsors and researchers detailed information about these strict requirements, urging them to be sure they were compliant with the required travel documents for entering and exiting Brazil. Each country had different requirements and I sent those as well. To cover all the bases, I also sent the information to the staff assistants of our senior executives and government bureaucrats.

One sponsor from IBM arrived on a flight from New York at 5am on the first day of the conference. He didn't have the proper documents and, although I tried to intervene on his behalf, he was put on the next plane back to the U.S., which happened to be going to Dallas, not New York City. Brazilian immigration didn't give a hoot: in fact, they savored putting a high level U.S. executive right back on the plane.

Two of our young Chinese researchers were living in Japan and studying at the University of Tokyo. Their advisor was one of our most esteemed faculty professors - revered in the academic world as well as the government, where he held a senior appointment at the Japan Ministry of International Trade and Industry (MITI). The researchers naively routed through JFK airport in New York City and since the U.S. had no diplomatic relations with China at the time, they were given a choice of being immediately deported to China or Brazil. They chose Brazil, and were greeted by immigration upon arrival and told they would not be allowed to leave the country without the proper travel documents. When I investigated it further the Brazilian customs office told me it would take six weeks to get the paperwork processed. Thinking it would make a difference if I went in person, the gentleman I spoke with said sure, he could expedite the process, and wrote on a piece of paper what amounted to USD $2,000: a bribe.

"That is against the law in the U.S.," I said. Although I knew the 'you-grease-my-palms-I'll-grease-your-palms' practice was alive and well in Corporate America, under the guise of 'consulting fees', it would not pass muster with MIT, or me.

"Well, that's what it will take. Otherwise you will have to stay here with the two students for six weeks and think how much that will cost." He was really enjoying himself, sticking it to an American.

Thankfully, I had taken the business card of a government official at a pre-meeting dinner the night before, and called his office. Although he was from a different province, he helped me break through the mounds of red tape. For three days I spent hours working through all the details. At 6am on the last day of the conference I was instructed to bring the two students to a local government office in the city, a ninety-minute drive from the conference site. There we met with a woman who happened to be Asian. The two students were communicating in Mandarin, not realizing the agent was fluent in the language. She reamed them over the coals for being so irresponsible, told them she couldn't believe they were so stupid to take such a risk with the penalty of imprisonment, and questioned their credentials as Ph.D. students. They were suitably humbled. She made them suffer as she continued to humiliate them, but she sure got her point across. Thankfully, she finally gave them their official travel documents. They were very quiet on the ride back to the conference.

All this came flooding back to me when I met my friends Karen and Maria for coffee and they told me about dealing with Brazil when their brother died in 1993. In their case, their brother was teaching in Brazil and was in a freak dune buggy accident with his new girlfriend. The driver of the dune buggy was unlicensed, although the rental company represented him otherwise.

They sued the rental company, paid exorbitant legal fees, and made frequent trips to Brazil for court appearances where the judge made them sit till the end of the day and then delayed the hearing for three months. The next time, he delayed it for six months and then he did this again. They were sure their lawyer was giving kickbacks to the judge as the clock kept ticking and the legal fees kept mounting – a fine example of dysfunctional DNA going global.

"They had no incentive to settle," Karen said. "They think all Americans are rich and they are masterful at playing this game. There is a whole sub-economy that works this way, with many people on the take. We experienced it everywhere. It wouldn't have surprised us if the rental company was paying the judge under the table to drag the whole case out in hopes we would drop the suits."

Maria added, "Our brother had been married to a Brazilian and divorced, and his ex-wife was, at that time, living in the U.S. She was wonderful. If it hadn't been for her, we would probably still be trying to resolve the law suits that resulted from his death."

When I returned from our meeting I immediately called Natalie at the U.S. Embassy in Brazil. She assured me all the funeral homes and other vendors they worked with did not engage in such practices – well, maybe not outright bribes but, as I soon discovered, there were 'gray areas'.

A GOOGLE BREAK
Story will resume shortly

"Publication is a self-invasion of privacy."

Marshall McLuhan

The quote from Mr. McLuhan was relevant before the Internet Age, but in today's world privacy regulations have been compromised and turned upside down with Facebook, Wikileaks, Twitter, LinkedIn and online GPS sites

– like Google Maps. It all depends on who is the hunter and who is being hunted.

Shortly after Natalie confirmed Kevin's burial in Silveiras, Brazil, there was a news frenzy surrounding Google's use of their GPS tracking capability to gather, warehouse, and use information on people's home sites. Back in 2007, shortly after we moved to our new home in Southwest Florida, Adam's Uncle Alvin found our street on Google Maps when we were visiting him and his wife in New Jersey. But it was an older site map of our development and didn't yet have houses built on several lots, including ours. The technology had advanced significantly in the intervening five years, was more widespread, and now had other competitors entering the field, like Apple's failed attempt at a map application. The media questioned this level of data mining, some viewing it as an invasion of privacy, and others as effective data sharing. Welcome to the Digital Divide: those championing totally open sharing of personal information and those demanding personal information privacy protection.

When we received the news from Natalie that Kevin was buried in conformance with Brazilian burial customs, thoughts about the Digital Divide were not keeping me awake, but it did open an opportunity. I crept out of bed, tiptoed to my office, sat down at my computer and logged on to Google Maps.

First I located the apartment building where Kevin and Makyla lived – the building that Robert owned. It was in a residential section of Rio de Janeiro. It took a bit of time, but I was able to locate Makyla's hometown of Silveiras and the street where the cemetery was supposed to be located. The address didn't exactly align with the map coordinates but with persistence and patience, I was able to virtually stand on the street facing the cemetery and view the gravesites across a small berm. No, it didn't look like a U.S. cemetery with funeral plots spread over grassed space, it looked like many of the cemeteries I saw in Greece, Italy, and Spain, with gravesites adjacent to each other, clustered together to make the best use of limited space, with a mix of above ground crypts, small mausoleums, and underground sites with small grave markers. Since Brazil is a Catholic country, many of the markers were adorned with crosses – large and small.

Google Maps has a feature that allows the mini-figure to pivot 360 degrees and zoom in and out of the viewing area. There I stood, in mini-fig form, feeling comforted that our son Kevin was laid to rest in this very place. I clicked on iTunes and played the first song that was in my Most Favorite Playlist, Eva Cassidy's version of "Songbird", and listened to it as I sat in silence and took in the scene 4400 miles away. That was followed by another of my favorites, Elton John singing "Daniel". I came close to actually crying... almost.

Then the Virtual Mini-fig Me continued walking into the center of town, strolled down the main street viewing the shops and small ma-and-pa restaurants and bistros, took a left and walked up to the house where Makyla and her daughter were temporarily living with her brother.

"Makyla, our Kevin is at rest, he has found peace," I whispered, "he is out of pain. May you someday be comforted by that and find strength to make a good life for yourself and your daughter."

> *"There's no way for them to take away my sadness, but they can make sure I am not empty of all the other feelings."*
>
> *David Levithan,* Love Is the Higher Law

Adam was up before the birds started chirping – and once again he was surprised to see the light on in my office. He came up behind me and gave me a shoulder rub, an affectionate gesture he does periodically and it always makes me purr.

"What's wrong? It's the middle of the night for you, what are you doing?" he asked.

"You're not going to believe what I found on Google Maps! I toured the street where Kevin and Makyla lived in Rio de Janeiro, found the town of Silveiras, and the cemetery where Kevin is buried. Want to see it?"

Adam's face said it all: It was clear he didn't. "It will just upset me," he said.

"Hun, I actually think it will do just the opposite. I think it will bring some comfort to you to know where he is laid to rest. For what it's worth, it did so for me. I feel much better now that I've actually viewed it. It's not like Rosewood Memorial or where your father and his family are buried, with space and lots of grass and flowers surrounding each grave, but it's like many of the cemeteries we saw in Italy."

I suggested he finish making his morning coffee and come back with it in hand and sit at my computer. "I need a bit of time to pull up the maps. I saved the coordinates."

I was right; it was comforting, but emotional, too, as I gave him a brief tour of the gravesites. For him, the tears flowed and it was my turn to gently run his shoulders and give him a hug. Then I showed him where Makyla's family lived, and the town center. He wasn't interested in seeing their apartment in Rio de Janeiro, and I respected that. The next time we spoke to Brian we mentioned it and I emailed him the map coordinates.

After a two-week break, I received an email from Robert. I hesitated to open it, fearing more gossip and gore.

Date: Tuesday, July 24, 2012 2:39:23 PM EDT
From: Robert
To: Deena
Subject: Contents of Kevin's apartment

Deena,

Today I visited Kevin's apartment for the first time. Makyla went to Silveiras and took the key, so I had another one made. The apt is full of nice little touches, including two menorahs on the kitchen counter, and his diploma from U. of Chicago and from another institution hanging on the wall. I have no idea what Makyla plans to do with these things, but it would be sad if she threw them away. I forgot to check if he put a mezuzah beside the front door, but since

your other stepson said that he was religious, perhaps he did. Ma-
kyla plans to move everything out of the apt on July 31.

Robert

I was torn by his actions: entering the apartment without Makyla's permission when it was still legally rented through July 31st, yet moved by his
concern about saving mementos that might have meaning for Kevin's family.
Yes, he owned the building but it was also his busybody nature that was at
work. I chose to take the high road.

Date: Tuesday, July 24, 2012, 4:21 PM
From: Deena
To: Robert

Robert - Thanks for letting me know. I ran this by my husband
and Kevin's brother and they don't want anything. It is fine to let
Makyla take all the contents of their apartment when she vacates it
on July 31st. Please promise me that you will <u>not</u> share the 'gory de-
tails' of Kevin's last day with my husband or Kevin's brother. Read-
ing it upset me and gave me nightmares, and it would really set
them back, as it did me. We are working hard to move forward as
best we can.

Thanks again,
Deena

Date: Tuesday, July 24, 2012 3:47:25 PM EDT
From: Robert
To: Deena

Deena, Don't worry. I don't intend to communicate with them. I
have decided to sell the apt building, since this was an upsetting ex-
perience for me.

Robert

Date: Tuesday, July 24, 2012 10:32:08 PM EDT
To: Robert
From: Deena
Subject: Thanks and my wishes for you

Robert - I am so very sorry to hear that, and to find that this tragedy has impacted so many people, including you. Again, thanks so very much for all you did to help us. I wish you well and I hope you live 25 more years with a great quality of life, too. You mentioned weeks ago during one of our chats that you will be celebrating a birthday soon. May you have a happy birthday, whenever that may be.

Kind regards,
Deena

TWO STEPS FORWARD, ONE STEP BACK

Four days later, Brian called to inform us he changed his mind about leaving Kevin's remains in Brazil. Since we purchased the cemetery plot at Rosewood Memorial Park, close to his mother's grave, he now wanted to bring Kevin home. Adam and I were emotionally exhausted from the volatility of the past 3+ weeks. We were united on this and told Brian we would not get involved with the Brazilian courts and felt it was unfair to push this with Makyla who was in an emotionally unstable state. To add a dose of reality to this, we limited the amount of money we were willing to invest in what would be at a minimum a three-year drawn out process. I provided Brian with the contact information for Natalie Martin at the Embassy's ACSU office and since he requested it, Robert's contact information as well. Brian immediately contacted both of them.

Date: Monday, July 30, 2012 10:56:19 PM EDT
From: Robert
To: Brian
CC: Deena

Subject: Kevin Baxter

Hello Brian,

I will try to help you to the best of my ability. I don't have an address for Makyla, nor do I expect to be speaking with her, since she moved out of the apt late last week. She may still have Kevin's cell phone working, but I don't know.

Frankly, I should warn you that I don't believe very much in what Makyla says. She told me that she would be willing to provide a power of attorney, to leave the family to make all of the decisions. Then Deena told me that she buried him in Silveiras, her home-town. According to Deena, the American consulate informed her that there is a law in Brazil stating that a body cannot be exhumed for three years after it is buried. I suppose the consulate knows this fact.

I have two attorneys that I can recommend. One is my current attorney, who claims to speak English, although I have never spoken with him in English. He is an elderly gent, whose address I have already sent to Deena, but I would be willing to send it to you. He is quite reasonable with his charges. The other is my former attorney that I dealt with when I was transferring my "modest" assets from the U.S. to Brazil. I know for sure that he speaks and writes English, because he can correspond in English. His problem is that he is not cheap, and that's why I changed attorneys. Let me know whether you want one or the other, or both addresses and phone numbers.

Should you decide to come down here to personally resolve the problem, you are welcome to stay in my guest bedroom, and I will act as your interpreter whenever necessary. There would be no charge for this, since if it were my family, I would do the same thing. Deena has been very nice to me.

Let me know.

Robert

Date: July 30, 2012 10:56:19 PM EDT
From: Deena
To: Robert
Subject: Your kind response to Brian Re: Kevin Baxter

Robert - Thanks for copying me and thanks for trying to help Brian. My husband and I are <u>not</u> encouraging him to pursue this but he feels strongly that he should at least try and we respect his decision. Your offer to help him should he come to Brazil was most generous and kind and not something you should feel obligated to do. You have done so much to help us and we are very appreciative.

Kindest regards,
Deena

Brian spoke with one of the recommended attorneys in Brazil and with Natalie at the Embassy and she was not encouraging. She told him if the lawyer was able to get Makyla to sign a release for Kevin's remains, it couldn't be brought before a judge for three years.

"During that time, she could change her mind or the judge could simply feel you had brought undue pressure on her when she was under extreme duress, and prevent you from exhuming his remains. You would also need to have his body embalmed and after three years it will be difficult to get any funeral company to handle that. All the paperwork will require additional delays and expenses and then there will be a long process to clear customs entering the U.S."

Natalie called me and delivered the same message, adding, "Deena, in all the years I have worked here, me and my colleagues have never seen this work favorably for the family unless there was a Will in place. And once again I'll stress that the Brazilian court system will favor Makyla, since she is legally his next-of-kin and a natural born citizen of Brazil. The legal fees and expenses involved will be astronomical, and a favorable outcome is highly unlikely."

Adam asked me to share with Brian, my friends' experience with their brother's death and the ten-year legal fight with marginal outcome, plus my own experience of the corruption and red tape, which I did. But in closing I added, "Brian, I encourage you to find your own peace of mind. I do not want you to live the rest of your life with regrets related to Kevin. Promise me, you will take the time you need to find that inner peace."

Two days later, Brian called and let Adam know he had spoken yet again with the lawyer and with Natalie. "I'm not going to pursue it. I would need to go through the process with Makyla and the court system now and three years from now and I don't want this dragging out for years."

Were we relieved? Not really. We were sad and resigned to the situation, as it existed not as Kevin wished it to be. It was out of our hands to make his wish a reality. What we did agree on was the possibility of moving Kevin to a single plot within the same cemetery, rather than have him in a shared gravesite with three other people.

But that wasn't as easy as we hoped. When I asked Natalie about this she got back to me with additional information.

"Some public cemeteries do have single plots as well as stacked plots similar to Kevin's. Unfortunately this particular cemetery doesn't have separate spaces. We asked the cemetery to recommend one or two private cemeteries for you to contact but there aren't any. The closest one is in the city of Rio de Janeiro, and that is three hours away. It is unlikely Makyla will allow this. It was very important to her and to her family to have him in Silveiras. And you would have to wait three years to start the process under any circumstances. Once again, you will run into the problem of getting her to agree and a judge to approve this."

We dropped that idea like a hot potato.

COMMUNICATION BREAK (DOWN)

Story will resume shortly

"We're sorry. You have reached an imaginary number. Please rotate your phone 90 degrees and try again."

Anonymous

On August 1st, I was unable to call any of the numbers in Brazil that worked the day before, not just Embassy phone lines but also Makyla's phone and several other numbers of Kevin's colleagues I was trying to contact. A recording came on – in Portuguese, not English. Maybe Venezuela's President Hugo Chavez invaded Brazil or a military coup took over the country in the dark of night? (Okay – this was a bit of a stretch by that's what happens when you are exhausted.) I checked online to see if there were any news updates about an infrastructure failure or cyber-attack, but nothing surfaced. I sent an email to Natalie and received an auto-reply that she was at a conference for the next three days. It wasn't until the next week that she got back to me with the news.

"They are rolling out new phone numbers over the next eight weeks, in stages. You have to add a nine before the city code. Most people live in the metropolitan Rio de Janeiro area and don't need to dial the extra digit and most don't even know this has happened. The phone company didn't do a very good job of communicating this change – many of our phone lines have been pretty quiet the past few days." No kidding!

Over the next couple of weeks, I dialed most numbers twice – with the extra nine and if that didn't work, without it. Makyla didn't even know about this change until I sent her an email with the update, and also mentioned that I was trying to call her.

Within days of losing Kevin, we asked Natalie to make sure Makyla was told about two of Kevin's assets: his bonus from work and a tax refund due from the Brazilian government. We had no information about his bank account(s) or anything having to do with his finances, but he had mentioned the bonus was sent by wire transfer to his personal checking account. At my suggestion, Makyla contacted his former employer to get the bank routing information. She provided an official death certificate for Kevin but the funds were impounded. It took eighteen months to get access to those funds.

Obstacles also came from the U.S. Adam knew Kevin had an account at Fidelity because the annual statements were being sent, care of our address. Kevin wasn't sure what it related to but it was $3,700 and he told us to just keep the statements so he would have a record of the account. We thought it would be a simple process, completing the paperwork with Fidelity and having them wire the money to Makyla. It ended up taking eight months and eighteen pages of forms, with most of the delays coming from the bank in Brazil, before Makyla had access to the funds. After her bank applied substantial "transfer fees", she received $1,700.

THE KEVIN TÚMULO

When Natalie gave me the brief tutorial about burial customs and traditions in Brazil she mentioned that Makyla planned to get a grave marker "in the future". Now that we had made what we hoped were final decisions about leaving Kevin's remains right where they rested in the stacked plot in Silveiras, Adam and I wanted to find out how we could go about having a marker made for him. Since we had just gone through the process of ordering one for Kevin's space at Rosewood Memorial Park, we hoped to get something similar for Kevin in Brazil.

We thought doing the right thing for Kevin and Makyla would be simple. Not so fast, sports fans…

Before contacting Makyla we thought it made sense to get more information from Natalie. On August 1st I contacted her. After several days she got back to me with the information.

"Since the cemetery where Kevin is buried does not create headstones, Makyla will need to place the order for that with an outside company. In Brazil, the custom is not to wait for a year to place a headstone and have an unveiling. Once the person is buried, then the order is placed and when it is finished it is installed over the grave without any ceremony. It is not unusual to wait to have the headstone ordered and put in place at a later time, when it is affordable, but there is no set time."

She also let me know the ACSU office would not be able to help us with this transaction since this was Makyla's right to do this as his wife.

That was helpful. There are only a few companies in the U.S. who manufacture bronze casting grave markers mounted in granite, one being the company who was doing it for Rosewood Memorial Park. There were several online companies who promoted engraved granite markers but when I contacted them, none had subsidiaries in Brazil and none could ship overseas. We could have it delivered to us and ship it, but most likely that would have been prohibitively expensive and we would have had to deal with customs delays and those infamous "fees".

I had been communicating with Makyla; checking with her periodically by email and phone, when possible, to see how she was doing and to check on the progress tracking down Kevin's bonus and tax refund. I always included that I hoped she would be able to get back on her feet, move back to Rio de Janeiro and resume her college studies.

The day I heard from Natalie about the grave marker, I also received a lengthy email from Makyla about missing 'my Kevin, the love of my life', how her whole family loved him and wanted him to remain in Brazil, and that it wasn't just her wish but the wishes of her family as well that made her reverse her decision on July 6th. What surprised me was her update about how the family paid for the burial. According to her, the family pooled their resources but it was only to cover the initial payment, 30 percent of the total that was the minimum required for the funeral company to enter into a contract. Makyla was responsible for the remaining payments and was working in a town nearby, that wasn't easy to get to, getting paid 'under the table'.

Although Adam was still upset about her not allowing Kevin to be buried in the U.S., we were in agreement that we didn't want Makyla dealing with this additional burden. I called her and although there was the language barrier some things did get through. Just to be sure, I followed up with an email in English with Portuguese translation.

Date: Thu, 16 Aug 2012 12:47:40 -0400

From: Deena

To: Makyla

Subject: Our gift to honor Kevin and to help you

Dear Makyla,

I am glad I called you and you are doing a little better. As you know, Brian, Adam and I hoped to have Kevin's remains returned to the U.S. We understand you and your family loved him and will find much comfort having him buried at Cemiterio Jardim da Angels in Silveiras, close to you. We are comforted knowing Kevin lies in peace in the country where he hoped to achieve all his dreams.

We would like to move forward with our life, and Adam and I would like you to be able to do that, too. To help you, we would like to send you Brazilian Reals $_____ to cover the full cost of Kevin's funeral. Please let me know the best way to wire transfer this to you. I believe this can be sent to the Western Union office closest to Silveiras. Please let me know their routing information.

We would also like to place a marker on Kevin's grave. Would you give us permission to do this? We would like to get a granite headstone that would be engraved with a simple inscription in English. We would need your permission to do this and we would cover the cost of ordering this and placing it on his grave. If this is acceptable to you, please let me know. We want you to be able to move on with your life and we hope this will help all of us honor Kevin's memory and move forward with our lives.

Love, Deena

Date: Thu, 16 Aug 2012 1:22:42 PM EDT

From: Makyla

To: Deena

Subject: Your gift

Hello dear family of my beloved Kevin! Every week I will visit the Kevin Túmulo. Yes I'd love to put a headstone in memory of him, but do not know how. You have to contact the cemetery for information for the Kevin Túmulo. THANKS A LOT FOR THE SUPPORT.

For Western Union (BANK OF BRAZIL), My Documents CP-Fxxxxyyyyyzzzz RG

HUGS AND LOVE!

AN EVEN BREAK
Story will resume shortly

"Sadness flies on the wings of the morning and out of the heart of darkness comes the light."

Jean Giraudoux

Compassion has its own rewards. By helping others we help ourselves. And in the process, Adam and I could only chuckle at the prospect of "The Kevin Túmulo" somewhere in Brazil – like The Great Pyramid of Giza – minus the Sphinx.

Since we had Makyla's permission in writing, we wasted no time in moving forward. I contacted the cemetery but could find nobody who spoke one word of English. We already knew from Natalie's update that we would have to contract the grave marker with an outside company, not the cemetery. But we had no idea whether they worked with their own preferred vendor, or what restrictions they had on the size and type of marker for a plot where four people were buried.

Perhaps the list of funeral homes Natalie had sent me in July would be able to guide me? No luck there - half of them had phone numbers that were no longer valid, and the two that were valid turned out to be personal cell phones of the people who owned the small Ma and Pa businesses but they, too, did not speak English, and they were all in Rio, not in Silvieras.

I called two of my colleagues from MIT who were Brazilians – one lived in the U.S. and one in Brazil. But after talking with them I ran into brick walls: my colleague in Brazil, Jose, was spending a sabbatical year in the UK, and Mario happened to be spending the month on vacation back home in Rio but his leads didn't work out, and I didn't want to bother him further.

As a last resort, I called and left a message for Natalie at the ACSU letting her know we had written permission from Makyla to get a marker, my failed attempts to locate a manufacturer, and if her office could just put me in contact with a company for the grave marker that had an English-speaking employee I would take it from there.

Her response arrived after the weekend and it took me by surprise. "I got your message on Friday and I wanted to let you know that we've contacted a few funeral homes on your behalf but unfortunately none of them can arrange for the headstone. Apparently, in Brazil this is typically done by specialty shops, which are often located near cemeteries. We contacted the specialty shop closest to the cemetery in Silveiras and when we hear back I'll let you know. We won't be able to handle the details of getting the permission from Makyla for approval of the specific marker or the payment, but we should be able to provide you with some samples and the contact information for the shop. At that point, it would be best if you could get a friend to translate or work through a local lawyer here."

I certainly hadn't expected her to do this on our behalf. But I was soon to find out why. As luck would have it, her boss had received my email thanking the ACSU office, and Natalie in particular, for the compassionate and outstanding service they had given Brian, Adam and me over the prior four weeks. In spite of the outcome, I told him we appreciated Natalie's responsiveness and professionalism. He not only sent me back a lovely email, but unbeknownst to me, let Natalie know she could continue helping us in any way we needed. And so, once again, her team helped us work with the vendor who, of course, happened to be a relative of the owner of the cemetery, and acted as our intermediary.

After much back-and-forth, we were able to work with Makyla and the company, to place the order for the marker. We wanted to keep it understated, not excessive like some of the monoliths that were visible when we viewed the cemetery on Google Maps. Makyla was leaning towards the latter for the Kevin Túmulo but we were able to reach a compromise.

There was a maximum size limit allowed, so that added a bit of reality, and the company recommended a porcelain plaque. What didn't make sense was how the plaque would be set on top of the grave. We wanted a granite base but they assured us they set it on the grave and all was included in the price. Just to be sure I included in the written order that the price *included* mounting and installation on the grave. They delayed the order until payment was received, which I sent by Western Union.

And then of course, there was yet another Brazilian Surprise...two, actually: one death-affirming (and no surprise), the other one life-affirming (big surprise).

Date: September 26, 2012 10:14:02 AM EDT
From: Natalie
To: Deena. CC: Theresa Mayeles

Hi Deena - I've attached several pictures of the grave marker. In order to install the plaque, the shop had to contract another worker to build a grave marker stand. They were unaware beforehand that they would have to do this. Unfortunately they didn't consult with us about the price or style beforehand, but I believe this is really the only style available for that cemetery. The cost for building the stand is Brazilian Reals $_____. They would like you to pay for the cost of the stand the same way you paid previously. They have already installed it over Kevin's grave. The flowers in the photograph they placed there as a gesture of their sympathy.

I'm also cc'ing my colleague Theresa Mayeles here, as this is my last day in the office before maternity leave. If you have any follow-up questions or concerns please feel free to get in touch with Theresa.

Best, Natalie

"Some people never go crazy. What truly horrible lives they must lead."

Charles Bukowski

RELIGION: BELIEVERS AND NON-BELIEVERS

"I know God won't give me anything I can't handle. I just wish he didn't trust me so much."

Mother Teresa

THE MEANING OF DEATH

Concepts of life and death and their respective meanings are influenced by a person's religious upbringing, education, and life experiences.

When I was a young child, our housekeeper, who was from Honduras, brought me to her AME church on a Sunday morning during a service that also included a funeral for a church elder. To this day I have never forgotten the impact of the spirituals, and gospel music brought from the home country. They were sung in a local patois by a choir whose voices were filled with such emotion, pain, reverence and majesty; I just stood in awe, holding tightly to our housekeeper's hand. The voices and music filled every inch of space and beyond: people swaying in unison with tears streaming down their faces.

On the bus ride home, I asked, "When I grow up, can I be black and sing like that? I really want to sing like that. Will you teach me?" She just smiled and tousled my hair. The closest I ever came to hearing music performed like that was when the Edwin Hawkins Singers released their single in 1967, "Oh Happy Day".

By being respectful and tolerant of diverse religious views, I have learned so much: met many interesting people, and come away with new ways of thinking. Often it has happened on an intellectual and abstract level: in discussion groups, forums, study groups and as part of social occasions.

No experience made it more real than losing Kevin. Suddenly I was faced with a hodgepodge of religious views, each pulling in a different direction and each framed as a well-intentioned desire to honor Kevin. More often than not, it really wasn't about Kevin because in the final analysis it is the living who struggle to come to terms with the loss of a loved one, especially one who chooses to exit early and suddenly, with no time to say good-bye.

The religious affiliations in our blended family cover a wide spectrum. In my case, I was raised in a liberal Reform Jewish home. I am now a member of the local Unitarian-Universalist (UU) congregation that anchors and connects me to community, but my spiritual connection to humanity comes through daily meditation and connection with Mother Nature. My first husband was raised in a devout Irish Catholic home, but when we met in college he defined himself as a 'recovering Catholic.' Our son Jonathan was raised celebrating Jewish and Christian holidays but is now a None – a person who does not embrace organized religion in any form but has a strong moral code. His wife, who was raised by a Jewish father and a Methodist mother, also considers herself a None. Their two daughters are being raised with strong moral codes practiced in daily living but with no religious affiliation; traditions and celebrations in their home center around a mix of secular, Jewish (Chanukah, Passover) and Christian (Easter, Advent, Christmas) holidays, all connecting them with family, friends and community.

My second husband, Adam, was raised in a liberal Jewish home. Adam's epiphany came at age nine when he asked the Rabbi, "Who was God's mother?" and the Rabbi answered, "God didn't have a mother." He has been an avowed atheist since then.

My epiphany came at age sixteen when I was crewing for my father on his sailboat, and we were in the middle of a weekend regatta on Cape Cod. Seas were quite rough, and my father 'took no prisoners' when he competed. The boat was heeling to one side – so far to the right that we were taking on water but we were about to "come about" round the marker and he wasn't going to give up first place. I loved these special times with him, but this particular time I had my boyfriend with me and developed a severe case of seasickness. At one point, I was clinging to the bow, retching over the side of the boat, and made a pact with God: "If you just let the horizon be steady for one minute I promise to go to temple every Friday." Well, God did not come through and I lost God, my lunch and a boyfriend that same day, a major bummer for a teenager.

Both Adam and I had paternal grandparents who were very devout, in my case Orthodox Jews and in his case a grandfather who was a cantor in a very Conservative Jewish congregation in Brooklyn, NY. Adam's son Brian was raised in a liberal Jewish home and married Sari who was from a devout French Catholic home. They are raising their two sons Catholic.

At the center of this eclectic mix was Kevin who considered himself Jewish. His wife Makyla was from a devout Catholic home grounded in the culture and traditions of Brazil. At the time of his death, he was dabbling in Orthodox Jewish traditions at the Chabad in Rio de Janeiro.

Extending beyond our blended family were relatives who were practicing Catholics, Jews, Ecumenical Humanists, and Spiritualists. Several of them were insinuating their religious demands into our life as well, cloaked "in Kevin's memory."

I placed a high priority on helping the family get through Kevin's death by handling the details of his burial and memorial arrangements. Staying true to my profession, program and events management, I tackled it like any other client effort - with one huge difference; this one was personal and infinitely painful. In addition to dealing with his back surgery recovery, Adam was dealing with anger and grief, as was Brian, and I felt a sense of responsibility to honor Kevin and hold things together until folks could reestablish a sense of equilibrium.

What becomes very challenging is the need to make decisive and long-reaching decisions in the midst of so much emotion and disparate tensions. Then I found a quote by Mahatma Gandhi and decided to enlist him as my Wing Man: "God has no religion." To this I added two important corollaries;

one from Hippocrates: "First, do no harm," and one adapted from Evangelical Christians: "With respect and reverence, what would Kevin do?"

A TIME FOR PRAYER AND REFLECTION
Story will resume shortly

"Forgive, O Lord, my little jokes on Thee And I'll forgive Thy great big one on me."

Robert Frost

"And God said: 'Let there be Satan, so people don't blame everything on me. And let there be lawyers, so people don't blame everything on Satan.'"

John Wing

"I do not feel obliged to believe that the same God who has endowed us with sense, reason and intellect has intended us to forgo their use."

Galileo Galilei

"I have wondered at times what the Ten Commandments would have looked like if Moses had run them through the US congress."

Ronald Reagan

"In high school I was voted the girl most likely to become a nun. That may not be impressive to you, but it was quite an accomplishment at the Hebrew Academy."

Rita Rudner

"I want to die before my wife. The reason is: If it is true that when you die, your soul goes up to judgment, I don't want my wife up there ahead of me to tell them things."

Bill Cosby

"The other day I saw a guy with a sign that said, WHERE WILL YOU SPEND ETERNITY? Which freaked me out because I was on my way to the Department of Motor Vehicles."

Arj Barker

Balancing the needs, wants and demands of different constituents requires a great deal of diplomacy under the best of circumstances. Add religion and death to the mix and it becomes a contortionist's delight.

When I was growing up in the 1960s there was a popular game called Twister[8]. It was made by Milton Bradley and caused quite a phenomenon by being the first game to use humans as playing pieces. Not surprisingly, it was quite popular with doctors, especially orthopedic surgeons. In fact it wouldn't surprise me if Twister had been invented by one, and given to patients for a holiday gift – an example of a perfect supply-and-demand business model. (Don't discount this: cotton candy was invented by a dentist!) That's how I felt – like I was playing Twister non-stop.

Original box design[8]

Alas, I confess to having a bad back, deteriorating joints and not enough Aleve to alleviate the pain.

"Sometimes, when one person is missing, the whole world seems depopulated."

Alphonse de Lamartine

ANGER MANAGEMENT

"If you can remain calm, you don't have all the facts."

Anonymous

It would be so great if coping skills could be ordered on Amazon.com in a ready-to-use gift box! When emotions range from one end of the spectrum to the other, it would be so convenient to have a selection of venting tools to choose from. I would consult it regularly for proper care and feeding of The Aarrgghh!

Left to my own defenses, I'll share with you some of the helpful tools I have collected over the years.

MR. AND MRS. BOZO MISUSE THE TEN ITEMS OR LESS CASH ONLY CHECKOUT LINE

It is late, I am tired, and the lady in front of me in the checkout line has her three young children with her, two of whom are pulling candy from the rack, which is strategically placed within easy reach for kids. She hits one of them, causing the baby strapped to the cart seat to scream. The toddler closest to me wets his pants and starts throwing a tantrum. They have thirty items on the conveyor belt and at least eight more in their cart. Dad is pretending he belongs to another family. The cashier says, "Sir, I am sorry but this cash register is for a maximum of ten items and cash only." Without missing a beat, he says in a thick foreign accent, "We have five people so that means we get fifty items." Ahhh, how creative! People behind me are complaining. I am feeling my 'cranky meter' rising by the minute. I decide to join the toddler – yup, I get right down on the floor with him and start throwing a tantrum. Let's just say that stops The Kid in mid-flail. Even the baby stopped screaming. The people behind me, fearful there is Very Bad Karma in this line, quickly move their carts to alternate checkout lines. One lady is so distressed she leaves her full cart in the aisle and exits the store. I feel refreshed, relaxed and ready to tackle whatever comes my way.

THE HEART ATTACK CREATORS

Adam is 'an aggressive driver'. Like Mork, played by Robin Williams in the popular TV series *Mork & Mindy*, a green light means "Go" and a yellow light means "Go Faster". This otherwise calm and gentle giant undergoes a Dr. Jekyll-Mr. Hyde transformation when he gets behind the wheel of a car. Often I remind him that the passenger seat where I am sitting is called 'the death seat'.

This is usually followed by a reprimand, "If you weren't always running 10-20 minutes late, I wouldn't need to rush." (He makes a valid point. I tend to run on Mean Jewish Time.) Then he adds, "I haven't had an accident, not lately anyway."

To which I respond, "That may be true, but you cause them, you're a carrier."

Lately, I have really made an effort to be on time, and I get into the back middle seat and buckle up. And when I do, Adam says with disdain, "Now I feel like the chauffeur."

"My favorite movie is *Driving Miss Daisy*," I say with a smile.

We make it to the concert; I am calm, he is pissed. It is called 'anger transference.'

THE WITCH AT THE CHINESE TAKE-OUT

More than once I've observed someone venting his or her rage on others and most of us have been on the receiving end of someone's anger management (or lack thereof). Adam called me as I left a meeting in town and asked me to stop in and pick up dinner at his favorite Chinese take-out. A big van parked in front was blocking a handicap parking sign and I pulled into the adjacent spot. When I entered the tiny take-out kiosk, a woman stared at me, took out her phone, and as she was talking she went outside. By then the van had pulled away to reveal the sign and it was then I realized I had parked in a handicap spot. After paying for my order, I exited the store to find The Witch blocking my car, taking a photo of it including a close-up of my license plate, and announcing, "I have called the police and they are coming to arrest you." To which I responded, "I wasn't aware it was a handicap spot. The van blocked the sign and I was in the spot for less than five minutes. I apologize – it was inadvertent." She wouldn't budge and started screaming. Two shop owners came out to see what was happening. I explained and they, too, tried to calm her down, to no avail.

"Who deputized you?" asked one of the shop owners. She just stood there as I started my car. With rush hour traffic and crime prevention on their list of priorities, I doubted 911 would be responding to her call within the next forty-eight hours. Adam would not wait that long for his dinner. It is wise to know when it's futile to try to reason with someone. When it became quite evident I was going to back out, I was grateful one of the shop owners took her arm and guided her to the curb. As I drove off, she shrieked, "Stop! Stop right now!" as she continued to take photos of my car, the handicap parking sign, and the two shop owners. I think she was a card-carrying member of the Taliban Car Patrol. I am not one to knowingly park in a handicap space and perhaps in her condition she needed the spot. Shaken to the core, I couldn't get out of there fast enough.

GIVE ME A BREAK
Story will resume shortly

"Experts say you should never hit your children in anger. When is a good time? When you're feeling festive?"

Roseanne Barr

152

THE ULTIMATE HOLIDAY DE-STRESSOR

Another joyous holiday season is here. How do you cope with the end-of-year holiday season when you feel as though you inhabit another planet? My "To Do List" was getting longer by the minute, stressing me to the max. To top it off, my ex-best-friend-for-life sent a holiday newsletter gloating about winning a Pulitzer for her debut novel and a Nobel Prize for curing world hunger. I needed a way to de-stress. First thing I did was toss out the "To Do List". The next thing I did was put pen to paper (well, how about fingers to the keyboard) and wrote the holiday family newsletter I *really* wanted to include in those greeting cards I wasn't in the mood to send.

HOLIDAY GREETINGS FROM BETTY AND HERB SMITH

As this year draws to a close, thanks to those who still spend money snail-mailing your lovely holiday cards and family newsletters. Since we are now an eco-friendly home, we are "re-carding". It's sort of like "re-gifting". We add our name below yours and "Pay It Forward", which is why there are multiple signatures on the enclosed greeting.

This has been yet another eventful year for the Smiths, filled with "challenges and opportunities". Thanks for sending all those Get Well cards to Herb in February. He is still doing physical therapy for a back injury suffered when he rear-ended that geezer driving twenty-five miles an hour in the left lane. He swore there was nobody behind the wheel, but the cop told him he just couldn't see the ninety-three-year-old driver because the poor guy could hardly reach the gas pedal, and he became distracted when his wife started screaming at him. Seems he refuses to wear a hearing aid (too vain or too cheap – you decide) and she was warning him to slow down because he was approaching an intersection – on I-75! She admitted being visually impaired but won't wear glasses (too vain or too cheap – you decide). To add insult to injury, Herb was fined

$750, got three points on his license, our insurance premium dou-bled, and he had to attend weekly anger management classes for two months.

In May we moved Herb's seventy-nine-year-old father here to be closer to us. It was the compassionate thing to do after his second wife passed. (No, she didn't pass away, just passed out of his life, having run off with his male nurse.) From his perspective, moving here was a form of torture and he's been on strike ever since. Prior to moving into our guestroom he was the first person ever kicked out of the local senior living community, after trying to unionize the resi-dents. He spends his days corresponding with Match.com thirty-somethings who think he's forty-something, and periodically calling 911 to complain that I am poisoning him with my cooking. We are now being charged $150 for each call.

Our daughter Flossie just sent us a wedding invitation to her third wedding. We encourage those who received one to disregard it. According to her, we should be happy she's "marrying up" but we figure this means up the alphabet, starting from Smith and working her way up - Martin, Green, and now Barkin. We were a bit disap-pointed her new last name wouldn't begin with "A" as that may mean there's one more in her future. Herb says she likes the ceremo-nies, receptions, and gifts more than her husbands. That may be true considering her first husband was Protestant, the second was Catholic, and her fiancé is Jewish. Since she is converting for a third time, the conversion service is being bundled in with the wedding ceremony, which will take place at The Wailing Wall in Jerusalem, a fitting location under the circumstances. We have informed Flossie that her wedding gift is being put in escrow for five years and it will be theirs provided this one lasts. We encourage you to do the same. She isn't talking to Herb, not because of this, but because after losing her job he suggested she teach a comparative religion course at the local university. By the way, we have no plans to attend the wedding if my sister Cici goes. For the third time, her wedding gift to her fa-

vorite niece will be her infamous cocktail hour concert of Broadway show tunes. This time, the wedding "Goodie Bags" will include a set of earplugs – our sole contribution.

As for our son Jack, we've saved the best for last. We were so proud when he left the family business to join the Peace Corps four years ago to "save the world". That was before Herb's auditor discovered Jack had invested the company's pension with Bernie Madoff. The lawsuits from our shareholders and employees just keep a-coming. Jack has truly given us "the gift that keeps on giving".

Hey, we're just kidding – all is hunky-dory on our end, well not quite, but we'll save that for next year. May your holiday be bright, the New Year filled with good health, and may laughter lighten your day.

Love,
Betty & Herb

THE MISFIRING MISSILE LAUNCHER

As I mentioned, Adam is an aggressive driver. Back in the late 1980s, one day I was thumbing through a catalog and came across a device that mounted on the dashboard of the car. It had three buttons; a missile launched into the air, slowing, descending, and landing in an explosive crash; a rapidly firing machine gun (*rat-a-tat-tat-tat-tat*); and a hand grenade with the pin removed whistling through the air and exploding upon impact. Everything was a la carte; batteries were separate and of course they were special lithium batteries that had to be ordered separately, and so did the handy-dandy mounting device. But I just knew it was the perfect gift for My #1 Guy. When it arrived in the mail, I put it together and mounted it on the dashboard of his car. He loved it; it was the perfect anger management device. He was suitably armed as a Road Warrior, waging his own private World War III as he virtually decimated the enemy without causing road rage.

A few months later I borrowed his car to cart supplies up to my son Jon who was at prep school. On the ride up, I got pulled over by a Speed Posse. This was something the New Hampshire Highway Patrol enlisted if they were running short on meeting their monthly revenue number. A plane would fly overhead and send by radio descriptions of cars exceeding the speed limit; they had a lineup of 4-5 patrol cars and a gaggle of officers pull them over. If a driver didn't stop, one of the officers would jump into his patrol car and pursue the offender with lights flashing. I didn't stop because I had my cruise control on and was going the speed limit maximum but not exceeding it. When the cop pulled me over he cited me not for speeding but for having a radar speed detector on the dashboard. Such devices were illegal in New Hampshire.

"Officer, this isn't a speed detector," I said. I was going to show him what it was but figured that wouldn't be wise. He was grumpy, had a gun holstered to his waist, and had no sense of humor but you'd be grumpy, too, doing this line of work on a cold, raw, Sunday morning instead of monitoring one of the infamous highway construction projects and earning time-and-a-half pay while eating free donuts and drinking fresh hot coffee. He gave me a ticket – for speeding!

I was so outraged I decided to contest it, which meant taking time off from work and driving forty-five minutes to the county courthouse, which was located in a town so small it was barely on the map. I headed off to the battle with the citation and the missile-launcher in hand, having removed it from the dashboard.

The courthouse was in the basement of this old converted church on a rural route that also housed the town hall offices and the jail. Walking down the stairs, the dampness seeped into my bones and the mold and mildew made me gag. As vertically challenged as I am, I was forced to bend down so my head would clear the door jamb at the bottom of the stairs. Blocking my path was my buddy, Officer Grump. His Tuesday disposition was even worse than his Sunday morning mood, but he did reluctantly let me by. I looked down just in case he put his foot out to trip me, walking on the vintage harvest gold shag carpeting that seemed to ooze mold with each step.

A big burley bailiff with two holstered guns dangling from his belt waved me into the room and directed me to the clerk. The room was at most twenty feet square and set up like a mini-courtroom out of the early 1960s; I expected to see Perry Mason sitting with the defense attorneys in the first row. Court was in session and I quietly showed my citation to the clerk and had my purse checked for weapons of mass destruction. The missile launcher was safely nestled in my coat pocket. It was so cold I kept my coat on and sat down on the back pew.

Have you ever sent or received a Tush Call? That's an accidental call dialed when a person sits on their mobile phone. Well, my tush landed on the missile launcher, and in a court room. Let's just say it took forever for it to peak, descend, and crash-and-burn. As I fumbled to find it, I accidently pressed the machine gun button. By this time the bailiff and every patrol officer in the room had their guns aimed – at me. The judge was under his desk.

In case there is any doubt, I lost my appeal.

LET'S GET PHYSICAL

I asked two friends how they managed their anger. My first friend said, "Once I was in a major funk back in the 1990s, a Big Time Funk that was really pulling me down. I have high blood pressure and need to be careful when I am under a lot of stress. When that's happened in the past my coping skills were often not the best. I was dealing with anger issues related to my mother and a therapist suggested I get a doll and diffuse my anger by yelling at her."

Rather harmless, right? Well, she went to Marshall's and bought a doll that was dressed in a workout suit with a T-shirt that read "Let's Get Physical". Sort of like that old Olivia Newton John song.

"And come to think of it she looked a little bit like Olivia," she said. "I took her home, clipped her to a hanger, hung it on the closet pole in the back of my closet and stuck pins in her heart when I was angry. A year later my mother died – of a massive heart attack and I was sure I caused it. Do Not Try That At Home. I honestly thought about calling my old therapist and requesting a refund."

Another friend had lost two husbands, both to debilitating illness requiring years of care giving. "I was exhausted and angry all the time - at God, at the angels, and at Satan - especially when my second husband got sick two years after we married. I had to quit a job that I loved to care for him 24x7 since we had no children or extended family close by. I saved every glass jar and beer, wine, and liquor bottle and when it got too much to bear, I moved the car out of the garage, closed the garage door, and tossed the bottles against the metal door."

"Weren't you afraid of being hurt from flying shards of glass?" I asked.

"No, I honestly didn't care. I stood back far enough and had a blanket on the floor to cushion the chards of glass."

"Did your neighbors call the police?" I asked.

"We lived in a small town where each lot was a minimum of five acres and nobody could see or hear their neighbors," she said.

"How long did you do this for?"

"About three months, and then I figured how much money I was losing by not cashing in the glass bottles. So I stopped smashing, cashed in the bottles and started buying a better quality of vodka. When he died, I joined AA."

I felt so much compassion for her, and that explained why she was a teetotaler.

As for me, when I am stressed I wish I could do what most other people do – pop a Happy Pill, eat a chocolate cake, a quart of ice cream or drink a bottle of wine, all by myself and with no guilt whatsoever: but since all of those options would make me deathly ill, that wouldn't work. What I'm left with is taking my aggression out on my treadmill or Nordic Track cross-country skier – for an hour a day when thirty minutes would suffice. At least it calms my nerves and gives me an endorphin high. And it allows me to read the letters-to-the-editor in our local newspaper without losing my sanity.

And then it's time to get back to reality but wouldn't it be nice to be able to banish those bad days, and I was having a lot of those… Sometime laughter just hurts too much. Sure, it might make you feel good for a nanosecond, but all too soon the pain bubbles around the edges and covers your mind, body and, soul with an ache so deep and thick, like molten tar, it smothers you and it's hard to breathe.

GOOD GRIEF!
Story will resume shortly

"*Grief isn't an abnormal condition. It's nature's way of healing our heart.*"

Melody Beattie

Sometimes we don't know what or whom we're missing. I found the following reading quite moving.

"How can I stop feeling so blue about being separated from my children?" a man asked his colleague when business had taken him away from home for a month. "You're asking the wrong person," his colleagues answered, "It has been eleven years since my son died, and I still miss him every day."[9]

Grief. It may strike suddenly, catching our heart by surprise. Or it may pound relentlessly and persistently for years, like ocean waves beating on the shore. Whether we're conscious of what or whom we're missing, our heart knows. We may never be happy about whom or what we have lost, but it is possible to be happy again.

"*The truth will set you free, but first it will piss you off.*"

Gloria Steinem

BURIAL TRADITIONS

"What is buried in the past of one generation falls to the next to claim."

Susan Griffin

To paraphrase Linda Ellis, the story of our life is written as the dash between our date of birth and our date of death. It is up to us how we live the dash.

That is so true; however, how we enter eternity is another story altogether.

A BRIEF HISTORY OF BURIAL TRADITIONS

In the distant past, death was honored as a natural part of the cycle of life. Grandpa and Grandma lived with the family and when they died, their loved ones washed them, dressed them in their Sunday finery, and laid them out on the dining room table. Other family members, friends and neighbors came 'round to pay their respects and mourn their loss together. They arrived with casseroles, baked hams, Grandma's favorite cakes, pies, and bottles of liquor to comfort the family - and themselves.

If the family was Jewish, the burial took place within twenty-four hours and 'Sitting Shiva' (the mourning period) lasted for seven days, with a Time Out for Sabbath services on Friday night and Saturday. For the Irish Catholics, 'wakes' (viewings) would last for days with the women loudly keening to honor their deceased loved one. Lots of crying, drinking, eating, and music accompanied this social rite signifying the group had lost a valued member. In some cases, keening hysterically became a competitive exercise as a sign of respect for the next of kin. If it was an untimely death - a young child dying from measles or small pox, or a stillbirth - the ritual was more somber. If a young wife died in childbirth, single women in the community came a-courting and were especially comforting and solicitous to the widower, hoping to replace Wife #1. For some, it was a time to party-hearty: a raucous send-off escorting the deceased's spirit to heaven. Children were present and saw birth and death, timely or untimely, as the natural order of things; seeing it in animals as well as loved ones. Burial was often in a small cemetery on the family farm or in the town or village where the deceased lived.

With the onset of the Industrial Revolution, families dispersed and family members moved from the small towns and farms to the cities. Capitalism entered the scene and saw death in a new light – Big Business ($$$$ *ka-ching, ka-ching, ka-ching*). Soon, mourning and burial were outsourced to funeral homes and federal and state regulations kicked in thanks to funeral association lobbyists. As my friend Janet said, "That's what happens when homes only have 'living rooms.'" Right on, Jan!

Caskets went from plain pine boxes to custom made works of art fashioned from exotic woods, bronze, silver, ivory or even gold. There are boutique casket designers who will replicate the deceased's favorite toy: imagine if you will Uncle Harry journeying heaven-bound in his mini-yacht or Dad motoring there in a red Ferrari.

Even cremation services were regulated, mandating that the deceased be transported in a casket. A friend told me you can go to Costco, buy a casket for $1,299 (keep the receipt!), transport Grandpa to the crematorium, and return the casket. When the customer service rep asks why you are returning it, you can say, "It didn't fit," "It was the wrong color," or "She didn't like it."

Your loved one's ashes can be put in an expensive urn on the high end, or a Cool Whip container on the budget plan. The Great Recession has brought a boom to the cremation industry as families look for economical ways to send their loved ones to their eternal resting place. Since profit margins for traditional funerals and cemetery burials are much higher than cremations, some of the traditional businesses are now offering custom designed cremation urns and fancy mausoleums in which to place them, with accompanying annual fees.

Entrepreneurs are entering the field, offering to encase ashes in artificial reefs designed to promote new coral growth in the ocean, or sending ashes into space on commercial rocket trips - $60,000 for a one-way adventure. A recently debuted product extension – "Destination Funerals" where the service is held in a locale that was especially meaningful to the deceased: the NAS-CAR race track, botanical gardens, the zoo, the museum, the local pub, the opportunities are limited only by the imagination – and the pocketbook.

An acquaintance told me, "My parents were atheists. They were both cremated and demanded that nobody could claim their ashes." Ahh, sweet simplicity...but definitely not for everybody. Meanwhile, traditionalists warn that these fads will deny future generations the comfort and continuity that comes from having a place to visit their ancestors – it erases family history. Who's to say? Perhaps some families don't care to preserve their history. Our modern society has little reverence or regard for elders – we worship our youth. Just look at the popularity of Botox treatments and plastic surgeries for men *and* women, starting in their twenties.

Just look at Ray Kurzweil, the sixty-five-year-old entrepreneur and recently hired Google employee who takes 150 pills and supplements a day and obsessively has his vital signs and blood monitored for the slightest signs of aging. His goal is to live forever. Just in case that doesn't work out, he plans to have his body frozen and DNA preserved so he can come back in the future. I'm not sure this qualifies as the biblical "Second Coming," but ya can't fault the guy for giving it The Ole College Try. If I'm going to live forever, I definitely want to trade in this body for a newer model with an array of custom features. In the not-too-distant future, ninety will be "the new fifty". But since I'm doubtful that will be achieved in my lifetime, I have a Will and Advanced Directive, just in case, and I sure hope Ray does, too.

Aging itself has become a crime against humanity, something to be denied and refuted, rather than accepted and respected. We outsource our aged parents to assisted living communities and nursing homes. Death has become an impersonal inconvenience, no longer integrated into the life cycle. Children fear death. In fact, some grow to adulthood before ever viewing a dead body.

The funeral industry shares my doubt and it isn't losing sleep over the fears that living forever will become a reality anytime soon. They're busy creatively addressing today's needs. To accommodate busy relatives and friends, some funeral parlors have drive-thru viewings of the deceased. That way, folks can get some cash at their bank drive-thru kiosk, stop at McDonald's drive-thru to pick up some Big Macs and shakes, and head to the drive-thru window for a final farewell to Grandma. Out of respect to the deceased, I do hope they stop texting for a few brief nanoseconds and have the kids stop playing their hand-held video games. Just past the viewing window is a collection box discretely positioned with a small sign suggesting a generous donation to Grandma's favorite charity. The catch is that a donation is required in order for the security gate to open so you can exit. Short on cash? No problem, they take Visa or Discover.

To accommodate family and friends living far away, a videographer can stream the funeral service and folks can be 'virtually present' in spirit if not in body. The only thing they can't do is partake of the delectable cuisine – artfully (and expensively) catered and beautifully presented at the church or funeral home. I recently attended a funeral service and reception at a senior center. There was so much food that residents of the center asked for large Styrofoam containers and heaped several with enough food to keep them sated for a week. I was astounded, especially when folks who never knew the deceased just stopped in to take a "Doggy Box".

As for mourning, it is Big Business, too. For $25.95, you can purchase a book on The Seven Stages of Grief: Shock & Denial, Pain & Guilt, Anger & Bargaining, Depression-Reflection-Loneliness, The Upward Turn, Reconstruction & Working Through, and Acceptance & Hope. Or for the bargain price of $19.95 you can buy one based on the Kübler-Ross "five stages of grief" model: denial, anger, bargaining, depression, and acceptance. Take your pick – or get even better bargains on eBay.

If all else fails, you can go the self-medication route: drowning your sorrows in alcohol, lighting a joint, or snorting cocaine. However, that can create other problems and I don't recommend it.

We're not done yet, my friends. Now we get to the topic of internment and grave markers and the continuation of my personal journey, accompanied by my Wing Man & The Corollaries - Gandhi ("God has no religion"), Hippocrates ("First, do no harm"), and my guiding principal ("With respect and reverence, what would Kevin do?").

A TIME OUT
Story will resume shortly

"To have or not to have: that is the question: When nobody is available is anybody listening?"

Adapted from Willie Shakespeare

We had The Kevin Túmulo in Brazil bringing comfort to Makyla and her family and honoring Kevin in his adopted homeland. Honoring him respectfully in the U.S. continued to bring new insights...and hurdles.

This brings us back to Rosewood Memorial Park and my buddy Joshua. We rushed to place the order for the cenotaph plaque before Joshua left for vacation in mid-July. This entailed umpteen phone calls and emails and leaping tall building in a single bound to get all the paperwork in place but I was determined to get this order processed so we could have the memorial service in mid-October.

Joshua and I were able to finalize the wording on the plaque, including my sign-off on the final proof. All I could hope for was that the portions in Hebrew were correct. Adam checked it, too, and said, "If there are any errors, we'll say they were intentional." (In my years working in high tech, when a software application had a 'bug' we told the customers it was a 'feature'.)

I also requested a mid-October memorial service - specifically Sunday, October 14th - and a canopy in case of rain, and put that all in writing to Joshua before he left. I knew that date was cutting it close, given the quoted 10-12 week lead-time, but Adam didn't want to chance bad weather later in October, especially since this would be outdoors.

Joshua's response was reasonable: he would have a better idea in late August about the delivery date for the plaque, he would add the canopy to our order, but he also said the memorial service details were handled by a different department. He said he would, however, forward my request on to them before he left.

I had maybe four days to feel relatively good that the pieces were slowly but surely coming together in a way that would meet everybody's needs, but that was short lived. When Brian returned to the office on Tuesday, after a long weekend in Maine with his family he sent an email letting me know he was not a "Happy Camper".

"I want the memorial service over Columbus Day weekend," he insisted.

I explained about the production schedule for the cenotaph and that pulling it in by a week would further compress the lead-time. Additionally, I knew Adam would resist this, since airfare would double over the holiday weekend as well as the car rental and hotel, and it would be a more crowded time to travel with Dorothy, which would make it more difficult for her, too.

"That's bullshit about a 10-12 week lead time. Why does the foundry need that much time? I'm going to call them myself," he threatened.

"Brian, the minute you do that, it will negate the contract and if anything is wrong with the order the liability becomes ours, not Rosewood Memorial Park's," I implored. "I will contact Joshua next week when he is back from vacation. He said he would give us a status on our order at the end of August. In the meantime, we can plan the details of the memorial service – the guest list, the program, and the reception. We don't need to send out the invitation until four weeks prior and that way nobody is booking flight reservations for an event with a tentative date."

I followed up that discussion with a tentative invitation list of people Adam and I considered inviting, and asked him and Sari to add their friends and other relatives they wished to include. We wanted to limit this to a manageable number since the service was going to be outdoors and graveside. For us, 'manageable' meant 15-20: but Brian wanted to include more of his friends so the list soon grew to thirty invitees. Adam was getting irritated, but I told him we needed to allow Brian and Sari to include the friends and family who would be there to comfort them.

Since Kevin's favorite cuisine was Chinese food, we wanted to host the luncheon after the memorial service at a good Chinese restaurant close to the cemetery.

A CHINESE FOOD BREAK
Story will resume shortly

"*Two Chinese men are walking out of Katz's Delicatessen. One says to the other, 'The problem with Jewish food is that two weeks later you're hungry again.'*"

Arthur Schwartz, The Food Maven[10]

It is a well-known stereotype that most Jewish people love Chinese food, and speaking for Adam's family and my family, that stereotype applied. In fact, Adam loves Chinese food so much he learned to cook it and we have an entire cabinet in our kitchen devoted to his culinary supplies: herbs, aromatics, cookbooks and online recipes. Wherever we live or travel he likes to go to the local Chinatown, if one exists, and order what the locals order, which most often is not on the menu.

Kevin inherited this love from his father, and on a family trip to Toronto we went to Chinatown for dinner seven nights out of eight. Leave it to Kevin to push the envelope by ordering shark fin soup, the most expensive item on the menu at $49 a bowl, to which his father informed the waitress that was no-go. True to form, Kevin made the same request every night.

"When you are paying for the meal you can order whatever you want, but while we are paying for it you will order nothing more expensive than what I order," said Adam, adding for good measure, "And since I am 'frugal', that won't ever include shark fin soup."

"Dad, you're not frugal, you're cheap." That was Kevin's response. He wasn't one to back down from getting what he wanted, even at the age of ten. Adam, Jon, and I just shook our heads and proceeded to sample other 'frugal' dishes and enjoyed each and every one, thanks to Adam's great guidance.

> *"If, according to the Jewish calendar, the year is 5764, and, according to the Chinese calendar, the year is 5724, what did the Jews eat for forty years?"*
>
> Arthur Schwartz, *The Food Maven*[10]

So it made sense to delegate the selection of the Chinese restaurant for the reception to my beloved husband Adam. I found three restaurants that were close to Rosewood Memorial Park and had private banquet rooms or separate areas for a group. Two had menus on their respective websites and I sent everything to Adam in an email for follow-up. He took this as seriously as doing our annual tax return, did due diligence and narrowed it down to two.

Adam made the final decision, choosing the place he liked best for the menu choices plus the banquet room ambience. I called the owner, Alice, and with a concession given to Brian's preferred date, we locked in our event with a tentative date of Sunday, October 7th. She understood our challenge regarding the final date, agreed to stay flexible, and was a pleasure to work with. Adam made the right choice.

PS – Shark fin soup was *not* on the menu but the banquet menu was outstanding, and included all of Kevin's favorites, and so much more.

I had sent an email to Joshua about Brian's wish to hold the memorial service on Columbus Day weekend, preferably Sunday, October 7th with Monday, October 8th as an alternative. So I wasn't surprised to see a call coming in from Rosewood Memorial Park. What was unexpected was that Joshua wasn't making the call. It came from a woman named Debby, with a question about the cenotaph order. Say whaaa? "Wasn't the order placed more than a week ago?" I asked.

"Well, no. Preference is given to unveilings and there were a lot of those in the queue," was the response from Debby. I was well aware of the Jewish tradition of having a grave marker unveiling a year after burial, but this was the first I heard about priority being given to them. I was learning lessons the hard way, and this was only the first of many: When there's no body, nobody seems to care.

It seemed there was a "pecking order" hierarchy in the funeral industry, or maybe it was just our experience at Rosewood. Top priority was given to internments, second priority was given to unveilings a year later, and cenotaph memorials were delegated as "fillers", scheduled in the remaining nooks and crannies.

"Our family jumped through hoops to get this order placed before Joshua left on vacation. I assumed it was placed on Friday, the day he left."

"Well, I'm just getting to it now, and Joshua is still away due to a death in the family."

Oh my goodness, I certainly wasn't going to call Joshua under the circumstances, but that explained why I hadn't heard from him in response to my email.

I was almost speechless, but rather than lose my cool, I answered her questions and told her to place the order by the end of the day – with Boyle, the preferred foundry recommended by Joshua. She did, and then called me back with more bad news: the foundry was on a two-week summer shut-down, the first time they had done so, and she wouldn't be able to place the order until the following week.

The universe was sending me a sign…I was beginning to listen, but there were others who weren't.

I updated Adam but chose to do this over dinner at his favorite Chinese restaurant. That appeased him…but only a little. Even Hunan Crispy Duck has its limits. We agreed not to tell Brian since it would just upset him. And possibly Joshua could get this expedited upon his return. I am not one who finds it easy to wait under such circumstances, but there was nothing to do but let the days tick by until I was able to make contact with Joshua the first week in August.

When Joshua was back in the office, I updated him on what happened during his absence and what we hoped he could expedite on our behalf. But before doing so, we had a long chat about the death of his family member and that included some compassionate sharing of losing a loved one. Two events bookend humanity: each of us is born and each of us will die. It's what happens in between that connects us.

He got back to me two days later, after following up with Boyle, and said he would check on the status of our order later in August. And he did: expediting the order would not be possible; they did this in the past and ended up with errors on the plaques. The Labor Day holiday was also added to the schedule. He spoke with their CEO Herb Hochman who agreed to allow us to book our memorial service for October 7th and we could host it without a plaque.

Adam was emphatically against that idea: "I do not want a service without a cenotaph, especially since Kevin's remains aren't there, either. It would be totally meaningless, and we would also need to fly up there over the holiday. Forget it. We'll wait till the spring – sometime in May."

Brian's response was swift – and emphatic: "I don't want to drag this out till May, I want to have a service on October 7th and put an end to this."

Adam wouldn't budge: "If there is no cenotaph on Kevin's grave then I don't want the service to be held there. We'll hold the service at your house." Left unsaid was Adam's discomfort being surrounded by his ex-wife's grave and her brother and other family, and having a service to honor Kevin over an empty gravesite with nothing to make it special for Kevin.

Brian agreed to host the October 7th service and added, "We can have another service in May when the cenotaph is installed and do that at Rosewood Memorial." We did not agree to that last part.

 # WE BREAK FOR AN ANNOUNCEMENT
Story will resume shortly

"Problem and Reality are different. Every Problem has a solution, while Reality has none. A Problem is meant to be solved and Reality is meant to be accepted."

Nishan Panwar

When I had time to think about all dependencies and preferences of the key stakeholders, I suggested to Adam that it might make more sense to let Brian do something at his home earlier in September when the weather would be better, and plan to host an unveiling service graveside in July 2013. This would be in keeping with the Jewish tradition: have the burial service soon after death and the unveiling of the headstone and/or grave marker (or in our case, the cenotaph) on the one-year anniversary of Kevin's death. It's known as the "yahrzeit" – a time to remember and honor the dead, recite the mourner's prayer (the Kaddish), and light a twenty-four-hour memorial candle. A reasonable solution, right? Not so fast, girlfriend…

Reality strikes in the form of Adam's response: "Brazil, Brian's house, Rosewood Memorial Park - how many times do I have to bury my son?"

Ouch!

"I don't know why they call it heartbreak. It feels like every other part of my body is broken too."

Missy Altijd

The sadness for Brian and his family seemed endless. In addition to losing Kevin in July, Sari's maternal grandmother died the day before Brian's August 29th birthday, and two days later Brian's maternal grandmother died. We were concerned about the amount of stress this was causing him, and did what we could to comfort him, Sari and our grandsons.

Sari comes from a large family. Her mother had eleven siblings but none were up to the challenge of delivering the eulogy. Sari did her family proud by taking on this responsibility and honored her grandmother with a beautiful tribute, which she delivered flawlessly at the funeral service. I was proud of her, too. I knew Sari wasn't totally comfortable speaking in public.

Brian and his grandmother's remaining son, Brian's Uncle Bernie, took care of the funeral arrangements and service for his grandmother. He and Sari hosted Bernie and his girlfriend, who flew in for several days over the Labor Day weekend. After the funeral, on September 3rd (Labor Day), family and friends were invited back to Brian and Sari's home.

When I called Brian's house to make sure he and Sari were doing okay, I didn't expect Bernie to pick up the phone, but it gave me a chance to express our deepest condolences. He was warm and gracious, and when I asked if by chance he and Brian had been able to walk over to view Kevin's gravesite as well as visit his sister's and brother's graves, I was not prepared for his response.

"We couldn't find them! That whole area was covered with Astroturf."

"Astroturf? You've got to be kidding!" I was incredulous.

"No, we couldn't believe it, either. Is that some kind of Jewish custom, to cover the graves of previously deceased relatives with artificial grass during an internment?" he asked.

All we could do was laugh. "Bernie, you've got me on that one. I'll contact Rosewood Memorial tomorrow and find out about that."

"There are just so many stories that are buried on family trees."

Henry Louis Gates, Jr.

When I got off the phone with Bernie, I realized how much Brian needed his family around him since he suffered so many losses in such a short timeframe. It reinforced for me the importance of doing something in October – for his benefit – whether we had a cenotaph or not.

And then…I had a brainstorm. As a compromise, what if we moved the date for the memorial service and unveiling for Kevin to Sunday, October 21st, when the cenotaph was sure to be installed? I confirmed the date with Joshua who did 'two thumbs up' and then I proposed it to Brian and Adam. That worked for all of us.

Since it was now just after Labor Day, Joshua and CEO Herb Hochman called Boyle and re-confirmed delivery for the first week in October: but as I had come to learn, it required about ten days to process the order, do a quality check, and schedule it for installation. Seems October is a favorable month for Jews to die and unveilings to take place one year later. Maybe it had something to do with wanting to get through the High Holidays, Rosh Hashana and Yom Kippur and the ten days of atonement in between, to cleanse the soul and make peace with God. Or maybe the thought of struggling through a cold, dreary winter made autumn, with all its glorious color, a better time to exit. Who knows how the universe flows…

As we quickly nailed down the details and finalized the invitation and list of invitees, I confirmed the date with Alice for the reception following the service at her Chinese restaurant, reserving the banquet room, which could hold a maximum of thirty people.

But soon the guest list was about to expand. At his grandmother's funeral, several relatives said they wanted to come to Kevin's memorial service and reception. Soon we went from a guest list of twenty-nine to forty-eight, and Adam's Tolerance Meter was rapidly running on low. I made a quick call to Alice to let her know our numbers might increase, and she let me know it would be snug but do-able if all showed up. Having run events professionally, I knew that would not be the case – not everybody who gets invited can attend. But I wasn't sure what other distant relatives and friends might surface from the depths and demand a seat at the table, or how about those compassionate folks who frequent cemeteries and self-invite to the reception for a free meal. One needs to keep an open mind about such possibilities – they seemed to be endless lately, it was getting tough to keep up.

One benefit of being anal-retentive like I am, is that when I find myself questioning if these events really did happen or were just my imagination at work, I can refer to the treasure trove of saved emails for a Reality Check. Honestly, sometimes I wish they weren't true. In fact I wish everything about this book wasn't true. But it really did happen, and as author and columnist Connie Schultz says, "We write from our wounds." Yes, we most certainly do.

And more wounds were soon to come. My son and his wife were twenty weeks into the pregnancy of their third daughter when there was an abnormal ultrasound. That was mid-August, as they were about to start their two-week summer vacation. Within the next four weeks, and after extensive testing, one moderate birth defect and a second severe abnormality surfaced, and on Rosh Hashana, September 18th, we lost little Baby Ladybug. Ten days later, Jacqueline was rushed to the hospital due to a hemorrhage from a complication from the lost pregnancy. And less than a week later she was scheduled to sit for her fellowship board exam, having attended the prep course over the summer, but certainly not able to study in the weeks leading up to the exam.

So much was happening to Brian and Jonathan and their families and it is especially painful when it happens to those we love and care about so deeply.

Therefore, I was more than happy to fly to Boston on very short notice – of all times, over Columbus Day weekend (Yes, God does have a sense of humor!) - to spend four nights and five days with my granddaughters while Jon and Jacqueline took a much-needed mini-vacation. It didn't matter that two weeks later I would fly up with Adam and Dorothy for Kevin's unveiling, that's just how life works out sometimes. You just go with the flow.

TIME OUT FOR A PLAY DATE

Story will resume shortly

"Adults are obsolete children."

Dr. Seuss

Dr. Seuss' lead-in quote may be right but I took it as a challenge to prove that it could be refuted. I find a great deal of healing being with my two yummy granddaughters, ages five and seven and my two handsome step-grandsons, ages ten and twelve. From the day they were born, their spirits have resonated with me – in mind, body, heart and soul.

Designing Super Hero costumes for Frank (age five at the time) and Caleb (age two) was a treat. When Frank first saw his, he said, "Deena, this is awesome!" Once he put it on, he didn't want to take it off. While Brian and Sari left for a three-day mini-vacation in Key West, Adam and I had dinner with the two boys and they spent the better part of the evening running around the condo where we lived at the time, pretending to be Super Frank and Super Caleb. The only way we got Frank to take his costume off was by promising to lay it at the bottom of his bed.

As I tucked him in and we lay there talking, he said, "Deena, when I wake up I'm going to put on my Super Frank costume and I'm going to fly."

OH MY GOSH: we lived on the top floor and I had visions of him getting up in the middle of the night, quietly putting on his costume, and testing its flight readiness by launching himself from the banister that dropped to the atrium fourteen floors below. Since I am a light sleeper, I decided to sleep next to him and insure his safety. I surely didn't want any grandchild of ours being hurt on our watch.

I am not one who embraces gender stereotyping but there definitely are differences between little boys and little girls, and I celebrate those differences. I loved raising my son Jonathan, in every way. Having stepsons in my life brought other dimensions of raising boys into my world, with all the joys and challenges that come with blended families.

And now, as my nuclear and blended family expands, time spent caring for my granddaughters, is nothing short of delicious. Human wake-up calls with not-so-gentle knocks on the door and then jumping into bed with Nonie (me!), and getting my camera and seeing who can make the goofiest face. They like to work out with me, trying out the treadmill and showing me how fast they can run and how many pounds they can lift with the hand weights. We make late breakfasts ("Nonie, we call this 'brunch'!") and that includes cutting shapes out of bread with cookie cutters and breaking an egg in the hole left behind – then frying it up golden brown and buttery but with the yoke cooked so it isn't runny (heaven forbid).

There is time for Rock-and-Roll and dancing and singing, and having friends and family come over to visit for tea parties and playdates. We take trips to the museum; and each and every day, rain or shine, there is time for a Treasure Hunt – searching and finding the hidden crafts projects we do together and let our creative juices flow in every direction.

We bake a cake or brownies together, measuring, pouring and mixing and then adding our own special extras like mint chips or extra sprinkles. And of course they get to lick the bowl and eat any extra chips and sprinkles. We take nature walks and explore the neighborhood, and then its bath time and story time just before "Lights Out". And lots and lots of hugs, laughter, some tears, bushels of love, and healing.

> *"My quest these days is to find my long lost inner child, but I'm afraid if I do, I'll end up with food in my hair and way too in love with the cats."*

> *Kenny Loggins*

As it turned out, the cenotaph arrived at Rosewood Memorial Park on October 3rd, which was a big relief. Provided there were no errors on the plaque, it would be installed in plenty of time for October 21st. But it definitely would not have been ready for our memorial service over Columbus Day weekend so our Plan B (or was it C, D, or E?) worked out well.

As we firmed up the memorial service program, we wanted to make this inclusive, with Adam being the first speaker, followed by me, Brian, Jon and several other family members we invited to participate. Kevin's and Brian's Uncle Bernie was coming from California but having just lost his mother as well as his nephew, we respected his wish not to speak or do a reading.

One of the biggest surprises was, after all was said and done Brian did not wish to say anything at the service.

"I don't actually have any positive memories of Kevin," he said.

That made me so sad. Adam, on the other hand, was angry, feeling we had done all this to help Brian and now he didn't want to participate. After venting a bit, in a loving way he cautioned Brian about how this would be perceived by his two sons if their father didn't say anything. Sari was supportive in allowing Brian to make whatever decision he was comfortable with, without any undue pressure.

"Remember, he not only lost his only brother but his grandmother and Sari's grandmother, too," I said. I offered to send Brian a couple of suggested poems and readings plus a couple of positive memories that might spark his interest and Adam encouraged me to do that. We also sent Brian a work-in-progress program for the memorial service including the music we planned to include.

We were very happy when Brian agreed to speak and sent me the two readings he chose, and he also added a song by the Dave Matthews Band. When I laid this all out with time slots for each speaker and song, we were well over an hour. Adam's speech was the longest and his chosen music was also very long – thirteen minutes - but I felt it was important to honor his priorities above all others. In the end, we cut out some other parts and brought it to around fifty minutes.

Just before I printed forty copies, I called to confirm the final details with Rosewood Memorial Park…and there were more lessons to learn (i.e., surprises). Unfortunately, Debby never sent the official final paperwork for the memorial service that included, in tiny print, "Internments are given priority and your unveiling may not be able to take place at the requested time." Our 11am time had been 'bumped' for a burial and another family had already reserved the noon timeslot for an unveiling since they were having a 'real' unveiling - one year after internment. We were at the bottom of the hierarchy in Funeral Land, with no body and only a cenotaph, so we were given the option of a 10am or 1pm timeslot.

PRIMAL SCREAM TIME

Story will resume shortly

"Speak when you are angry and you will make the best speech you will ever regret."

Ambrose Bierce

"The greatest remedy for anger is delay."

Thomas Paine

"Arghhhhhhhh..."

Me

"God's voice is still and quiet and easily buried under an avalanche of clamour."

Dr. Charles Stanley

Sometimes it is wise to know when the odds are not in your favor and it just isn't worth trying to take a stand. The office faxed me a copy of the official paperwork and I was informed that Debby had been fired. No kidding! This obviously wasn't her only screw-up with us as she was the one who had delayed placing the order for the cenotaph back in July. But we weren't in a strong position to argue. Starting the service at 1pm would mean running up against our flight departure time so there was no other option but the 10am slot.

However, I did call the president of Rosewood, Herb Hochman, and he was extremely apologetic. He accepted full responsibility, took ownership of the problem and said they don't usually allow unveiling services to include a graveside memorial service. Unveilings are booked thirty minutes apart. He made an exception for us, promised we could have the 10am slot as long as we were out by 11am for the internment, confirmed we would have a small canopy no matter what, but only six chairs would be available.

"And please, no Astroturf!" I demanded. It turns out this is not a rare Jewish custom it is something that is done at Rosewood when a grave is dug for an internment. The adjacent plots are covered over with Astroturf to protect them from getting damaged.

I won't even get into the reactions from Adam and Brian about the change to 10am – it would be censored. Alice, bless her heart, agreed to open her restaurant thirty minutes early to accommodate the reception. I sent an urgent email to all our guests, apologizing for the late notice about the time change and encouraging folks to bring folding chairs and an umbrella in case of inclement weather. Brian wanted to set up his own large tent but we nixed that idea. We didn't want to tempt the fates with some other detail that could go wrong, and I didn't want to ask Rosewood for permission to do something that would need lord only knows how many approval cycles and restrictions. Most assuredly, the folks attending the 11am internment would not appreciate a tent tear down effort coinciding with their service. I also didn't want a tent pole skewering some other guest and risking getting sued.

Two days before we departed for Boston, as I was printing out copies of the program, Adam came into my office visibly upset. He had been doing some final edits on his speech and was practicing it in front of the mirror to feel more comfortable delivering it.

"Deena, I know you feel this is the right thing to be doing for Brian and the family but you are ripping a scab off my wound."

I stopped what I was doing and just went over to him and hugged him dearly, not wanting to let go. I ached for my beloved husband and what came to mind was a quote I read from Rosa Parks: "Have you ever been hurt and the place tries to heal a bit, and you just pull the scar off of it over and over again."

"There are two types of people in the world: those who prefer to be sad among others, and those who prefer to be sad alone."

Nicole Krauss, The History of Love

THE UNVEILING AND MEMORIAL SERVICE

Date: Thursday, October 25, 2012
From: Deena
To: Dear Diary

Sunday's Memorial Service & Unveiling was a very emotionally draining, but necessary day. We arrived early to set up the chairs and check the cenotaph and it was understated and perfect – just as we hoped it would be.

Adam had a tough time getting through his speech; he broke down about four times and it just broke my heart, but he regrouped and soldiered through, as I knew he would. Brian and Jon also spoke and although they did their best to mask their anger it came through loud and clear. After the service I acknowledged their ambivalent feelings – love mixed with frustration at the years of volatile ups and downs with Kevin - and respected that they were being authentic and true to themselves. Perhaps it was good to have a Reality Check

during the service, given that everybody who attended was estranged from Kevin due to his illness – with the exception of Adam
and me. To do otherwise would be to ignore "the elephant in the
room".

This was a lay service led by Adam and me, and since his speech
focused on memories of Kevin, my speech was more like a brief ser-
mon helping family and friends gain a degree of closure. It was very
moving to have Kevin's friend Tanner there as well as his Uncle Bernie from California. All of Brian's wife's family was there as well as
several friends whom we hadn't seen in years.

After my speech, my nephew Jeremy did a lovely job singing my
Tribute to Kevin. Adam came up and stood with me while Jeremy
sang it. That was tough for him but I loved him for doing that and
I'm glad I did it as my musical message for Kevin. It was inspired by
the early morning Google Maps viewing of Kevin's final resting place
in Brazil, when I listened to Elton John's song on iTunes. Perhaps it
was my own Reality Check, because it was a very sad song.

MUSICAL TRIBUTE TO KEVIN
Adapted By Deena from Original song "Daniel"
by Elton John and Bernie Taupin

Kevin is traveling tonight on a plane.
I can see the red taillights heading south in the rain.
I think I see Kevin waving goodbye.
No, that's not Kevin - that's just the clouds in my eyes.
Brazil was the place where he searched for his dreams.
Kevin said it's the best place that he's ever seen.
He should know, he's been there enough.
Yes, I miss Kevin. Oh I miss him so much.
Kevin my stepson, fueled by passion and pain.
But you just found this world way too hard to explain.
Your flame burned bright, but you gave up the fight.

Kevin you're a star in the heavenly night.
Kevin my stepson, fueled by passion and pain.
But you sure found this world just too hard to explain.
Your dreams - they died. You left with no "Goodbye".
Kevin you're a star in the infinite sky.
Kevin is traveling tonight on a plane.
I can see the red taillights heading out in the rain.
I think I see Kevin waving goodbye.
Yes it looks like Kevin is now a star in the sky.
I'm sure that must be Kevin - he's that bright star in the sky.

The service ended with Adam's brother Steven reading the Mourner's Kaddish (prayer), followed by the classical music Adam chose for the finale – "Lark Ascending".

The weather was perfect – a crisp, cool, sunny, and colorful autumn day. After all the warnings we were given to be done with the service before 11am, it turns out the closest unveilings and burials were in sections far from where we were. So there was ample time to linger after the service without any need to feel rushed, which also was a blessing. There was no need for the staff to have put such pressure on us – we could have had the service at 11am; however, by having it at 10am we had extra time to visit with family and friends before heading to the reception.

Alice was waiting for us upon arrival at her restaurant. The separate party room was just the right size. Brian and Sari brought photos of Kevin, and Alice set up a small display table. Everybody enjoyed the meal. Adam and Brian and his family were surrounded by people who cared for them and loved them. Although this was a tiring short trip for my mother-in-law, Dorothy loved being with her two sons, two surviving grandchildren, and her two great-grandsons. I sat with Jon, my daughter-in-law Jacqueline, plus Jeremy, and Tanner, loving every minute listening to their stories: and Adam joined us, too. Warmth and laughter filled the room. I wished there was a way to bottle it and bring it home.

Our flights were on schedule – no problem on arrival or departure. That made it easier for Dorothy. We were so glad she was able to come with us, and so was she.

After we dropped Dorothy at her apartment and got her resettled, we drove home and Adam held my hand and said, "Thank you – I am so grateful for all you did. It was the right thing to do after all." That was the most meaningful and priceless gift I'd had in a long time – the one that counted the most.

The Baxter Family Love Boat narrowly avoided capsizing in the storm: Despite its tattered sails, missing rudder and damaged boom, the hull was strong and watertight and we had safely navigated through the turbulent, angry sea to find a safe harbor.

Music by Diegoberto
The artist loves music and karaoke.
NAMI Anything Goes: Art-From-The-Heart Project
(Author's note: It was poignant how he included 'Father' in this creative collage.)

A few days after we came home from the service, Adam and I were talking over dinner. He was struck by the number of people who attended the service that found comfort from their belief in heaven, where they would be reunited with their loved ones. In his case, being an avowed atheist, he never thought about the down side: the utter finality when something, like your child taking his life so young, happens and you have no belief in an afterlife. The experience of losing Kevin to suicide did not change his belief system in any way, so I don't expect him to be heading off to Friday night services at the temple or Sunday services in a church anytime soon; but I found it beneficial that he gained at least a broader perspective of the value of religion.

On Death & Dying
"Death be not proud, though some have called thee
Mighty and dreadful, for, thou art not so,
For, those, whom thou think'st, thou dost overthrow,
Die not, poor death, nor yet canst thou kill me."

John Donne

A parent's loss of a child, whether in utero, infancy, or any other time up to and including adulthood, carries with it an additional dose of pain. Suicide adds yet another dimension. As Gilda Radner faced the end of her battle with ovarian cancer she said, "Cancer is probably the most unfunny thing in the world..."[11]; the same can be said about suicide. As we dealt with the losses that book-ended our summer of 2012 – Kevin's suicide and Jacqueline's pregnancy - we had friends dealing with losses of a very different kind, with dark humor surfacing in the most unexpected ways and mocking human suffering with absurdity.

Two friends of mine lost their mothers. Peggy's mother was ninety-five and succumbed to cancer as did Suzie's mother who died at eighty-five from a long list of illnesses, including lung cancer.

Peggy was her mother's primary caretaker when she was diagnosed with cancer, and she moved her into her home in Michigan when she could no longer live independently. Sadly, her mom was too sick to come to her Florida condo, but that was where she always planned to spend her final days. Her Florida condo faced the Gulf of Mexico and she loved the view during the day and the sunsets at dusk.

Peggy was very close with her mother and had eight other siblings; however, she was the only one who was single and she was able to set up a separate room in her home with a hospital bed and additional space for a home health aide.

"Deena, I was so blessed to have that time with my mother," she said. "But my mother was a difficult woman and could be a handful. As the cancer spread, she got angry a lot and would take it out on me as well as the home health aide. At the end she was sedated a lot with morphine, which managed her pain, but she was often delusional as she drifted in and out of consciousness. She was also very religious – a devout Irish Catholic – and sometimes she ranted at God or would tell me she spoke to my father and other friends in heaven.

"The last week she was mostly unconscious but every time she wasn't she asked, 'Peggy, am I dead yet?' and I would hold her hand and assure her she wasn't. But after the 50th time asking me this, I was so frustrated I told her, 'No, mother, but if you keep asking me I'm going to accelerate the process.' With that, the home health aide burst out laughing and mom thankfully drifted back to Never Never Land."

"At my age I do what Mark Twain did. I get my daily paper, look at the obituaries page and if I'm not there I carry on as usual."

Sir Patrick Moore

Suzie's mother was ailing for years and misdiagnosed as well. Her mother took so many medications each day that the interaction of all the side effects significantly impacted her quality of life. So she would pick and choose which meds to favor each day by announcing, "Hello kidney! You are getting a break today so I can poison my liver and melt my stomach, so please behave and just do your thing. I'll get back to you tomorrow."

By the time her lung cancer was properly diagnosed it had already metastasized and she deteriorated within a matter of a few weeks. Like Peggy, Suzie was her mother's primary caregiver. She and her husband live in London in a small home. Suzie's twenty-something daughter also lives with them so space was at a minimum. Not wanting to put her mother in a nursing home, she moved her mom into her home, set up a hospital bed in their dining room, and put the furniture in storage. It was a stressful time for the family.

Suzie and her husband were taking a much-needed weekend away at a country inn, when she got an urgent call from her daughter saying she needed to come home. "Grand mummy is unconscious, and her breathing is very shallow." she said.

Suzie promptly called her sister and other family members and within a few hours they were all standing vigil around her mother's bed. "Everybody made it, and we were packed tightly into the dining room, holding hands, and everybody was crying. Mum looked really terrible. The hospice doctor stopped by and after examining mum he said, 'It won't be long.' And with that, mum opened her eyes wide, stared at all of us, bolted upright and shouted, 'Oh, Piss off everybody! Get me some supper.' She was just not ready to go yet, and as much as it would have been a blessing to have her die that day, she hung on for another two months."

"My grandmother was a very tough woman. She buried three husbands and two of them were just napping."

Rita Rudner

My good friend Marj died from lung cancer after being a dedicated chain-smoker for sixty years. She and her husband had no children or close family and the last thirteen years of her life was non-stop stress ruled by her husband's disease – Alzheimer's. She wasn't afraid to die, not at all, in fact she often told me she welcomed it. That always made me sad, but she felt she was living hell on earth.

Although she was raised Catholic, she gave that up in her twenties and had no use for religion. Some of her dearest friends in the neighborhood were an ex-priest and ex-nun who were married. Marj's caregiver was her hair stylist Amy, whom she treated like a daughter. Amy and four other close friends of Marj's were taking turns staying with her in her home, with hospice also providing nursing care and pain management. As the end drew near, Amy, who was a devout Catholic, called the ex-priest and asked him to come over to administer the last rites. He still had his old vestments and as he headed out the door he grabbed his old stole – the sacred vestment worn around his neck when he would conduct masses and administer to the sick.

"I'm not sure this counts, since I'm an ex-priest," he told Amy and the other friends upon arrival.

"That's okay. I talked with Marj when she was lucid and she said she was willing to compromise, just in case, and who better to do that with than an ex-priest," Amy responded.

He sat down on the edge of Marj's bed, and when she felt the bed move she opened her eyes and said, "Oh Father, I must be in heaven. I've waited all my life to get a priest into my bed."

> *"There are worse things in life than death. Have you ever spent an evening with an insurance salesman?"*
>
> *Woody Allen*

And I tell Adam I have found the perfect inscription for his tombstone:

> *"Here lies an Atheist. All dressed up and nowhere to go."*
>
> *A real inscription found on a grave marker*

PART II

THE VOICES OF
THE MIND SPEAK

The Message by Heather
NAMI of Collier County art program artis

MENTAL ILLNESS SPEAKS

"The mind is its own place, and in itself can make a heaven of hell, a hell of heaven."

John Milton, Paradise Lost

I achieved my goal of "presenting the best of Kevin" - in the initial notice to family and friends, the obituaries that were published in the newspapers, and to the extent possible, at Kevin's memorial service. However, the reality of what Adam and I had been dealing with on a day-to-day basis over many years with Kevin was quite a different story.

It's this clash that is hard to deal with – how to reconcile these opposing views. The work ahead for Adam and me included getting our feet back on the ground post-Kevin and establishing our New Normal. Adam has been traveling that path mostly in private, knowing he has my love and support. For me, the journey includes facing the reality of mental illness and its significant reach into the DNA of our respective families and our society. It has rocked my family of origin's boat, The Baxter Family Love Boat and The Humanity Ship – it is ubiquitous. My hope is that in writing this story it will dispel some of the stigma that shrouds it in darkness. It is time to let the mind speak when it is healthy and when it is ill – to give it a voice and to listen.

ACCEPTANCE OF ILLNESS

I am convinced that the way we deal with illness has a lot to do with how illness was treated when we were young. I grew up in a large family with four siblings and other visitors of all shapes and sizes coming and going. My mother had a hectic, busy life with little time to tend to sick children. She had zero tolerance for anyone slowing down the pace so she sent us to school even when we were sick. We could forget about faking sick days: feigning a sore throat or upset stomach. Often, the school nurse would have to call home and have my mother come to school to pick us up if we had a fever or were vomiting. That brought little relief, since she took her time coming to get us and stopped to do errands on the ride home. We quickly learned that we had to be close to death to have a Sick Day. As an adult, this makes you pretty adept at going to work even when you are sick. If you are also a single parent, like I was for a couple of years, you use your sick days when your children are ill and drag yourself into work when you are ailing. The down side is there is little concern about giving a cold or the flu - or worse - to your colleagues and anyone else in your sphere.

That's because American culture is ambivalent about illness: on the one hand we promote Big Pharma in every other media ad and every doctor's office but we are reluctant to face the reality of how our lifestyle encourages – even celebrates – unhealthy living.

My experience has also been that most workplaces are unforgiving and unsympathetic toward illness. Business metrics favor increased productivity and lower costs. Despite the enormous amounts of money spent on physical and mental health it is not something we have fully integrated into our mindset or the workplace. And yet health related costs – in real dollars and lost productivity – are ever present in every federal, state and local government budget as well as those of corporations, non-profits, small businesses and families. It presents itself as a visible line item or as a hidden cost of doing business.

OUR CULTURE OF HUMILIATION...AND DENIAL

Every day millions of people are affected by major and minor health challenges. Caregivers are some of the most overworked, underpaid, and undervalued resources and they have few advocates fighting for support services. Illness often does not become real in the public square until a celebrity or prominent person is stricken with a critical illness and uses their fame to shine a light on it. People like Michael J. Fox and Robin Roberts have brought that type of focus to Parkinson's and myelodysplastic syndromes, known as M.D.S.: a rare and debilitating blood disorder. They deserve praise for their courage and for the positive impact their celebrity advocacy has had on research funding and bone marrow donors.

What about mental illness? Although many celebrities and prominent people are impacted by it, my experience has been that our culture is unforgiving whenever it is disclosed.

I was a young twenty-something in 1972 when Tom Eagleton, the United States Senator from Missouri, was Democratic presidential candidate George McGovern's nominee for vice president. What wasn't disclosed to McGovern's staff during the vetting process was that between 1960 and 1966, Eagleton, who suffered from bouts of depression, had received electroconvulsive therapy twice. The media had a field day and eighteen days later McGovern requested his withdrawal and replaced him on the ticket with Kennedy in-law, Sargent Shriver. The Republicans used this as a campaign issue, questioning McGovern's judgment during the election. It sent a loud message to the American electorate that mental illness was shameful.

TIME OUT FOR A
MENTAL HEALTH UPDATE
Story will resume shortly

"There is a thin line between genius and insanity. I have erased this line."

Oscar Levant

Fast-forward to today; here are some sobering statistics[12] on how mental illness impacts all of us:

1. *Size: The United States spends $113 billion on mental health treatment, or about 5.6 percent of the national health-care spending (2011, Health Affairs journal).*

2. *Focus on meds: According to the Kaiser Family Foundation, mental health dollars mostly go toward prescription drugs and outpatient treatment - a big shift away from inpatient treatments (1986 – 2005).*

3. *Limited access: Access to mental health care is more limited than other types of medical services. In 2010, the Bureau of Labor Statistics estimated there were 156,300 mental health counselors in the U.S. and 89.3 million residents live in areas with limited or no access to mental health services, 61 percent more than the 55.3 million people lacking access to primary-care, and 100 percent more than the 44.6 million lacking access to dental health.*

4. *Cost: Mental health care is costly and presents a barrier to treatment for 45 percent of those who go untreated. A quarter of the 15.7 million Americans who received mental health care listed themselves as the main payer for the services; outpatient treatment out-of-pocket costs between $100 and $5,000. This highlights the significant limitations on insurance coverage for mental health services.*

5. *Stigma: Attitudes about mental health services are another big barrier to care. In a 2007 study of 303 untreated mental health*

patients, "66 percent thought the problem would get better on its own, 71 percent wanted to solve the problem on their own, and 47 percent cited financial obstacles as a reason not to seek treatment. Still, attitudinal barriers about the value of mental health care seemed to be the biggest obstacle."

6. State fiscal constraints: According to the National Alliance on Mental Illness, states cut $1.8 billion from their mental health budgets during the 2008-9 recession, and legislate more oversight for mental health services than for physical health. The biggest budget cuts were made to long-term, inpatient care facilities and this shifts treatment of the mentally ill toward other places in the health-care system. NAMI reports that Rhode Island has seen "a 65 percent increase in the number of children living with mental illness, boarding in public emergency rooms" after a series of budget cuts.

7. Federal mandates: Recent federal legislation requires more expansive insurance coverage for mental health services. The Mental Health Parity and Addiction Act of 2008 (MHPA) bars insurers from putting up financial barriers to mental health care that are greater than those created for physical treatments. The Affordable Care Act creates more mental health mandates, by requiring all insurers who sell on the exchanges to include such treatments in their benefit packages.

And yet the loopholes in the MHPA requiring prior authorization and proof of medical necessity end up being discriminating: a patient seeking treatment for acute mental illness, like attempted suicide, has to wait for treatment while their doctor submits voluminous paperwork and waits for approval. A patient showing up in the ER with signs of a heart attack would be treated immediately. Those loopholes are only now being addressed with new legislation – more than five years after MHPA was enacted.[13]

According to Rachel Howard, Health policy intern with the Center for American Progress: "Over half of the U.S. prison population is mentally ill, and people who suffer from mental illnesses are represented in the criminal justice system at rates between two and four times higher than in the general population. Given that studies find people with mental illnesses to be no more prone to violence than those without mental illnesses, the root of this overrepresentation in prison clearly lies in our mental health system's short-comings. Instead of treating the underlying biological and environmental causes of these disorders, we are criminalizing and incarcerating the mentally ill."[14]

Gary Fields and Erica Phillips writing in The Wall Street Journal, say "American prisons have replaced state mental hospitals as a place to warehouse the mentally ill. The country's three biggest jail systems – Cook County, Ill., Los Angeles County, and New York City – are treating more than 11,000 prisoners for mental illness on a typical day. By comparison, the three largest state-run mental hospitals have a combined 4,000 beds."[15]

"Knowledge speaks, but wisdom listens."

Anonymous

Despite these numbers, it is worthwhile taking a look at how the media portrays mental illness.

It is my belief that an overwhelming majority of people in twelve-step and other types of addiction recovery programs dealing with substance abuse (alcohol, prescription and non-prescription drugs, and illegal drugs), overeating, hoarding, over-shopping, gambling, cutting, shop-lifting, and many dealing with obsessive-compulsive disorders, suffer from depression and other mental illnesses. The particular addiction starts out as a coping mechanism and over time becomes a habit with yet another set of problems. Dual diagnoses of addiction and mental illness are common.

Yet schlocky talk shows, reality TV, network, cable and tabloid news services, and the Internet have raised it to the level of entertainment and the sensationalism brings shame and ridicule. The only thing this helps is program ratings.

What is changing is that Baby Boomers (typically defined by demographers as those born between 1946 and 1964) are aging and they give voice, $$$ and numbers to issues that are important to them. Folks like Gail Sheehy are using their talents to advocate for caregivers while others like AARP are lobbying for access to quality healthcare for seniors. Thankfully, they are all including mental health as well as physical health services in their respective agendas. Glenn Close is another woman who is using her talent to change the attitude of people toward mental illness, through her advocacy work with *Bring Change 2 Mind*. Another way this is being brought front-and-center are the high percent of Iraq and Afghanistan war veterans returning home after numerous deployments with serious war injuries – physical as well as emotional.

Boomers are also making their presence known in other ways:

According to Catey Hill, "Boomers are the least happy of all age groups, according to a 2008 study published in the American Sociological Review journal. 'The generation as a group was so large, and their expectations were so great,' Yang Yang, the author of the study, told the American Sociological Association, 'not everyone in the group could get what he or she wanted due to competition for opportunities.' Another report from the Pew Research Center concludes the boomers – even when they were younger – have been consistently less happy than other generations for the past 20 years."

Hill goes on to say, "Maybe it's because so many grew up in the '60s, but whatever the excuse, boomers are drinking and drugging their way into old age at a rate much higher than their parents' generation. The number of people fifty and over who were admitted to substance-abuse treatment programs increased 136 percent between 1992 and 2010, according to the latest data from the Substance Abuse and Mental Health Services Administration.

"Alcohol is the most common reason that boomers seek treatment, but the proportion of admissions of people over fifty for heroin abuse nearly doubled and for cocaine use more than tripled over that period.

"Because of the magnitude of these changes and their potential impact, it is increasingly important to understand and plan for health-care needs, including substance-use-prevention and treatment needs, of this population," the administration writes."[16]

Despite increasing numbers of Americans dealing with depression, ADHD, and many forms of addictions often rooted in mental illness, brain and mental disorders still carry a stigma. Perhaps it is because so little is really known about the brain, how it works, and the genetic, environmental, and lifestyle impacts on its optimal functioning. There is so much mystery surrounding it. Humans don't deal well with mysteries that cannot easily be solved in a one-hour TV episode, a movie, or between the front and back cover of a good novel. Unless we are masochists, we don't like prolonged or unresolved pain and suffering. Thankfully, brain imaging technologies and the Human Genome Project (HGP) are advancing the knowledge of brain science through collaborative research.

Am I overly optimistic? I don't think so. Eric R. Kandel is one who gives me hope and he is well credentialed - an American neuro-psychiatrist who received the 2000 Nobel Prize in Physiology.

Kandel highlights the problem of pinpointing "the underlying biological bases of most psychiatric disorders". Although much research still needs to be done to bring it to the same level as heart disorders, the gap is closing, thanks to recent research efforts.

Specific to the biology of depression, scientists used brain-scanning techniques to identify several components of brain circuitry. The research revealed four important findings:

1. *The neural circuits disturbed by psychiatric disorders are likely to be very complex.*

2. *Specific, measurable markers of a mental disorder can be identified and can predict the outcome of two different treatments: psychotherapy and medication.*

3. *Psychotherapy is a brain therapy: It produces lasting, detectable physical changes in our brain.*

4. *The effects of psychotherapy can be studied empirically; it is a science.*

Viewed as a biological science, psychiatric disorders must include genetics and researchers are slowly fitting together the pieces of the puzzle, bringing promising new insights of how brain development is influenced by genetic mutations.

Research is showing that continuous division and copying of DNA leads to errors, and the rate of error increases with age. "These mutations are one reason older fathers are more likely to have children with autism and schizophrenia."

"Our understanding of the biology of mental disorders has been slow in coming, but recent advances like these have shown us that mental disorders are biological in nature, that people are not responsible for having schizophrenia or depression, and that individual biology and genetics make significant contributions… This new science of the mind is based on the principle that our mind and our brain are inseparable."[17]

I would add to that: our body chemistry and the environment in which we live are also critical factors, and until we treat *the whole person,* there are risks in focusing too narrowly on one part of the system that makes each of us perfectly imperfect human beings.

As we await further brain imaging and HGP breakthroughs, we're left with this fear of the unknown that fuels the stigma. Is mental illness contagious? Is that why it is so easy for individuals, families and society at large to deny its existence? Friends and colleagues who deal with diabetes, heart disease, and cancer rightfully deserve our compassion, understanding, and support. I have friends who died of lung cancer after a lifetime of chain smoking, and family members, friends and colleagues dealing with drug and alcohol addiction who received compassion, understanding and support. Those who are from generations ahead of me told me cancer carried a stigma that kept it 'in the closet' fifty years ago, so there is hope for mental illness finding the light.

TIME OUT FOR A COOTIE BUG BREAK
Story will resume shortly

"Mental illness is the last frontier. The gay thing is part of every-day life now on a show like 'Modern Family,' but mental illness is still full of stigma. Maybe it is time for that to change."

Eric McCormack

Let's take a look at stigma. I grew up playing the popular children's game called Cootie Bug. On the playground during recess in first grade, the boys would chase the girls, and if they successfully caught up with you the guy would tap you on the head and shout, "Oooh, you've got cooties." That was a most undesirable label and once you were labeled, you could only rid your-self of the distinction by tagging the one who tagged you. Otherwise, you were marked for life – at least it seemed that way to six-year-old girls.

In reality, cooties were head lice and it wasn't at all funny when my cous-in gave it to me and my siblings; we were scratching our heads and having kerosene hair washes three times a day, burning our scalps, followed by combing with fine-tooth combs meant to capture the fried, dead critters.

By the end of eighth grade, the games at recess had matured significant-ly – sort of. You can decide for yourself. During science class we were sepa-rated by gender, taken into separate classrooms, and shown a film on human sexuality and venereal disease. For some reason the producer of the docu-mentary chose a parochial high school, of all places, as the setting (we were in public school). In showing how VD could spread, they put a hash tag on a person who had and was transmitting syphilis (red#) or gonorrhea (green#). This was obviously long before Twitter was ever imagined. My best friend

Cindy, who was Catholic, was sitting behind me and muttered, "I wonder if one of the nuns or priests will get tagged." That sure cut the tension but our teacher was less than amused. Just before recess, some of the boys stole paper, red and green markers, and a roll of masking tape. They drew big hash tags on them and went around slapping select girls on the back with them. Most of us didn't know they were on our backs until a friend would inform us. It was humiliating to say the least.

> *"I don't have any stigma attached to my body. When I'm in my own private space, I have very little on."*
>
> *Padma Lakshmi*

HOW MENTAL ILLNESS SPEAKS TO ME

Breakout by Diana
NAMI of Collier County art program artist
(Author's Note: I identified with the blue figure hidden but trying to emerge.)

The Reluctance to Reveal

Let it start with me. I had a maternal and paternal grandparent who suffered from depression and substance abuse – mostly alcohol. I was raised in an alcoholic, co-dependent home, with substance abuse, depression, addictions, and many family secrets: which is common in such households. I call the secret-keeping "the reluctance to reveal". From the time I was a child I have experienced bouts of depression, and I self-managed it using coping skills – some positive and some negative, as well as therapy and support groups in adulthood. It was made more difficult due to my low tolerance for medication: more like zero tolerance.

After a particularly traumatic experience in my teens when I personally experienced life-threatening violence, I begged my mother for permission to get counseling. Her response was to ridicule me and tell me to just "tough it out". I was suffering from what would be called today post-traumatic stress disorder (PTSD). Periodically, I envied friends and family members who buried their sorrows in recreational drugs or found relief in a good stiff drink, but my body simply does not handle any of that well, and it has never been an option for me. Al-Anon, talk therapy, meditation, and the right support group and resources have been invaluable, as well as having the love and support of my second husband, Adam.

My maternal uncle and godfather died by suicide back in the mid-1990s, leaving his four daughters and second wife to deal with his unexpected and sudden exit. I ached for my cousins after the funeral as they gathered upstairs during the reception to read the note their father left for them: such sadness and pain. I found it quite interesting that my cousins had very different opinions about sharing the real cause of their father's death, with their own children. Of the three who had children, one told her sons that grandpa committed suicide, and the other two did not share that information with the kids. As a consequence, the sibling who told her two sons the truth was ostracized for a long time by her sisters. This added yet another dimension to the loss: the reluctance to reveal.

Illness – mental and physical – can impact family planning as well. My younger brother and his wife did not have children, in part because my sister-in-law had parents and many relatives who suffered from debilitating depression, and alcoholism. She simply did not want to risk "the depression gene" being carried forward. In their mid-thirties my brother developed autoimmune disease and that was also something they did not wish to pay forward. Ironically, when they were in their late forties they adopted a beautiful little two-year-old girl, whose parents suffered from such extreme mental illnesses, Child Protection Services had removed her from the home. She was put in two different loving foster homes by the time my brother and his wife were given custody and it took two more years – until she was four – for the adoption to be official. My niece, now fifteen, is thriving and my hope is that she will continue to do so.

Adam's ex-wife, Kevin's mother, suffered her whole life from debilitating depression. It impacted their marriage, and since she had custody of their two sons, it impacted both of them in different ways. Early in our relationship Adam told me he never filed one of her therapy or medication bills through his firm's insurance, though they ran into the tens of thousands of dollars. This is how he and many others were dealing with it in the 1970s and '80s. Only a handful of large companies offered mental health coverage and those who did had caps on coverage. In Adam's case it was a combination of limited coverage and the reluctance to reveal. He was concerned about the possible impact this would have on his own career advancement.

Her mental illness also impacted our marriage in profound ways. Adam did not like to 'rock the boat' with her since it made things more difficult for Brian and Kevin. However, in doing so, he often didn't appreciate how much that impacted our relationship and our home life with my son Jonathan. At first, he got close to Jon; but when his ex-wife told Brian and Kevin, "Your father is replacing you with his new stepson," he pulled back. She sent notes with the boys every time they visited on alternate weekends, many addressed to me, telling me what I needed to buy or provide for the boys. She took us to court three years after our marriage, when we enforced a work provision in the divorce decree, and made sure the lawsuit papers were served the evening before Jon's Bar Mitzvah service.

Whenever I tried to set healthy boundaries, Adam resisted "in the interest of maintaining harmony" with her. She would manipulate the situation, time and time again, and use it as a wedge between the boys and us. As Kevin grew up, he also became quite adept at this same type of manipulation, and he seemed to pick up where his mother left off after she died in 2001. He would endear himself to Adam and drive a wedge between Adam and me, and Adam allowed that to happen.

I often felt alone, despondent and very depressed, and turned it inward. Many times I thought about ending the marriage but then Adam and I would find a level of détente or some other life crisis would take priority, as often happens in life: my father had frequent illnesses, Adam's father was undergoing electroconvulsive therapy for depression, a risky investment tanked and Adam and 70+ other partners in his firm were facing possible bankruptcy, and my ex-husband lost his job in Jon's senior year of prep school just as he was applying to all top tier colleges, etc. During this time, Kevin continued to need an inordinate amount of 'care-and-feeding'. I chose to channel my energies into getting my MBA, mid-career; as a part-time student at night after work, I felt I was at least doing something constructive.

Kevin's maternal uncle also ended his life by committing suicide when Kevin was in college. His brother Brian found him at the family's home, and it was a scene I wish he had never had to discover. I could never understand why his mother asked him to go to the house, since she suspected this might be the case, but perhaps this lack of judgment was a result of her own mental illness. The whole tragedy was made worse by the local paper sensationalizing it in a tabloid-style exposé the day of the funeral. In this instance, too much was revealed about their uncle's mental state in the public square and Brian and Kevin took it especially hard since their names were also included in the article. In defense of my stepsons, I called the reporter, brought her to task for her insensitivity, and questioned her sense of decency. To which she responded, "What are you so upset about? That's yesterday's news."

Yesterday's news for the general public but not for those who are humiliated by that news – it is lasting. All I could think about was the movie, *Absence of Malice* starring Sally Field and Paul Newman. Boy, could I relate to the consequences of innuendo and defamation!

 **(IN)SANITY BREAK**

Story will resume shortly

"I don't suffer from insanity. I enjoy every minute of it."

Anonymous

Eckhart Tolle has one workshop where he talks about the madness surrounding us, and you come away asking yourself, "Who is *really* insane?"

This is at the top of my mind as I stand before the mirror, freshly showered, and dressed to go out. It is just a few days after losing Kevin. My spirit is numb, my mind is grieving over our loss and my heart is aching. Yet I have an important appointment to keep and I don't want to be late. And so I prepare to face the world by undertaking that daily ritual practiced by women all over the world, and more and more men, too – the act of 'putting on my face'.

(Confession: I sometimes I do this at stoplights while driving. I was born twenty minutes late and have been trying to catch up ever since. I am making slow but steady progress, having cut it down to ten minutes. By the end of my life, perhaps I will be on time…maybe not. I tend to agree with Woody Allen: "I'm not afraid to die; I just don't want to be there when it happens." So don't wait up for me, I may be late for that too.)

On this particular day, I am 'putting on my face' at the vanity mirror in our bathroom, not my car. That means I glop green eye shadow on my eyelids ($15.00), black goo the consistency of bat guano on my eyelashes ($15.00), pink blush on my cheeks ($20.00), and two different colors of grease-paint on my lips (total = $30.00) in order to present my 'best self' to this insane world.

Really now, is this a good use of funds…or my time? Couldn't I put that $80.00 (plus another $5 tax that benefits the State of Florida), to better use, like writing a donation to the National Alliance on Mental Illness (NAMI)?

I can only laugh at myself for allowing corporate America to define what 'looking good' means. And that's the point – it is how our culture focuses on the exterior. And when you think about it, it is nothing more than a mask. It's what's inside that really matters.

Photo source: Susan Joy Smellie
NAMI art program artists display their colorful masks.

"The most important kind of freedom is to be what you really are. You trade in your reality for a role. You give up your ability to feel, and in exchange, put on a mask."

Jim Morrison

The appointment I was rushing to attend was a suicide support group meeting. Upon introducing myself, the group leader brought me to task for saying, "Our son committed suicide." The group referred to suicide as "death by mental illness." According to the group leader, the word, 'committed' aligns suicide with committing a crime - like murder, rape or theft. From a purely legal definition, it does share common characteristics such as pre-meditation and intent to cause injury, but is it illegal? Is it committing mur-der to take one's own life? Or is that a right? I leave it to the legal eagles and theologians to sort that out - it is above my pay grade.

However, being the curious person that I am, I came home after the meeting and did a bit of research. According to The Free Dictionary by Farlex:

> *Under Common Law, suicide, or the intentional taking of one's own life, was a felony that was punished by forfeiture of all the goods and chattels of the offender. Under modern U.S. law, suicide is no longer a crime. Some states, however, classify attempted suicide as a criminal act, but prosecutions are rare, especially when the offender is terminally ill. Instead, some jurisdictions require a person who attempts suicide to undergo temporary hospitalization and psychological observation. A person who causes the death of an innocent bystander or would-be rescuer while in the process of attempting suicide may be guilty of murder or manslaughter. More problematic is the situation in which someone helps another to commit suicide. Aiding or abetting a suicide or an attempted suicide is a crime in all states, but prosecutions are rare. Since the 1980s the question of whether physician-assisted suicide should be permitted for persons with terminal illnesses has been the subject of much debate, but as yet this issue has not been resolved.[18]*

Notice the sentence, "Some states, however, classify attempted suicide as a criminal act, but prosecutions are rare, *especially when the offender is terminally ill.*" Since Kevin's death I have had people tell me the very act of taking one's life means the person is mentally ill. Who determines when mental illness is terminal? A medical doctor is able to do this with physical illness, but who gets to decide when mental illness is involved? I feel it is at least important to raise this question. I have no answer. I am less concerned with the legalities of suicide and far more concerned with the ways in which modern society stigmatizes it, making it difficult for those dealing with it as well as their family members, friends, employers and colleagues.

Having learned to be stoic about illness was not just the norm in my family, but Adam's as well, and that included both physical as well as mental illness. Our culture seems to function the same way in the subtle and explicit messages that bombard us daily. Few people can tolerate being around hypochondriacs but on the other end of the spectrum, stoicism in the extreme equals denial – a refusal to, 'listen to our bodies': and that can prove to be life threatening. My younger brother denied his back pain and by the time kidney cancer was discovered it had already metastasized and he was dead within eight weeks, at age fifty-one. My former brother-in-law's wife had a sister who kept her colon cancer a secret and shortly after her death, his wife was diagnosed with the same disease and lost her battle at age fifty.

My family has long denied the prevalence of mental illness in our family tree. The same applies to Adam's: He has family members who dealt with bouts of depression and had electroconvulsive therapy (better known as shock therapy), and we both come from addictive families and know it is really tough to be labeled, 'mentally ill'.

One of my greatest challenges has been accepting just how ill Kevin was and the length of time mental illness had been the root cause of so many of his behavior problems. It was made harder by the lack of a correct diagnosis, which is common with bi-polar disorder, coupled with Adam's years of denial and Kevin's as well. Given what they experienced with close family members, especially Kevin's mother, they simply found it easier to dismiss it. Whenever I brought it up or other family members did so, we were met with resistance and anger – a brick fortress of denial. This was a form of dysfunctional DNA that frequently destabilized The Baxter Family Love Boat, with Adam and Kevin on one side of the boat, and me alone on the other side.

One of the few exceptions was during Kevin's senior year in high school. He applied early action to Fenton College and was accepted. Soon after, he experience a bad case of 'Senior-itis', skipping classes, hanging out with an unsavory group of guys, not completing assignments, and letting his grades fall. What was in jeopardy was his acceptance to Fenton and he simply didn't seem to care. After much coaxing, Adam convinced Kevin to move to our home and commute to school, succeeding only after promising to buy him a new car in exchange for getting counseling. That lasted for less than six weeks. His behavior was extremely disruptive, testing boundaries like most other teens and staying out well past curfew.

He often didn't show up for therapy appointments and his anger and aggression were often directed at me – the parent who was around the most since Adam got home from work later than I did. It came to a head when he came home at 4am one Sunday, with his car towed to the front door, totaled in a one-car accident. Despite Kevin's elaborate fabrication about what happened, the truth is more likely that he was drunk, fell asleep behind the wheel, swerved off the highway, and waited a while to get help till he had sobered up a bit. The police report and forensics (skid marks, no markings on his car) did not match his story at all – that he was hit by another car, making him swerve off the road. Looking at his wrecked car in the light of day, he was lucky to have survived. He refused to take responsibility for his actions, and out of frustration, he vented his anger at me one evening to such a high degree that I feared for my safety and demanded that he leave until his father came home an hour later.

Kevin returned to Worcester to live with his mother but a couple of months later, this same anger and defiance resurfaced during his high school graduation. We received a call from the principal informing us that Kevin refused to follow the school rules when he insisted on memorializing a classmate who had taken his own life half way through their sophomore year. Kevin went so far as to call his deceased friend's parents and invite them to the graduation, telling them he was going to honor their son Shawn during the ceremony. The school administration barred him from the awards ceremony and convocation service prior to graduation and threatened to call Fenton College and have his acceptance revoked. Adam had to keep Kevin in his car during the ceremonies, parked outside the building, to prevent him from entering as he had threatened to do. But he still defiantly inscribed Shawn's name on the top of his mortarboard and bowed his head for the principal to see it when he walked up to get his diploma. Later, he refused to drop the matter and decided to sue the Worcester School Board. It took a visit from the state lieutenant governor to work out a resolution with him. Whenever Adam or I tried to reason with him, he pushed back hard. He was steadfast in his termination that his friend Shawn would not be forgotten. More than twenty years later, I ask myself if this was, perhaps, an early sign that Kevin viewed suicide as an honorable way to exit when life got too painful and that the decision to do so should not be shunned by society. I wish he were here to answer that for me now.

About a year later we received a call from Fenton College in the spring of Kevin's freshman year, informing us that Kevin had had a breakdown. Against our wishes, he signed a franchise agreement with a house painting company. We had ample experience with the same company from my son's experience during his freshman year. The company intentionally targets eighteen-year-old college students who can legally enter into a contract. They woo them with the promise of high returns for a summer job as a "business owner": except that they start these kids out with less lucrative locations, less-than-reputable leads for paint equipment and cargo vans for sale, and they don't explain that those high returns come in the last few contracts. Most college freshman have no clue about cash flow or the realities of running a business. My son ended the summer more than $3000 in debt and spent ten months working tables at a college café to pay us back.

Like Jon, Kevin was sucked in by the hype. Although Fenton was located in Connecticut, Kevin planned to spend the summer living at home, so he requested a territory in the greater Boston area. The problem was the business model was quite clear that students needed to spend their weekends from February to May, plus Spring Break, going door-to-door and getting contracts signed up in order to be 80 percent committed before June. Kevin was busy with classes and although he bought a van, he trusted the referral from the company and ended up with a VW bus covered with Grateful Dead psychedelics. He thought his Dead-Mobile was too cool for words and we told him he needed to cover his own insurance.

The first weekend, instead of coming to Boston to work on contract engagement, he took his "too cool for words" VW van to Vermont on a ski weekend, and called us when the van died, a fitting tribute to Grateful Dead leader Jerry Garcia. Within twelve days he maxed out our AAA emergency road service and we refused to cover his repairs. He spent Spring Break skiing with his classmates at Whistler Resort in Canada, putting his expenses on a credit card he got in his own name (another way industry plays on eighteen-year-olds), and as exams neared and without any franchise contracts he was unable to handle the stress. In April, he came home to live with us, humbled by the experience, and Adam agreed to contact the paint company and negotiate an early termination with the proviso that Kevin would pay us back for advancing him the settlement. We also worked with the college to make it possible for him to complete his coursework and take his final exams as take-home exams.

Kevin spent the rest of the spring and summer working menial jobs and paying back the loan and paying off his credit card. We also insisted he get counseling and although he was put on medication, he didn't like the sexual side effects and soon stopped taking them. Sadly, the side effects of many mental health drugs are numerous, and it doesn't help when the person is also self-medicating – and not disclosing that. Having Kevin live with us was a stressful time for Adam and me.

It happened again in 1998, following his graduation from Fenton College. Against Adam's wise counsel, Kevin insisted on accepting a two-year paid internship with Lehman Brothers in New York City. He saw it as his ticket to a future in private equity on Wall Street but Adam warned him the salary looked great on paper but would not go far in New York City, and the hours would be brutal – upwards of 120+ per week. Kevin refused to listen. He was the only non-Ivy League intern to be selected for this highly competitive opportunity and he was dazzled by the generous signing bonus.

"You'd earn more per hour working at Burger King, even factoring in the signing bonus," Adam warned.

Kevin got defiant and said he could handle it. He envisioned working hard Monday through Friday, living it up in New York City during the weekends, and totally discounted the impact stress had on him. Two months after he started, his mother was diagnosed with emphysema and was ill. Kevin took time off on weekends to visit her in Worcester but his boss still required him to keep up with a full workload – upwards of 120 hours per week, including the weekends and most evenings. After four months, he arrived on our doorstep, literally, with his suitcases and boxes, having resigned from Lehman.

When the doorbell rang, I opened the door to find him standing there with all his belongings, with a smile on his face as he announced, "Hi, I'm home."

I was shocked. I had left MIT and was working from home as a consultant. Adam, taking the path of least resistance, neglected to tell me he had given Kevin permission to live with us – in our small apartment in Boston. So Kevin was upset that I didn't welcome him "home" with open arms.

I called Adam at work and said, "Is there something you didn't tell me? Kevin just arrived with all his stuff and announced he was 'home'. I told him he wasn't 'home', his 'home' was in New York. And he told me what happened."

He said, "Oh, didn't I tell you? I guess I forgot."

After two weeks, our home environment was impossible. Kevin's belongs were all over the living room and he was a slob. His lifestyle was itinerant and unaccountable, which would have been fine in his own apartment in NYC, but didn't work for us in Boston. His mother was calling 3-4 times a day, shouting at me if I answered the phone, which I often did for client calls. When I would put Kevin on the phone the two of them would engage in shouting matches, with him often slamming down the receiver, and the situation became untenable. I was unable to work at home and ended up spending time working at the public library, but it was far from optimal. Meanwhile, Adam was at work, often traveling for the entire week, safe in his world with an ability to block it all out. I envied him, but it also angered me.

I longed for, and needed, a stable home: a Baxter Family Love Boat that provided a peaceful oasis where each member, and the family as a unit, could thrive in harmony and weather the storms of life. I never gave up in that quest, but you can only do that if each member seeks a similar outcome and is willing to do their share of the heavy lifting. It's also elusive when you don't have all the facts.

It got worse when Lehman insisted Kevin pay them back for a pro rata portion of his signing bonus, which he had mostly used on his NYC apartment, signing a lease he ended up breaking and losing his security deposit plus two months' rent. I got so depressed I finally gave Adam an ultimatum: We would cover the cost of a studio apartment or furnished room and either

Kevin would move out or I would move out. I was grateful when Adam said Kevin would leave. We found him a very comfortable, bright furnished room a short walk from our Boston apartment and covered the cost for six months, until he found a job; however, Kevin held a grudge against me for years, saying I had "kicked him out" as if he was tossed on the street to fend for himself when that was not the case at all.

When we got him counseling, the therapist told me, "Kevin projects most all of his anger at you because he doesn't want to anger the one parent he feels aligned with – his father. He is also very angry with his mother because she is so helpless. So you are the beneficiary of these dynamics." I tried to remember that – often – but it was not always easy and I turned that frustration inward. By this time I had survived rupturing my back and cancer, burned through three Nordic Track Pro Skiers and was on my fourth one.

Especially in the last five years of Kevin's life, I stopped raising the need for psychiatric counseling but was always supportive on the rare occasions when Kevin would seek it. Prior to that, we found out he did this in the form of doctor-shopping, visiting psychiatrists mostly to get prescriptions for the drugs he was taking illegally – on campus, during college and grad school (Ritalin), and from friends and from colleagues at work. But he also got anti-anxiety medication to help him sleep. Another time we intervened was in 2007, when Kevin's anxiety and erratic behavior were again at an all-time high.

DR. PHILLIP HERMAN

In 2007, after we moved to Florida, we asked my son Jon to refer us to a top psychiatrist in Boston, where he was doing his residency. Kevin had been fired from his job in Boston in June 2006 and although he maintained his apartment in Boston, he was spending more and more time in Brazil, living off unemployment checks and dipping into his retirement savings. In late August, he returned to Boston for six weeks. He was acting erratically: showing up at my brother's office looking disheveled and demanding to see him, scheduling dinners with Jon and my nephew Jeremy and not showing up, and disrupting his brother Brian's life. We were able to encourage Kevin to start therapy with Dr. Herman by offering to cover the cost, since his medical coverage had expired. Adam flew to Boston in October for a joint appointment with Kevin and Dr. Herman the day after my brother's call about Kevin's unsettling behavior.

Kevin showed up late to the appointment and it was apparent to Dr. Herman that he was self-medicating. Ninety minutes into the session he abruptly left, leaving Adam and Dr. Herman behind. That was the last time the doctor saw Kevin. Adam left Dr. Herman's office, drove to Brian's house to spend the afternoon and evening, and Kevin dropped by to talk to his father, showing up at close to 10pm. He demanded his inheritance – on the spot he wanted Adam to write him a check for an amount based on…fantasy. The conversation did not go well and Kevin left in a highly agitated state, telling his father he didn't want to see him again. Brian was as astounded as his father.

Later that night Kevin sent an eBlast to everyone in his address book, including many members of Adam's family, my family, and many of our friends. Also included were several colleagues of mine with whom I had corresponded on Kevin's behalf regarding job leads. It was an engagement announcement and included an invitation to his Engagement Party/Open House – the next day! It also included a rambling monologue of his and Makyla's three-year courtship, "spanning two continents," his grandiose plans as a successful international businessman, and their future life together - spending six months of the year in Brazil and six months in Boston. He included a photo of himself and Makyla at sunset on a beach in Bahia, Brazil. To those who hadn't seen Kevin recently, he was barely recognizable with his shaggy hair, goatee and crazed expression. It was nothing short of frightening.

My phone started ringing immediately and my email Inbox was jammed by Sunday morning with friends and family not sure how to respond. Was this legit? Were we up in Boston and planning to go to the party? Should they go? I responded no, we were not going, we had never met Makyla, she would not be at the party, she was in Brazil, but they should go if they wanted to. It was a tough time for us – with Adam in Boston and me in Florida.

Kevin bought generous platters of food and wine for the afternoon Open House/Engagement Party and not surprisingly, only four people showed up – Brian, Sari and their two sons. Meanwhile, Adam was on his way back home. When I met him at the airport I found a despondent father hurting deeply from what had just transpired.

What Adam failed to share with me was Dr. Herman's diagnosis: Kevin was suffering from Bipolar Disease and was in a full manic phase. Adam didn't reveal that nugget of information until five years later, on the night we received the call about Kevin's suicide.

Interestingly, when Makyla and Kevin came for their only visit together, in August 2011, she told me that she didn't know anything about their engagement until Kevin returned to Brazil shortly after the Open House/Engagement Party. "He came back to Brazil and showed up at my house announcing we were getting married. That was the first I had heard about it. He said we were going to get married the next month." She loved him, and given her circumstances she was only too eager to marry a man who promised her such an exciting future.

A week after Kevin's obituary ran in the newspaper, Dr. Herman sent us a lovely letter with a poignant message. I called and left him a voice-mail, thanking him for his kind and comforting words. It had been close to five years since our last interaction with him – the session with him, Adam and Kevin in October 2007. Two days after that session, Kevin emptied his apartment, put his belongings in storage, flew to Brazil and Dr. Herman never saw or heard from him again.

Close to five years later, on July 22nd, Dr. Herman called. It was a Sunday afternoon and I was surprised he would take the time to call – on a weekend no less. We spoke for over an hour.

"I don't want you to think I study the obituaries, but I happened to see Kevin's photo and that's what drew me to the announcement," he revealed.

I confirmed his suspicion that Kevin had taken his life. He asked me to fill him in on Kevin's life in the intervening five years, which I did, and he said his saddest memory was not being able to get him to take medication. When I told him about the self-medicating with alcohol and marijuana, he said that was a particularly lethal combination for bi-polar disorder and could very well have brought on a psychotic episode that enabled him to end his life. His most helpful words were, "You and Adam did everything you could have done for Kevin. The guilt you are feeling is very normal: it is because you are really experiencing hopelessness at the situation you were unable to prevent despite your most earnest efforts. And it is much easier to blame yourselves than it is to accept that the situation was hopeless. It's human nature." I really appreciated both of these insights.

Dr. Herman's call came seventeen days after Kevin's death and soon after talking to Kevin's uncle from California. Bernie mentioned he never married because he feared passing on the suicide gene to his heirs. It seemed so unfair – carrying such a heavy weight throughout one's life: the long dark reach of mental illness, and the DNA connection.

After talking to Dr. Herman, I wrote the following entry in my journal: "I have boiled it down to two sentences: Kevin's mental illness coupled with bad choices about money, medication, marriage, career, and relationships, converged in The Perfect Storm, and left him no options in his own mind but to end his life. Thankfully he is out of pain but he has left behind so much pain and unbearable heartache."

Despite Dr. Herman's parting words earlier in the day, I was also feeling a lot of guilt at not insisting we send Kevin a one-way ticket home from Brazil to live with us and get treatment. I wasn't sure, based on history, if the disruption to our life and the impact on our marriage could take such sustained stress. Given Adam's frequent health challenges and path-of-least-resistance approach to conflict, I knew most of that stress would fall on my shoulders; but if we had him here in Florida, we could employ the Baker Act and get him into treatment for his own safety. That is the long, unresolved reach of suicide – death by mental illness. It slams reality in your face, forcing you to admit your own limitations and humanness as well as those you love. It is very humbling and painful. Whose responsibility is it to shoulder the burden of an adult child with severe mental illness – the adult child, the adult child's spouse, the adult child's employer, the adult child's parents or society?

ON SANITY – REALLY?

Therapists attempt to "make us well" so we can function in an insane world that pressures us to pursue a grand and elusive future without taking a nanosecond to enjoy the journey. It is all about The Quest for Success: Human-Doing versus Human-Being.

A WATER COOLER BREAK
Story will resume shortly

"Laughter and tears are both responses to frustration and exhaustion. I myself prefer to laugh, since there is less cleaning up to do afterward".

Kurt Vonnegut

My attempt to take a nanosecond was most certainly not to enjoy the journey I was on, but simply to get through it. One way my Eckhart Tolle meditation tutorial was helping me, was to reconnect me with Mother Nature. I have always found deep spirituality and connection to humankind in the magnificence of nature.

Right outside my back door, the deer come out of the preserve of thick, saw palmetto and vines, to dine nightly on our hibiscus bushes. The baby fawns cautiously venture towards the lower flowers and buds, tentatively smelling them, taking a little nibble, savoring that first bite, and devouring the rest with a bit more energy. The bolder bucks and does are card-carrying Frequent Diners; they head for the buffet of red and yellow blooms with gusto, sating their appetites. Ahh, the sacrifices we make – this garden offering to Mother Nature which soon comes to an end when my beloved Adam charges out the back door and rudely interrupts their feast by clanging two pots together. Nature meets man. My man.

In the morning, the day awakens to the sounds of birds and insects calling to each other. Above all, I feel most at peace around water – the ocean, a lake, and in our case, the Gulf of Mexico in all its glory, including magnificent sunsets (but I can do without the periodic Red Tide). At sunset, the dolphins crest as they feast on schools of fish, pelicans compete with fisherman along the town center pier for their catch of the day, little sandpipers scoot along the shoreline, and the occasional eagle perches in the nearby pine grove, scouting for unsuspecting prey.

On the way home from one sunset visit to the beach, I had a brainstorm, inspired by a feature article on Fallingwater in Architectural Digest. Fallingwater is the name of a very special house that is built over a waterfall. Frank Lloyd Wright, America's most famous architect, designed the house for his clients, the Kaufmann family. Fallingwater was built between 1936 and 1939. It instantly became famous, and today it is a National Historic Landmark.[19]

Why not create my own Fallingwater? Maybe having a fountain in our home would soothe my aching heart and perhaps even encourage those elusive tears to flow. I stopped at the mall and one of the big box stores had an entire section of decorative indoor fountains. The collective sound from their display was lyrical. I chose one with a distinctly feng shui feel, and as soon as I got home I set it up on the table in our entryway. The water flowed serenely over the tiered rocks…but there was no sound. None at all. It was obviously the sound from nearby fountains at the store that made me think this model would fill our home with similar tranquility. And after two days, an algae bloom was turning the water green and covering the rocks with matching green fuzz. It wasn't quite what I had in mind. I disassembled it and returned it for a second model.

This one was larger and distinctly anti-feng shui, in fact so much so, that the water flowed…everywhere. Adam went ballistic when the mist settled on his favorite rosewood table, so model #2 went back to the store.

Model #3 was a perfect fit: nice flowing fountain, soothing sound, and a controlled water flow. Adam suggested moving it into my office so I could enjoy it during the day. And I did, but the sound of the water did not bring tears to my eyes, it encouraged my bladder to flow and I spent most of the time in the bathroom peeing rather than working. Talk about unintended consequences!

So much for my own Fallingwater: I packed up Model #3 and returned it to the store. By this time I was on a first-name basis with the sales clerk.

"A case of 'Three Strikes, You're Out,'" I said. "I promise this is it, I give up."

"What should I write down for the reason *this* one is being returned?" asked the sales clerk.

"How about 'Product – okay. Customer's plumbing: defective.'"

"You have made my day," she said.

> *"It's okay to cry if you are in pain. Remember, tears are prayers too. They travel to God when we can't speak..."*
>
> Anonymous

HOW MENTAL ILLNESS SPEAKS TO MY COMMUNITY

You Try To Look Your Best Even Though Your Brain Is A Mess by Tim
NAMI Anything Goes: Art-From-The-Heart Project
Tim's favorite artist is Andy Warhol. He traced a photo that
looked a bit like a Warhol painting, then used color to emphasize his point.

Shortly after arriving in Southwest Florida in the late '90s, I joined several volunteer organizations that helped me quickly integrate and acclimate to my new home. I left the cold New England winters behind and came to the sunshine seeking physical and mental healing and a healthier living environment. Adam was still working in Boston, and came down on alternate weekends; six months later he was able to transfer to his firm's Miami office. Nine months after that he was offered early retirement and grabbed that opportunity. I continued doing consulting work full time, and then part time.

Until Adam retired, I had weekdays and evenings to myself and used that time to immerse myself in work and volunteer projects. At the local Newcomers Club I met many "newbies" and at one luncheon there were five social workers sitting at the table, all recent arrivals, and all launching new practices.

"Am I the only one at this table who isn't a social worker or psychotherapist?" I joked. "Is there some reason you all decided to move here?"

The woman to my right said, "Southwest Florida is 'The Recovery Capital of the World." She had recently been hired as a social worker for the David Lawrence Center (DLC), a mental health institution that focused mostly on substance abuse: alcohol and other addictions. The center was established in 1968 and was expanding and changing its focus. She had expertise in substance abuse intervention and recovery for individuals, and also worked with corporations and non-profits setting up their substance abuse recovery services. Her name was Charlotte.

Rumors circulated around town from time to time that certain celebrities were receiving treatment at DLC and I was glad she maintained her professionalism when another person at the table inappropriately asked for confirmation. But Charlotte did confirm there were high levels of alcoholism and drug addiction among the wealthy retirees flocking to the area. "It crosses all socio-economic boundaries," she said, "and there are plenty of doctors and pharmacists who are part of the problem, running pill-mills, writing illegal prescriptions and involved in illegal distribution of controlled substances and pain medication of all types."

By the time dessert was served all five of these therapists had given me their business cards. Since I wanted to have leads for both primary care and mental health care providers, I kept all of them, but I put Charlotte's at the top of the pile.

As the years rolled by, our city grew exponentially during the boom years. The DLC expanded its residential treatment facility, and more psychiatrists, psychologists and social workers were moving to the area and were joining existing group practices or launching their own. In 2010, Hazelden opened a new residential and outpatient treatment facility in Southwest Florida for alcohol and substance abuse. I have no doubt their due diligence for selecting this area was due to its projected growth as a retirement destination for Baby Boomers. Through the boom and bust years, the need for these services has continued to grow. In fact, the Great Recession has created an enormous pool of residents of all ages – young families, middle-agers as well as seniors - facing job loss, foreclosure, and economic insecurity, with resulting increases in substance abuse, depression, and domestic violence.

I started seeing a local mental health professional in 2000 and had first-hand experience with the limitations and side effects of medications for depression. I have been med-intolerant all my life so I was sensitive to Kevin's complaints about the side effects of the meds he was unable to tolerate. I tried other ways to manage my physical and mental health challenges - healthy diet, high quality vitamin supplements, regular exercise, and some not-so-constructive ways that weren't helpful.

Kevin chose a different route - alcohol and self-medicating. In my teens I got the drinking thing out of my system and by my mid-twenties I gave up all alcohol since it brought on chronic bladder infections. Yes, I did try pot four times, and unlike Bubba Clinton I did inhale, but I really didn't like it and wondered what all the hoopla was about.

Cocaine? Fuggedaboutit! Given my med-intolerance, I knew intuitively my heart would go South on me and I never had the desire. That was reinforced when Leonard "Len" Bias died at age twenty-two. Len was a first team All-American college basketball forward at the University of Maryland. He was selected by the Boston Celtics as the second overall pick in the 1986

NBA Draft on June 17th, but died two days later from cardiac arrhythmia induced by a cocaine overdose.[20] His untimely death impacted me deeply, and it obviously was a loss to his family. Len is considered by some sportswriters to have been one of the greatest players not to play at the professional level, so it was a loss to basketball as well.

Ironically, his legacy lived on not in the way he lived but in the way he died. House Speaker Tip O'Neill from Massachusetts sponsored the Anti-Drug Abuse Act and pushed it through Congress. The result was mandatory sentencing: five years for first-time offenders caught with 5 grams, ten years for those caught with 50 grams, and those dealing drugs received twenty year sentences. The unintended consequences were the arbitrary way the law was applied, and the enormous increase in the cost and infrastructure of incarcerating millions of offenders.[21]

I had friends from high school and college who ended up strung out on drugs. Closer to home, I attended a family wedding and several of my siblings, their spouses and many of my cousins disappeared. Turns out they were with the bride and groom celebrating by doing lines of coke. I was no saint, I had my own drugs of choice and at the top was trying to be a people-pleaser and if I couldn't perfect that I tried to be invisible – how's that for insanity! Dysfunctional DNA is alive and well in my family.

Over the years I saw my therapist off and on for individual counseling. Several times Adam and I saw her for couples counseling, most always for guidance on ways to handle Kevin's ongoing problems. Occasionally Adam saw her for individual counseling, too, and she was one of the first people I called the night Kevin died. Just like the Angie's List commercial, I have her on speed-dial if I need her and I am grateful for that.

After 9/11 I called Charlotte for guidance. By that time I was managing the MIT program on a consulting basis from my home office in Southwest Florida. We were hosting our annual conference in Boston on September 10th-11th, 2001. The city was on lockdown for a week following the 9/11 terrorist attacks since two of the planes departed from Boston's Logan Airport. For the next two weeks I partnered with our host hotel to take care of our international sponsors and students who were stranded in Boston. Returning home to Florida, I was totally drained. Charlotte received a call from a former client in Washington, DC, and she flew there to do a post-trauma intervention. Upon her return she was doing similar outreach programs in our community and I attended one of her local sessions. It was very helpful for me, and I sent some helpful handouts to my MIT colleagues as well. Over time, she and her husband became friends of ours; when Adam returned from Boston in 2007 after his session with Kevin and Dr. Herman, we contacted Charlotte for guidance, too.

NAMI

I also had the pleasure of meeting Kathryn Leib Hunter, Executive Director for the National Alliance on Mental Illness (NAMI) of Collier County. Active in the local branch of a women's advocacy organization, I was on the Women of Achievement Committee, and in 2006 Kathryn was one of our honorees. I contacted her in 2007 upon Adam's return from Boston when we were seeking support services for Kevin. We were considering having him committed but since he was no longer a minor, we weren't sure what we could do. She invited us to an evening program two days after Adam's return, where we learned about the Baker Act.

The Baker Act[22], as it is commonly known, is officially The Florida Mental Health Act of 1971. It allows for emergency or involuntary commitment. Judges, law enforcement officials, physicians, or mental health professionals can initiate The Baker Act when there is evidence that the person: 1) has a mental illness (as defined in the Baker Act) or 2) is a harm to self, a harm to others, or self-neglectful (as defined in the Baker Act.)

At the very time we were attending the NAMI program, little did we know that Kevin was on a plane headed to Brazil, soon to marry Makyla and settle there. Since he was now out of the U.S. and outside the national or state medical and legal jurisdictions, we didn't attend any further NAMI programs. But I did keep in contact with Kathryn and she was one of the people I called within days of Kevin's death.

When I called the local NAMI office, a woman named Rosemarie was working the reception desk over lunch. Kathryn wasn't available, but she asked if she could help. I poured out the reason for my call, about having just lost Kevin to suicide and how I needed to connect with Kathryn. As I was about to give her my name and phone number, it suddenly dawned on me that Rosemarie was one of the adult students my women's organization honored with a local scholarship – for two years running! I had met her in April at the spring awards luncheon and had written an article about our twelve local scholars. I remembered that Rosemarie worked at NAMI.

"Oh my goodness, Rosemarie – it's me, Deena Baxter! I'm the one who wrote the magazine article about the adult women local scholars!"

And with that she spent a good thirty minutes on the phone talking to me about what had happened and what I was going through. I could not believe how this call was turning out.

"Rosemarie, never in a million years did I expect that this was how we would connect," I said as we ended the call.

"Deena, how I wish it weren't for this reason," she said, with much professionalism and compassion.

Leave it to her, she hand-delivered my message to Kathryn and filled her in on what had happened. Kathryn called me the next afternoon. Over the next three months Kathryn and I met three different times at her office, and she encouraged me to keep in contact by email. She has become a friend and colleague beyond measure.

During my first visit with Kathryn, within ten days of losing Kevin, I was still numb with shock as I shared with her the craziness that seemed to be surrounding my life since his death. In the midst of sharing my heartache we also were laughing because…well, what else could you do with some of this stuff? And at that very moment, Rosemarie knocked on the door with a crisis-in-progress. When she saw me there, we hugged and I told her why we were laughing in the midst of such a tough time. She laughed right along with us, and soon left to manage the issue at hand.

As she headed out the door she said, "Deena, I'm glad you haven't lost your sense of humor!" Kathryn agreed.

I said, "I'm counting on you to tell me if I do because life's not worth living if you can't occasionally laugh at it. It will keep me going until I can learn how to cry again."

As Kathryn and I resumed our conversation, one thing I knew for sure was that I needed to find a purpose for all this pain and heartache.

"Kathryn, I'm not sure what form it will take, but I feel compelled to use Kevin's death to help dispel the stigma that surrounds mental illness. I can't let him die in vain and I want to end the legacy of suicide in the family. My stepson Brian has been through too much loss associated with mental illness."

She encouraged me to start keeping a journal and suggested I wait a year before deciding what to do. "It takes a long time to work through this and you'll be in shock for a while. Don't rush it when it's still so raw. You are still in shock."

As we wrapped up the first meeting Kathryn handed me a package that included NAMI resources and a NAMI video on DVD. She also grabbed some books off her shelf that she thought would be helpful. I wasn't ready to immerse myself in reading about mental illness at that point (understatement), and I told her so.

"I know myself well enough to know intuitively that whatever road I choose will not include going out on the stump speaking as an expert on suicide prevention or mental health. That's not what I could ever do. I lack the professional credentials and it would be too depressing," I confessed.

"I can understand that, but you could consider being a speaker at our law enforcement training programs for new law enforcement recruits. All city police and county sheriff's department new recruits are required to go through a training program to learn about handling mental illness and Baker Act situations. It is a public safety issue and it comes up frequently. Invariably it is a person diagnosed with mental illness and the question comes up about why these folks can't just take their medications. You could definitely address that. Often Baker Act incidents include alcohol or substance abuse and not always mental illness, but frequently it is all three," was Kathryn's response.

As I was leaving, she handed me one book she felt would definitely be of help, and she gave it to me as a gift, not on loan – a book titled *MIND ON THE RUN – A Bipolar Chronicle* by Dottie Pacharis.

"Deena, Dottie is like you in several ways. She lost her youngest stepson to suicide and shortly thereafter her oldest stepson died from the effects of alcoholism. Their birthmother suffered from severe depression and alcoholism and took her own life. Dottie spends part of the year in Southwest Florida and when she's here, she is a NAMI volunteer. She is advocating for changes to the legal system that prevented her family from dealing with her youngest stepson's bipolar disorder."

This was a gift, and so as not to be ungrateful I took it and said, "Thanks. I hope you won't be offended if I find that I'm incapable of reading a book that would be so depressing, especially after losing Kevin." She understood – and put no pressure on me other than hugging me tight. Kathryn is more than six feet tall, and I'm a little over five feet, so you can imagine how that looked – and felt. Yummy comes to mind…and a funny Kodak Moment too.

"Can I use your restroom? I never pass up a free one," I chirped.

We burst out laughing – it felt good. As she led me to the Ladies Room I added, "Since you gave me the gifts of your time plus these helpful resources as well as a copy of Dottie's book I am going send you a copy of a book I wrote. It was published two years ago and is about the joys of volunteering. I use humor to tell the story about a woman who volunteers in a charity thrift shop and some of the hilarious and bizarre characters that shop there. The underlying message is 'when you volunteer, you get more than you give'. It's a short read - perfect bathroom reading. It might be helpful to you for recruiting future volunteers and if nothing more, it will make you laugh."

"I look forward to reading it," she said.

A BRIEF PAUSE
FOR A BRAINSTORM
Story will resume shortly

"Those who dance are considered insane by those who cannot hear the music."

George Carlin

As I was using the restroom, I had an Ah Ha Moment. I would use my writing talent to write a book about the crazy aftermath I was living after losing Kevin. Kathryn was waiting for me at the front door, ready to lock it and close up for the day, and I shared my idea with her.

And then I added, "Kathryn, I'm going to write it and it could be used as a fundraiser for NAMI."

'I love it!! And I love that you are leaving with that sparkle back in your eyes and the energy that has always been your strength."

And she was right.

"Of all the things I've lost, I miss my mind the most."

Mark Twain

As I drove home, the book idea took hold and by the time I arrived I had a working title: *THE FUNNY FARM – Surviving Suicide.* I ran into my office, dashed off a thank you email to Kathryn - including the book title - and packaged up a copy of my book on volunteering so it would go out in the next day's mail. Then I made up a new file folder for the NAMI resources she had given me, and as I put Dottie's book in there, I noticed that Kathryn's endorsement was included on the back cover.

In August, my women's organization honored our local scholars at an afternoon pool party celebrating publication of the article featuring these local women who were earning their undergraduate degrees. This took place at my home, and Rosemarie arrived with her friend Richard. I was soon to find out that Rick wasn't just her friend but her husband – they were newlyweds! From writing the article I knew Rosemarie had artistic talent and so does Richard. They are a lovely couple and I am glad he was there to celebrate when we honored Rosemarie and the other scholars, and the publisher was there to give them copies of the magazine – hot off the press.

As this book began to take shape, Kathryn and I kept in contact periodically. She was busy with a grant opportunity from the State of Florida that was awarded to her team and I was busy with work, volunteering, and writing. In late February we reconnected by phone and I tossed out the idea of having children, teens, and adults who benefit from NAMI's wonderful programs and services do the artwork. This resonated with Kathryn and over the next six weeks I worked with Rosemarie, Lisa, another great staff member, and Susan Joy, a local licensed art therapist who is involved with some NAMI programs. What evolved from our brainstorming meeting was the *Anything Goes: Art-From-The-Heart Project*. I am grateful for their support and leadership in making this project a reality, and the inspiration for an even bigger project.

Self-expression of My Favorite Things by Alice
Alice's flowers and feminine designs are definitely a self-expression of her favorite things.
NAMI Anything Goes: Art-From-The-Heart Project

INTRODUCING DOTTIE PACHARIS

(Photo by Deena Baxter)

The first Thanksgiving after losing Kevin was a difficult holiday for Adam and me. Traditionally we had hosted a Thanksgiving Dinner For Our Orphan Friends – those who don't have family in the area. I've always preferred to have Thanksgiving at home with the turkey and all the fixings roasting in the oven and filling the house with fragrant aromas coupled with good friends and family gathered round the table; but coming home from Kevin's memorial service in late October, emotionally drained, I took one look at the turkey roaster and simply couldn't face doing all the planning and cooking. We spent the holiday quietly, taking my mother-in-law Dorothy to dinner at our social club for their delicious Thanksgiving feast. The club was warm and inviting and nobody left hungry.

After taking Dorothy to her apartment we came home and called our sons Brian and Jon and spoke with the grandkids, and watched a Netflix movie. My bedtime ritual is an hour of reading accompanied by a big bowl of popcorn. I wandered into my office and Dottie's book was sitting on top of the folder. Since I was feeling blue anyway, I thought of the expression "misery loves company," so why not read it.

MIND ON THE RUN – A Bipolar Chronical is not 'light reading', but I couldn't put it down. I read until 3am and finished it on Friday. Kathryn was right – Dottie and I had a lot in common since we both blended families with children from prior marriages. Her stepson Scotty had struggled with bipolar disease significantly more serious than our Kevin did, and yet there were many parallels. Sadly, both ended their lives the same way – by suicide. Her oldest stepson Buddy was so devastated about being unable to save his younger brother Scotty, he drank himself to death shortly thereafter. According to Dottie, the family never saw him sober after Scotty's death: Such a painful legacy, given their birth mother's depression, alcoholism and suicide.

Dottie was inspired to write this story of the family's struggle with the medical system as well as the judicial system in order to launch her advocacy campaign. Due to patient privacy laws and other health law restrictions, the family kept running into roadblocks that prevented them from helping their adult son get the treatment he desperately needed. Scotty's was an extreme example, but I recognized many of the behaviors in Kevin, though to a lesser degree.

I was even more depressed over the long holiday weekend from reading the book, but it also renewed my commitment to end the legacy of suicide in our family. I also felt an instant bond with Dottie - our shared desire to chip away at the stigma surrounding mental illness that prevents it from being treated. Her focus was on judicial barriers and restrictions; my focus was on the cost of shame, secrecy and denial.

I also asked Adam to read the book. He initially resisted but I implored, "Please do this for Kevin, for Brian and Jon, for our grandchildren, and for me."

He honored that request by reading it on Saturday. That evening we talked over dinner. As I've said before, Adam sees the world in black and white and that makes him an outstanding tax attorney. He also has an enormous capacity to forgive and forget and I admire him so much for that – most of the time. I tend to see the world in full-spectrum Technicolor, and I am extremely sensitive to pain and suffering. He saw few connections between Scotty's and Kevin's behavior but I accept that he simply couldn't go there – it served no useful purpose now that we'd lost our Kevin.

What we did agree on is to talk with Brian, Sari, Jon and Jacqueline about the impact Kevin's illness had on all of us, and our hope that should they or any of the grandchildren need mental health treatment, they have our full support and we encouraged them to get the best care available. I loved Adam for being willing to do that, but I knew it would be up to me to initiate those discussions and that proved to be the case.

However, I wanted and needed much more than that. I also needed to track down this woman named Dottie and thank her for writing the book and sharing her family's heartache. Theirs was a nightmare that lasted for thirteen years and, unlike a movie, it was real and they were unable to turn off the projector. I also I wanted her to know I hoped to join her quest to dispel the stigma surrounding mental illness but would accomplish that in a different 'voice'.

Once again, the Internet came in handy and I was able to find Dottie's contact information for her northern home and her residence in SW Florida. On Sunday of Thanksgiving weekend, she returned my call and we spoke at length. After exchanging emails we continued to keep in contact and share each other's progress. She has launched her advocacy crusade and is being invited to speak at medical and legal conferences. She has written many articles and opinion pieces that have been published and are making a difference by engaging legislators and the mental health community in discussions about the unintended consequences of patient privacy laws.

I was blessed to spend an afternoon with her on Monday, April 15th, when she stopped by for a visit. Dottie is a delightful lady, articulate, compassionate, and committed to changing our mental health laws. It has been an honor to cross paths with her. She brought me a lovely plant in full bloom. Since I have a habit of killing silk plants, I wanted to send it back home with her – for the plant's sake; but I am happy to say it is safe and thriving – at my neighbor's house. I do have visiting privileges. I can only stay for fifteen minutes because the leaves start to wilt if I linger.

REALITY STRIKES... AGAIN

Story will resume shortly

"I object to violence because when it appears to do good, the good is only temporary; the evil it does is permanent."

Mahatma Gandhi

As Dottie and I were doing a 'deep dive', sharing our experiences and perspectives on losing children to mental illness, Adam stepped out of his office with an update.

"There's been an explosion at the finish line of the Boston Marathon," he said. "This just happened and there's not much information available but there were a lot of people injured."

This stopped us cold. Adam and I had lots of family up that way and although we weren't aware of any who were running the marathon it was hard to know if they were in the crowd cheering those at the finish line. I was relieved that Brian and his family were on vacation in the Dominican Republic, but Jon and his family were not away – their girls had a different spring vacation schedule. Nobody was answering their cellphones but Adam dashed off a quick email to everybody up that way, hoping they were all okay.

Adam kept us updated as the media frenzy began – with information (and misinformation) flying across the news ticker scrolling across the bottom of the TV screen.

I was quite shaken and reached for Dottie's hand when suddenly it dawned on me why this was hitting me so hard on so many levels.

"Dottie, Kevin was the youngest person to run the marathon. He ran it when he was twelve years old. When Kevin died, our original plan was to bring him home, have him cremated and sprinkle some of his remains at the Boston Marathon finish line. As much as I wish we had been granted custody of his remains, I am grateful we were not up there with family and friends surrounding us and potentially putting everybody in harms' way. Things happened just the way they were meant to be."

After Dottie left, I sent a separate email to other family, friends, and colleagues in Boston, sending our deepest condolences and hoping everybody was safe. As it turned out, my niece Jessica was at the finish line and left seven minutes before the explosions to return to campus to meet up with friends. She sent me an email, quite shaken but letting me know she was safe in her dorm room and the college was on lockdown. My daughter-in-law Jacqueline took the day off to bring the grandkids to their first Boston Marathon and they were three blocks from the explosions. When the bombs detonated, she immediately grabbed the girls, ran to the car and left the area. She and my son Jon were at medical school in NYC on 9/11 and she said it reminded her of that scene. Thankfully they were physically okay but the girls are five and seven and they were quite shaken.

Jon works as a surgeon at one of the major hospitals in Boston and he called and said they had twenty-six of the injured there. His specialty is micro-nerve reconstruction. He told me he and his team would be working on many of these cases once they are stabilized. To think his dream of being a surgeon would include an experience such as this! I have such respect for him and his team.

The night of April 15th, as I went to bed, I sent an email to Dottie, thanking her for coming to visit. I closed with these thoughts, "I have a heavy heart tonight – trying to understand such senseless loss of life. My heart goes out to all the injured, and the families who are dealing with this; but I also know that this is just part of our modern day life, and tonight when I count my blessings I will be including you and your visit today."

As our Boston area family, friends and colleagues continued to check in, I was to learn that one of the victims, Lingzi Lu, was a graduate student in mathematics and statistics at my alma mater, Boston University. An undergraduate student was also severely injured. Friends of ours knew one of the other victims well, Krystle Campbell. As the next several days played out with the mayhem in Cambridge, at MIT, and in Watertown: family, friends, and colleagues continued to live in lockdown mode, and send frequent updates. A cousin of mine who writes for The Huffington Post lives and works in the neighborhood where the final show-down with Dzhokhar Tsarnaev took place, and reading her live feeds were surreal – and frightening - considering this was my cousin authoring these updates.

Talk about insanity – seems this is part of our New Normal.

"I can calculate the motion of heavenly bodies, but not the madness of people."

Isaac Newton

NEXT TO NORMAL

As our theater subscriptions were coming to the end of what is considered "the busy season," in Florida lingo, I read a review of the musical we were about to see – a local production of the Broadway hit titled *Next to Normal*. According to the review, the story line was about bipolar disease and what it does to the patient and the family. Say whaaa? A musical? Come to think of it, was that any more unthinkable than writing a book about surviving suicide and including humor?

"Hun, I'm not sure this is a good idea," I said to Adam as we drove to the theater. "Obviously when we ordered our subscription last year it was before we lost Kevin. And besides, I had no idea mental illness was the subject of the play until I read the review." (Note: We arrived at the theater with time to spare. I'm getting better with age.)

The theme of the play didn't seem to bother him. We planned to meet friends for dinner afterwards and he enjoys that combination as our datetime. Me too: but the subject matter of the play sure didn't resonate with me.

Adam wept through the first half and I was fully prepared to leave at intermission and call our friends and postpone dinner for another night.

But at intermission I was surprised when he said, "Yes, it's brutal but we'll stay for the second act and meet Michelle and Don for dinner."

I deferred to Adam, but would have preferred leaving before the second act and going home. The show was just too brutally raw for me – hitting home on too many levels. That's the difference between us – Adam has this marvelous capacity to take some things at face value. Often he'll say, "It's just a movie, it's not reality." Not me – I'm living the story, experiencing each and every one of the characters, finding similarities in myself or people I know, and wondering if I could be married to the jerk who is the main character. After the show I imagine what happens to each character, afterwards. They have a life - and an afterlife - far into the future. You get the picture. And yet, Adam cries every time he watches the final race in *Chariots of Fire* and *Secretariat*. I'm still waiting to cry. I leave it to you to figure out, I've stopped trying.

As much as I wanted to leave, it was not meant to be. And that's because what was meant to be was that I stood in line to use the Ladies Room during intermission and started up a conversation with the four women on either side of me. All were struggling with the play on different levels, but the woman in front of me told me her friend who was in the restroom had lost her son only a month ago – to suicide. I mentioned our loss, and she shared that her own son had bipolar disease and all that she had done to advocate for him. As she spoke, I detected a bit of a Boston accent and sure enough, it turns out she had roots in New England, and her son was now living in New Hampshire, not far from where I had spent my elementary school years. We clicked immediately, on several levels, and by the end of intermission she had written her email and phone number on my Playbill. Her name was Ginger.

Adam and I got through the second act and I was so drained as we left the theater, I just wanted to go home and be alone with him; but it was too late to cancel our dinner and besides, Adam wanted to go. He loves food and he has plenty of company: there are those who live to eat, those who eat to live, and then there is me. I enjoy everything about food except the eating part due to severe food allergies. In my next life, I am coming back as Adam. As it turned out, we had a delightful dinner with our friends and came home to receive Sunday evening phone calls from our sons. Lovely.

It was meant to be – the six degrees of freedom that separate us all. I sent Ginger an email the next day and didn't hear back but I kept her contact information on my desk. A couple of weeks passed and I reached her by phone. What ensued was an hour of hilarity and heartache as we talked about our New Hampshire and Boston connections, mental illness, her Irish Catholic roots, my Irish Catholic connections with my first husband's family in Boston, growing up with alcoholism, bipolar sons, guilt, etc.

And the best and final piece de resistance was when I asked, "So what do you do in your spare time, Girlfriend?"

"I tap dance!" said Ginger. "In fact, I lead a co-ed tap dancing troupe called The Senior Tappers."

"Are you kidding? I read all about you in the local paper! They did this big front page feature story on your group and I was tempted to sign up."

"Well, why didn't you? We'd love to have you!"

And then I told her my sad tale.

"Well, when I was growing up I took ballet lessons until I was sixteen. When I started out at age seven, I really wanted to take tap lessons. The studio I went to held classes for ballet, jazz and tap and at the recitals I thought the tap dancers had the coolest costumes – with glittery top hats and tails, small batons, and those cool tap shoes that clicked with each step. Classical ballet was so staid and formal by comparison, and even our teachers were tight-ass compared to the free spirits who taught tap. I went home and over dinner I asked my mother if I could switch to tap and she said, 'No, Jewish girls take ballet, not tap.' So here's the bottom line and you can take it from me, 'Jews Don't Tap.'"

We haven't stopped laughing over that one and I don't think Ginger will ever be the same.

> *"If you don't do anything stupid when you're young, you won't remember something funny when you're old."*
>
> *Anonymous*

HOW MENTAL ILLNESS SPEAKS TO OUR SOCIETY

Tower by John E.
John E. copied the black and white tower from a picture.
It was a really powerful symbol of mental illness: There is no door to get in or out.
NAMI Anything Goes: Art-From-The-Heart Project

Here are just a few of the ways society defines mental illness: how that plays to our fears, and humiliates and ridicules those who are dealing with mental illness and brain disorders.

A Screw Loose	*Loony*
Basket Case	*Lunatic*
Crazy	*Mad Hatter*
Cuckoo	*Nut case*
Deranged	*Off Your Rocker*
Ding-a-ling	*Psycho*
Freak	*Wack-a-Doodle*
Fruitcake	*Weirdo*
Head Case	*Whack Job*
Insane	*Whack-O*
Kook	*Wingnut*

The language of treatment isn't much kinder: Common terms for psychiatrists (medical doctors who treat the mind), and psychoanalysts and therapists (who treat mental illness but are not doctors), include: head doctor, headshrinker ("shrink" for short), quack, and charlatan. They speak in a foreign language - psychological nonsense referred to as "psychobabble." Movies such as *Analyze This*, starring Robert De Nero and Billy Crystal, play to those stereotypes.

When I was growing up, I felt there was a prestige hierarchy among medical professionals that placed psychiatrists at or near the bottom, along with radiologists and pediatricians. This influenced how the public viewed the profession. Like any other profession, there are reputable mental health practitioners who base their work on scientific fact and analyses, and those who hang out a shingle and are far less credentialed. It is wise to remember that 50 percent of all medical professionals in all specialties graduated in the bottom half of their class. The same applies to every other profession: lawyers, accountants, economists, scientists, engineers, etc.

A close friend of mine told her ninety-year-old grandmother she was seeing a psychiatrist. Her grandmother responded, "Why can't you just go talk to our minister, for goodness sake. You don't need to be wasting money on that hocus-pocus." Ouch!

EXPERIENCING MENTAL ILLNESS

"I have my own little world, but it's okay - they know me here."

Anonymous

This book is not intended to be a primer on mental illness. There are credentialed researchers and medical experts who are trained in brain science and I encourage you to seek them out.

What I will include is a brief summary of Bipolar Disorder[23]. According to the National Institute of Mental Health (NIMH):

Bipolar disorder, also known as manic-depressive illness, is a brain disorder that causes unusual shifts in mood, energy, activity levels, and the ability to carry out day-to-day tasks. Symptoms of bipolar disorder are severe. They are different from the normal ups and downs that everyone goes through from time to time. Bipolar disorder symptoms can result in damaged relationships, poor job or school performance, and even suicide. But bipolar disorder can be treated, and people with this illness can lead full and productive lives.

Bipolar disorder often develops in a person's late teens or early adult years. At least half of all cases start before age twenty-five. Some people have their first symptoms during childhood, while others may develop symptoms late in life.

Bipolar disorder is not easy to spot when it starts. The symptoms may seem like separate problems, not recognized as parts of a larger problem. Some people suffer for years before they are properly diagnosed and treated. Like diabetes or heart disease, bipolar disorder is a long-term illness that must be carefully managed throughout a person's life."

The symptoms of Bipolar Disorder:

Extreme mood swings: Unusually intense emotional states that occur in distinct periods called "mood episodes." An overly joyful or overexcited state is called a manic episode, and an extremely sad or hopeless state is called a depressive episode. People with bipolar disorder also may be explosive and irritable during a mood episode.

Extreme changes in energy, activity, sleep, and behavior - sometimes symptoms are so severe that the person cannot function normally at work, school, or home.

Symptoms of mania or a manic episode include:

Mood Changes

• A long period of feeling "high," or an overly happy or outgoing mood

- *Extremely irritable mood, agitation, feeling "jumpy" or "wired."*

Behavioral Changes

- *Talking very fast, jumping from one idea to another, racing thoughts*

- *Being easily distracted*

- *Increasing goal-directed activities, such as taking on new projects*

- *Being restless*

- *Sleeping little*

- *Having an unrealistic belief in one's abilities*

- *Behaving impulsively and taking part in a lot of pleasurable, high-risk behaviors, such as spending sprees, impulsive sex, and impulsive business investments.*

Symptoms of depression or a depressive episode include:

Mood Changes

- *A long period of feeling worried or empty*

- *Loss of interest in activities once enjoyed, including sex.*

Behavioral Changes

- *Feeling tired or "slowed down"*

- *Having problems concentrating, remembering, and making decisions*

- *Being restless or irritable*

- *Changing eating, sleeping, or other habits*

- *Thinking of death or suicide, or attempting suicide.*

In the above summary, the most important statement is: "Like diabetes or heart disease, bipolar disorder is a long-term illness that must be carefully managed throughout a person's life."

It is worth deconstructing this statement: it assumes four critical success factors – proper diagnosis, affordable quality health care services, a pro-active patient and a support system that can help the person when a crisis arises.

Before any physical or mental illness can be treated, a person needs to be correctly diagnosed. Kevin exhibited all the classic symptoms of bipolar disorder to varying degrees before he reached puberty, but he wasn't diagnosed until he was thirty-one years old and in a full manic episode in 2007. This means that he, his family, his teachers, classmates, friends, employers, and colleagues had no context in which to understand his swings in behavior and collectively work as a team to help Kevin manage it and achieve his full potential. That would have been the perfect scenario. However, we live in an imperfect world.

In reality because there is still so much that is unknown about mental illness, this fear of the unknown makes it seem overwhelming and prevents society from finding workable solutions. It takes resources, time and money, and all three are at a premium in today's political and economic environment: but they were in short supply even during the boom years.

Another reality is that there are limits to diagnosis and treatment of mental health disorders, and even the 'experts' don't agree on diagnoses and treatments. In fact, from my extensive reading on the subject they can't agree on what is 'normal'.

> *"Psychoanalysis is that mental illness for which it regards itself as therapy."*
>
> *Karl Kraus*

Here's more proof: The American Psychiatric Association publishes a manual that is considered the bible of mental illness diagnosis, the Diagnostic and Statistical Manual of Mental Disorders (DSM). This tome catalogues close to 300 categories of mental disorders. It is an important publication because it determines which mental disorders are eligible for insurance coverage, legal standing, and visibility and discussion in The Public Square. DSM version four was published nineteen years ago, and in May 2013, the much anticipated DSM-5 was released.

According to William Falk, editor of *THE WEEK* magazine:

> *Critics of all kinds have lined up to assail this dictionary of disorders as subjective and lacking in scientific validity – assembled primarily to justify the prescribing of pills of dubious value. About 50 percent of the population, the APA admits, will have one of its listed disorders at some point in their lives…To be skeptical of these neat categories isn't to deny that minds get broken, stuck, or lost, and need help finding their way out of misery. But psychotherapy remains an art, not a science; there is no bright line between nuts and not. If you're an old lady who lives amid piles of newspapers and personal treasures, you have "hoarding disorder". If you're a CEO who exploits sweatshop labor to pile up countless billions, you're on the cover of Forbes.* [24]

A separate article highlights the clear conflict of interest since sale of the DSM is the APA's cash cow and the latest version is based on "questionable scientific methods". In fact, one of the most vocal critics of the DMS-5 is retired Duke University psychiatrist Allen Frances, the lead author of DSM-4. According to Benjamin Nugent in Slate.com, "Frances regrets the way much of that work was produced, and has waged a fierce campaign to discredit DSM-5 and persuade the APA to order a rewrite."[25]

Ethan Watters authored an article titled *Mad Fashion* (Pacific Standard, July/August 2013), in which he highlights the need for the science of psychiatry to recognize the important role culture plays in how mental disorders are defined. If a DSM had been published in 1880, it would have included hysteria, since thousands of women were experiencing the symptoms at that time. "Practically speaking, the criteria by which something is declared a mental illness are virtually the same now as they were a hundred years ago." The science simply isn't there yet to diagnose based on hard science: genetic modeling, brain imaging, and cognitive science. So we end up with a system where psychiatric theories and diagnostic categories shape the symptoms of patients. As the doctors' ideas change, so will the symptoms of the patients. "What changes, it seems, is that they get categorized differently depending upon the cultural landscape of the moment." A person with "anxiety" in the 1970s, "depression" in the 1980s and "social anxiety disorder or ADHD" in the 1990s, may be presenting the same symptoms. And when they seek help from a psychiatrist, there is a human dynamic at play that makes us "uniquely susceptible to being influenced by the psychiatric certainties of the moment." [26]

It isn't surprising that mental health practitioners – psychiatrists, psycho-pharmacologists, psychotherapists, psychoanalysts, and all other mental health therapists and specialists – have an image problem. Brandon Gaudiano published an opinion essay in *The New York Times* highlighting that very issue. He is clinical psychologist and assistant professor of psychiatry and human behavior at the Alpert Medical School at Brown University and when I contacted him, he sent me the research paper on which his essay was based. Gaudiano highlights the tension that exists between psychotherapy versus medication use: how "[t]raditional psychotherapy use is on the decline while medication use is rising;" and how the profession must "address diagnosis, treatment development, and training issues," to bring it on par with biological treatment models.[27] These are sorely lacking and the APA has only recently formed a committee to develop treatment guidelines, lagging biological medicine by two decades. Gaudiano is a strong advocate for science-based methods that can inform treatment alternatives, and how this will be increasingly important as the health care system moves toward evidence-based treatments.

He indicts those within the profession as well: "There has been a disappointing reluctance among psychotherapists to make the hard choices about which therapies are effective and which — like some old-fashioned Freudian therapies — should be abandoned."[28]

Several days after his opinion piece ran in *The New York Times*, letters from four of his colleagues in the profession were published and they all defended their turf – traditional psychotherapy, psychopharmacology, etc. Most all highlighted the need for a balanced approach, a mix of psychotherapy and medication. My concern is that the move toward specialists and sub-specialties pits one approach against another and leaves the whole patient out of the equation: the mind, body and soul of each of us that makes us perfectly imperfect humans. Our body is a system – when we "tweak" one part, it impacts the whole. How can we mere mortals contribute to the discussion? We can do it by giving mental illness a voice - by letting it speak and advocating for what we need – for loved ones who are suffering, and for caregivers and caretakers who suffer as well.

The APA isn't alone in facing disruption from within as well as from without. A similar controversy is underway with the recent American Medical Association (AMA) decision to classify obesity as an illness. Many critics of this decision come from both the AMA and the APA. However, unlike mental illness, there will be plenty of lobbyists setting up offices in Washington advocating for obesity treatment centers, new drugs, and a myriad of other companies seeking a piece of the funding; I have no doubt that they *will* get that funding. The difference is, an obese person is obviously and measurably overweight while a person struggling with mental health issues is not; and yet, both obesity and mental illness significantly drive real U.S. health care costs for which we all pay.

"Show me a sane man and I will cure him for you."

Carl Gustav Jung

As in any other health challenge, a person can shop around until he or she finds a doctor who either agrees with their self-diagnosis (and denial), or attributes the patient's symptoms to a different cause. It takes a skilled psychiatrist, psychotherapist, or social worker to correctly diagnosis bipolar disease and see through a patient's manipulation and self-delusion.

Kevin was extremely adept at turning therapy sessions into fifty-minute discussions about what was wrong with his boss, his girlfriend or wife, me, his father, and the world at large. He could be quite engaging, and if there was any pushback, he simply terminated treatment: in some cases walking out mid-session as he did when Dr. Herman and Adam were meeting with him. Reputable doctors of any specialty have limits to what they can do without full cooperation of the patient. Ideally, a team including a psychopharmacologist, primary care physician, psychiatrist, nutritionist, and therapist would be working with a patient who is committed to pro-active management of their bipolar disorder. That includes a willingness to fully disclose all symptoms and reveal any alcohol or recreational drug use. Kevin was what's known in the medical profession as a "non-compliant patient."

Patient privacy also has placed a burden on families of adult children who are dealing with mental illness and/or addiction. As soon as the person is of legal age (eighteen in the U.S.), HIPPA comes into play. The Health Insurance Portability and Accountability Act of 1996 (HIPAA) has three rules: the HIPAA Privacy Rule protects the privacy of individually identifiable health information, the HIPAA Security Rule sets national standards for the security of electronically protected health information, and the confidentiality provisions of the Patient Safety Rule protect identifiable information being used to analyze patient safety events and improve patient safety.

We were limited with respect to the information any treating physician or psychiatrist could share even when we were often covering the fees. This is the law Dottie Pacharis is focused on changing since her family was barred from helping Scotty numerous times as he self-destructed. These privacy laws, though well-intended, sometimes have unintended consequences that have negative outcomes, including death. It's a double-edged sword.

According to NAMI of Collier County Executive Director Kathryn Leib-Hunter, there is a stop-gap solution - the Advanced Directive. It doesn't totally eliminate the barriers but it designates a healthcare surrogate who is authorized to make health care decisions for an adult child suffering from serious brain illness and disorders. The limitation is the adult child needs to be willing to execute a legal directive assigning treatment, including hospitalization and medication, to a designated representative (i.e., a parent, a partner, etc.) when the patient is deemed by a physician to present a danger to him/herself or society. The directive can be very specific in terms of what it allows, and this can override HIPPA barriers when needed.

Three other major cogs in the wheel are Big Insurance, Big Pharma, and Big Media. To keep health care costs down, limits were placed on talk therapy and appointments with psychiatrists limited to twenty-five-minute sessions ending with a prescription for medication. I experienced this first-hand. It has taken many decades for insurance coverage for mental health to reach parity with coverage for physical illness - and we're not there yet. The Health Care for America Plan ("Obamacare") has addressed pre-existing conditions but the future of mental health insurance continues to be a work-in-progress.

Big Media also plays a role shaping our culture and giving illness a voice. Print and broadcast journalists "love to broadcast new mental-health epidemics. The dramatic rise of bulimia in the United Kingdom neatly coincided with the media frenzy surrounding the rumors and subsequent revelation that Princess Di suffered from the condition. Similarly, an American form of anorexia hit Hong Kong in the mid-1990s just after a wave of local media coverage brought attention to the disorder."[29]

Social media has further amplified the voice, and accelerated the speed of communicating these disorders and the subconscious mind can be easily influenced by these suggestive cues. Hoarding and cutting were not on the radar screen a generation ago, but are now in the spotlight. DMS-IV lead author Dr. Frances writes, "We are always just one blockbuster movie and some weekend therapist's workshops away from a new fad. Look for another epidemic beginning in a decade or two as a new generation of therapists forgets the lessons of the past."[30]

Is suicide epidemic? Perhaps it is worth asking if the media's obsession with all things macabre coupled with the global reach of technology-enabled social media, gives tacit approval for taking one's life. There are, after all, stories through the ages about suicide pacts and copy-cat episodes. In Kevin's case, there most likely were genetic, family history, cultural, and societal factors; however, meds were also a factor.

In seeking help for Kevin we found doctors whose first course of treatment was medication. This wasn't a total surprise, but I did find it unsettling that the pens in their office, their notepads and prescription pads often were from drug companies promoting the very medications being prescribed.

I'll share one personal experience of how this worked. My endocrinologist referred me to a psychiatrist for hair loss and she immediately asked me to fill out a card provided by GlaxoSmithKline. It had twenty leading questions and only one choice of answers - "Yes" or "No". The entire questionnaire had one short instruction at the top: "Check the appropriate box for each question *based on your lifetime.*" Questions like "Have you ever thought about taking your own life?" Who hasn't – especially anyone who survived puberty? If the person answered "Yes" to eight questions or more, they were diagnosed by the drug company whose medication was then prescribed, not by the psychiatrist. Conflict of interest, you think? I was so outraged I sent a letter to both my endocrinologist and the psychiatrist expressing my anger, and to drive home the point I faxed it to every member of the GlaxoSmith-Kline board of directors.

My nephew Jeremy and his wife Gail gave me other examples of the influence of Big Pharma in our modern day society. Gail is a school psychologist; she told me 60-70 percent of her students have been diagnosed with ADHD and are on prescription medications of various sorts. In the summer, at the exclusive summer camp Jeremy runs, he said about 75-80 percent of the 350 campers go to the infirmary every morning for their medications, mostly for ADHD. The three of us have had long discussions on this topic and share a concern that we are over-medicating our children in the interest of "taming" their creative and energetic nature to make parenting and classrooms less stressful.

In Kevin's case, even without a firm bipolar diagnosis, often a minimum of 2-4 meds were prescribed to manage his various symptoms-of-the-moment, and that was due to the unique nature of bipolar disorder: since there are a range of mood swings and intensity, there are meds to manage the manic as well as the depressive episodes.

Here's a short list of the medications used to treat bipolar disorder.

- *Antipsychotic and antidepression medications: Haldol, Risperdal, Abilify, Geodon, Saphris, Zyprexa, Symbyax, Seroquel, Lithium, Lamictal, Prozac, Wellbutrin, Zoloft*
- *Mania medications: Lithium, Klonopin, Ativan, Xanax, and Valium (diazepam).*

Most all these medications by themselves have major and minor side effects, and drug interactions are often not understood or recognized. Significant weight gain, tremors, impotency, GERD, and lower intestinal track impacts are just a few of the negative reactions. It takes patience and a willingness to try different medications before the right blend is found, and this trial-and-error process may only help for a limited time as the patient builds up resistance or a reaction. Sadly, many of these drugs also carry the risk of being habit-forming/addictive medications, setting in motion a whole additional set of problems.

LET'S GET HIGH

Story will resume shortly

"Scientists say that the universe is made up of Electrons, Protons and Neutrons...They forgot to mention Morons..."

Anonymous

Did you ever read the teeny-tiny fine print accompanying any prescription drug? The warnings and side effects can sometimes take up three-quarters of the space. The same applies to ads on TV. Adam and I frequently laugh when the announcer's message at the end of medication ads is like a speed-reading contest with the closing line, "severe bleeding, kidney failure, seizures, brain tumors, heart and liver damage, and death may occur." Every ad for erectile dysfunction medication that runs during the weekly four-day golf tournament Adam watches (i.e. 60 percent of the ads in Florida due to the senior demographic), ends with this alert: "For an erection lasting more than four hours, go to the emergency room immediately." And our response is, "Ha - that's the last place most guys in this state are rushing to." For them, such a happening would qualify as the resurrection quickly followed by the rapture and meeting new sustainability standards all rolled into one little pill – "Better Living Through Chemistry" at its finest.

And yet the ubiquitous ads for medications are flashed before our eyes – on TV, radio, in print and online - 24x7, urging us to self-diagnose and demand that our doctors write a script for our every ache and pain, whether imagined or real. We are allowing Big Pharma to define us by our diseases and by their definition of what is "normal". They and their shareholders are laughing all the way to the bank.

We would be wise to listen to Hippocrates:

> *"It's more important to know what sort of person has a disease than to know what sort of disease that person has."*

Equally challenging is that research trials for psychotropic drugs are rarely independent: there are frequent cases of researchers whose funding is dependent on Big Pharma distorting the outcomes by suppressing or minimizing negative results and magnifying or overstating positive results.

In our situation, Kevin was having side effects from prescription medication but he was also binge drinking, self-medicating with Ritalin and recreational drugs, and eating an unhealthy diet. When I would ask him about his therapy sessions he would tell me, "I'm okay, Makyla is the one who has the problem and that's what we've been talking about – how to get her into treatment." Other times he would tell me he didn't like the doctor and stopped going. Further complicating the situation was that Kevin was outside the U.S. healthcare system, often without medical insurance coverage, and seeing doctors with limited fluency in English. We had no idea what their credentials were and which medications they were prescribing.

What I do know is what he shared with me: On occasion he was taking pain medication for various medical ailments and Vicodin was one such drug he took. It is a powerful painkiller, which contains the narcotic hydrocodone.

What I also know is recently the Food and Drug Administration recommended tighter controls on how doctors prescribe the most commonly used narcotic painkillers, changes that are expected to take place as early as 2014, and Vicodin will be one of a number of drugs included. The move, which represents a major policy shift, follows a decade-long debate over whether the widely abused drugs, which contain the narcotic hydrocodone, should be controlled as tightly as more powerful painkillers like OxyContin.

Prescription drugs account for about three-quarters of all drug overdose deaths in the United States, with the number of deaths from narcotic pain-killers, or opioids, quadrupling since 1999, according to federal data. Drugs containing hydrocodone represent a huge share — about 70 percent — of all opioid prescriptions, and the looser rules governing them, some experts say, have contributed to their abuse.

Dr. Janet Woodcock, director of the F.D.A.'s Center for Drug Evaluation and Research, said, "These are very difficult trade-offs that our society has to make. The reason we approve these drugs is for people in pain, but we can't ignore the epidemic on the other side."[31]

This isn't sitting well with Big Pharma and pharmacy groups like the National Community Pharmacists Association, and they have mobilized their legions of lobbyists to derail legislation in the Senate that would mandate the type restrictions that the F.D.A. is now recommending. They are claiming that the new rules could make it harder for some patients to find doctors to prescribe the drugs or pharmacies to fill the prescriptions. [31]

> *"We're friends, you laugh, I laugh, you cry, I cry, you jump off a bridge, I get in my boat and save your butt!"*
>
> *Anonymous*

This isn't to say there aren't many people who benefit from Big Pharm medications, even those with side effects; however, this story is about our experience and my Shout Out to Big Pharma is to remind them that the Hippocratic Oath says, "First, Do No Harm," not, "First, Do No Harm To The Bottom Line." Putting profits before patients may satisfy shareholders and compensate Big Pharma executives handsomely, but Johnson & Johnson's recent $2.2 billion settlement turned out to be a bad business model: promoting powerful psychiatric drugs for unapproved uses in children, seniors and disabled patients, according to a Department of Justice announcement on Nov. 4, 2013.

There are people who have earned the right to make such statements – about the benefits and risks of medications. These people have walked-the-walk in their personal search for what society deems a "normal life" while living with a bifurcated self – one manic or hypermanic, one depressed. One qualified person is Linda Logan, who wrote about her 25+ year struggle with Bipolar Disorder II, the hard truths that surfaced during that long, hard journey, the limits of psychotropic medications, and the importance of finding the lost sense of self, which was critical to her recovery, and not something that can be remedied with a pill or injection of meds.

Philip Yanos, an associate professor of psychology at John Jay College of Criminal Justice in New York, told Logan his grant review team was skeptical about his research on "illness identity," i.e., patients over-identifying with their mental disorder. Illness identity was viewed as less important than "serious symptoms that patients experience, like cognitive impairment and thoughts of suicide." Yanos believes there is an important identity shift that needs to take place, from "patient" to "person", and that shift takes time. For Logan, the shift from "patient" to "person," was only one part of the process and far easier than the second part - reconstructing the "person." In other words, reclaiming personhood and defining personhood, were necessary for Logan's sense of identity.

She gained further insights from Amy Barnhorst, a psychiatrist at the University of California, Davis, who helped her better understand the "unique set of challenges facing people who have experienced mania and hypomania." It can be very hard for the reconstructed, healthier person to reconcile their manic and hypomanic behaviors with their emerging identity. When mental illness takes over, there is a loss of accountability; the healing self is left with a need to explain and apologize for the damage wrought by the sick self. There is mourning and loss involved, and for many people who are healing, this creates a sense of despair when doctors discount its significance and don't help the person deal with it.

Logan was encouraged when Janina Fisher, a psychologist and the assistant director of the Sensorimotor Psychotherapy Institute in Broomfield, Colo., told her this is rapidly changing. The role of the self is increasingly playing a role in new therapies and treatments being designed by clinical psychologists. As an example, Fisher helps her patients integrate their mental trauma into their life without having it dominate their life.[32]

Rorschach Test
NAMI of Collier County art program artist

THE LEGACY OF KEVIN

In addition to the memories we had of Kevin – the joys mixed with the sorrows – what saddened me most was the trail he left behind. One was The Marijuana Trail. When Kevin and Makyla visited us in August 2011, and we discovered they were using our phone and our car to make daily round trips to Miami to transact marijuana deals. Adam gave him a choice: "Give me all the drugs and stop doing drug deals from our home, or leave."

His defiant response was, "No, I have too much invested in this." And for good measure he added, "It's no big deal, Dad. Your cousin Peter and others in our family smoke pot and other more potent stuff and Brian and Sari are looking forward to me bringing some to them next week when we fly to Boston."

"What anybody else does in their own home is their business. I'm talking about you using our phone, our home, and our car, and you getting caught on I-75 and the impact that will have on us. As for taking it on the plane to Boston, are you an idiot, Kevin? What are you thinking? You're risking getting caught by airport security with a foreign wife? Do you have any idea what's at stake for her, not to mention you? Don't you have enough problems in your life?"

"Don't worry, Dad. I know how to do this."

"Oh, so you do this all the time?" queried Adam.

"No, pot is illegal in Brazil. I don't do it there."

To which Adam responded, "It's illegal here in Florida and in Massachusetts, too, Kevin, and it sure isn't legal to take it on the plane anywhere."

Within hours they were packed and Adam moved them to a motel at the beach that had cheap summer rates. They stayed there for the remainder of their time with us – five days and four nights. We called Brian and Sari to warn them about Kevin's behavior – and the pot – and they were firm about their "no drugs" policy. They planned to take Kevin and Makyla with them and their boys to their camp in Maine and were adamant they would not allow any drugs. Brian called Kevin to try to talk some sense into his brother, but he was met with the same obstinacy and resistance as Adam.

Two days after he left for Boston I got a call from the hotel manager saying they checked out without settling their bill. I gave him Kevin's email and cell phone and ended the call. Tough love – yes, it's tough to love toughly.

So it came as no surprise to me that shortly after Kevin's death, more pieces of this puzzle came together. The first was in an email from Makyla, where she revealed her anger and frustration about Kevin's chronic use of marijuana and the impact that had on their relationship. According to her, he and Carlos, his friend and work colleague, spent every weekend night smoking and drinking.

The second piece was when Natalie Martin from the Embassy faxed me the police report – four pages that I retyped and translated from Portuguese. Seems they found marijuana in the apartment and when they interviewed the apartment concierge he stated that Kevin asked him for frequent leads on buying marijuana.

The third piece came eight months after Kevin's death, when I finally connected with Kevin's former girlfriend Marcelina. When I told her how much Kevin loved her, she said one of the things that came between them was his frequent use of marijuana. "I was a very naïve and innocent sheltered Italian girl coming to the U.S. for the first time, and here was this worldly older guy doing these things that I simply had never been exposed to, and never wanted to try." They were together back in 2002-3 so it seems Kevin had been using marijuana consistently for at least the last ten years of his life.

Whether he was addicted to marijuana or not will never be known but what matters is that regular use plus binge drinking, which he did tell me about (e.g. "I got wasted last night"), were a toxic and possibly lethal combination, according to Dr. Herman, given his bipolar disorder.

Shortly after connecting with Marcelina and her information about Kevin's pot use, a collection agency sent Kevin a letter (c/o Brian) seeking to collect more than $1,600 in outstanding parking fines – twelve citations plus fees, interest and fines dating back to 2003-04 when he was at the University of Chicago: It was yet another classic symptom of his mental illness reaching us long after his death.

Adam was unable to handle the news about the marijuana trail and did not wish to read the police report. He told Brian to just ignore the collection letter but my reaction was very different. I did not want Brian or us to continue receiving these types of debt notifications from Kevin's long list of creditors. I had already sent his death notice to the IRS and the student loan collection agencies, and contacted the City of Chicago to inform them of Kevin's death, following up with a copy of his death notice.

> "The lessons we learn from pain will always make us the strongest."

> Anonymous

That may be true, but those lessons can also wear us out. In my case the forces of patient and family denial, the limits of medicine, availability of recreational and prescription drugs, society's competing priorities and constraints, and international borders converged, leaving a trail of marijuana, bad debts, lost friendships, and broken hearts.

This journey through heartache and loss has also impacted my view on legalizing marijuana. Years ago, my younger brother, who was diagnosed with Multiple Sclerosis but kept it a secret for thirteen years, told me he got relief for his symptoms from bee venom and marijuana. That explained why he kept a beehive outside the kitchen window, and why some of his ashes after he died were stored in a 35mm film tube. I was later to find out this was a common way recreational drugs were hidden. So I was influenced by his experience when the legality of medical marijuana became a hot political topic in the 2000s, and supported its legalization.

However, after experiencing Kevin's chronic use and the significant negative impact that had on his bipolar disorder and magnification of his symptoms, I have yet another perspective tugging me in the opposite direction. According to recent reports, marijuana's purity has increased 160 percent over the past 20+ years, and it is 85 percent cheaper. It's not the same "weed" that was popular during the Counter Culture years in the late 1960s/early 70s.

Speaking of unintended consequences, there have been stories surfacing in the media of late about the unintended consequences of California's legalization of medical marijuana: According to Bill Keller, "The state's medical marijuana is such a free-for-all, that in Los Angeles there are now said to be more pot dispensaries than Starbucks outlets. Even advocates of full legalization say things have gotten out of hand."[33] Keller also highlights how the profit motive promotes demand, and there is a need for regulation for potency, contamination, labeling and use of pot for pastries, candies, beverages, ice cream, and inhalers.

Ironically, in yet another twist, the medical profession and Big Pharma benefit from marijuana: with physicians charging $150 - $300 for patient visits for medical marijuana prescriptions and psychiatrists and Big Pharma benefitting when patients become addicted.

As Bob Curley writes:

> *Also new to the DSM-V are diagnostic criteria for "cannabis with-drawal," which the APA says is caused by "cessation of cannabis use that has been heavy and prolonged," results in "clinically significant distress or impairment in social, occupational, or other important areas of functioning," and is characterized by at least three of these symptoms: irritability, anger or aggression, nervousness or anxiety, sleep difficulties (insomnia), decreased appetite or weight loss, rest-lessness, depressed mood, and or physical symptoms such as stom-ach pain, shakiness or tremors, sweating, fever, chills, and head-ache.[34]*

In Kevin's case, he exhibited every single symptom of "cannabis with-drawal," so this is yet another impact of Kevin's death – I am torn about pre-venting those who might benefit from doing so yet I am concerned about the unintended consequences.

I do not want Kevin's legacy to be this: "Bipolar disorder won!"

A MENTAL HEALTH BREAK

Story will resume shortly

"*All I want to be is normally insane.*"

Marlon Brando

Bipolar disorder and other mental illnesses don't always have to win. Yes, I have read inspiring stories like Linda Logan's, and I have also met some re-markably strong people like her who live fulfilling, successful lives because they accept and proactively manage their illness. They do not allow the illness to define them: they have successfully separated their identity of who they are from their diagnosis, and see it as one part of their whole being.

One of these people was a student who came into my life in 1998 when I was managing the international research program at MIT. Kirsten was a Ph.D. economics student and recent recipient of a research grant from our program. She knocked on my office door early one morning and I could sense she was very nervous.

"May I talk to you for a minute?" she asked.

"Sure, come on in and have a seat," I said.

"I really need to ask you a huge favor. I have bipolar disease. Before I came back to get my Ph.D. I was working on Wall Street, earning a great salary. I would go home and watch QVC and by the end of each week packages were arriving for stuff I had no recollection of ordering. I'm talking about $400-$500 per delivery. I was also drinking a lot and not getting any sleep. It was really bad. I maxed out seven different credit cards, each to the tune of $10,000 or more, and finally had a total breakdown and that's when it was diagnosed."

"Are you okay now?" I asked.

"Yes, but I have to manage my medications every day and I have to monitor my moods because I have times when I am anxious and restless, and times when I feel myself getting out of control."

"How can I help you?"

"I need you to be on my support team. You've just given me a generous research grant for this year, and I am grateful. I need you to tell me if I am focusing on my work and the required deliverables, so I don't lose this grant."

We talked further about the specific ways I could help her, and I told her how much courage she demonstrated by taking me into her confidence and being part of her support system. What she feared most is that she would have a manic phase and be out of control and nobody would call her on it.

"I start talking too loud, laughing inappropriately, and spending wildly." And then she said something I will never forget; "And you can't believe how invincible I feel – I stop sleeping, stop eating, and feel like I could win an Ironman competition and go on to climb Mount Everest. And then…I stop taking my meds, because the feeling is just so incredible; but then I crash-and-burn."

And there you have it. The manic feeling feeds on itself.

As she got up to leave, I came around my desk, gave her a big hug and said, "You can count on my support, and if QVC deliveries start showing up at my door, you will definitely be getting a visit from me."

Kirsten spent the year working hard, successfully completing her research, and graduating in June of the following year. In her case, bipolar disorder did not win.

For graduation, I sent her a gift, courtesy of QVC.

My son once told me after talking to Kevin, who was on one of his spending jaunts in Brazil during graduate school, "Mom, Kevin loves the Kevin that he is in Brazil. The women, the high life, it is so different from the Kevin who has to function in the U.S. That's why he loves to go there."

Floral Bouquet by Alice
NAMI Anything Goes: Art-From-The-Heart Project

SURVIVING THE SANDY HOOK ELEMENTARY SCHOOL MASSACRE

There are too many times in our world when people suffering from brain disorders and serious mental illnesses (i.e., extreme depression, bipolar, psychosis or schizophrenia), feel "different," and as a consequence are bullied and marginalized by society. Sometimes they are also groomed by a home environment filled with guns, fears of Armageddon, and violent video games; and rather than channeling their loneliness, frustration and anger inward, they channel it outward. In the rare instance when that happens, it can end like Friday, December 14, 2012: To coin Franklin D. Roosevelt's famous quote, "a date that will live in infamy."

This email says it best.

Date: Fri, Dec 14, 2012 at 11:31 PM
To: Friends and Family
From: Deena
Subject: Friends & Family - Treasured moments amidst today's carnage

I was totally devastated by the senseless Connecticut elementary school carnage today. I imagined those innocent 20 first graders who were the same age as my granddaughter, being sent off to school with excitement building around the holidays, and the six courageous teachers and administrators, like one of my daughters-in-law and several of you, who were there to teach our next generation of movers-and-shakers. I was off-kilter at all my afternoon meetings, starting each one with a moment of silence on behalf of the victims. Several of my clients hadn't yet heard the news.

On my way home this afternoon I needed to stop at Trader Joe's for some holiday groceries. Just as I entered the store, I was greeted by this adorable little 2-year-old girl dressed in a pink ballet skirt, pink top, and silver glitter-sparkled Maryjanes, pushing her little shopping cart. I asked her father if I could talk to his little girl and he said that was fine. Then I asked her if she loved to dance because

*she looked like a beautiful pink flower, and she invited me to join
her. So there we were, dancing together in the aisle of Trader Joe's.
Afterwards, her parents let me buy her a treat she got to choose, and
she took a long time to select just the right one. It was so life affirm-
ing and I pass that energy on to all of you.*

*It is with a heavy heart that I send you holiday sunshine and
best wishes.*

Love,
Deena

I had been making slow but steady progress working through my grief
and sadness over losing Kevin, but I am a citizen of the world and what was
coming at me from the media was the August cinema shooting in Aurora,
Colorado, non-stop chatter about the 2012 presidential, state and local elections, and shortly after Kevin's October 21st memorial and unveiling, Hurricane Sandy, followed by Sandy Hook.

Many people have said it is tough to get through the first holiday season
after losing a loved one, and that rang true for me. It just seemed to make it
harder with the media's news focus throughout November and December. Sandy Hook was particularly difficult for me because it involved so many innocent
children and adults. As the year was coming to an end, I was actually looking
forward to kissing 2012 goodbye, but unlike other years, this year would *not*
include one ritual - organizing our annual New Year's Party Poopers Party for
40-60 friends at our favorite Chinese restaurant. I was just too drained.

Shortly before Christmas it helped to write down my thoughts and submit a
commentary to several newspapers. It was published shortly before Christmas.

The Legacy of "The Sandys"
By Deena Baxter
Published December 23, 2012 by Scripps News

*The convergence of "The Sandys" has impacted me on many lev-
els, all pointing to the need for prudent legislation, action, and advocacy on climate-related safety, gun safety, and mental illness. First,*

Mother Nature displayed her wrath so visibly with Hurricane Sandy, leaving a path of devastation and destruction in NY City and surrounding shoreline communities. And months later, those same communities are experiencing record levels of mental illness by those still struggling to recover and rebuild their shattered lives. Then came the carnage at Sandy Hook Elementary School, leaving in its wake the loss of so many innocent lives.

Why have I taken the convergence of "The Sandys" so personally? Because I live close to the SW Florida coast in an area prone to hurricanes and flooding: because I have two granddaughters the same ages as the children killed at Sandy Hook, plus a daughter-in-law and other family members who are educators dedicated to teaching our future movers-and-shakers, and because I have a stepson who suffered from mental illness and took his life this summer. Officially it is called, "Death by Suicide," but in reality it is, "Death by Mental Illness."

Perhaps now is the time for us to find common ground in the wake of so much collective and personal heartache. We can believe in or refute climate change and recognize that unregulated development along the coast has consequences for personal safety and property. We can be a member of the NRA, or not and support reasonable restrictions on access to firearms, assault weapons, and high-capacity ammunition clips. We don't personally need to experience mental illness to recognize that denying its existence has enormous consequences to the person dealing with it, their family, and the community.

We can honor the holiday by tapping into our humanity and embracing the spirit of the season most by embracing our loved ones and holding them dear. The gift of time and being present are the best presents of all, and we can give gifts that keep on giving: financial donations to The Red Cross, the National Alliance on Mental Illness (NAMI), The American Foundation for Suicide Prevention (AFSP), and organizations championing and protecting our envi-

ronment and wetlands like the National Audubon Society and the Sierra Club. We can couple that with calls to our legislators advocating for responsible regulations of coastline development, gun safety, and access to mental health services, with accompanying funding to make those regulations a reality.

We have the power to change "The Sandys" legacies from ones of death and destruction to ones of action, advocacy, and hope. May so many innocent people not have died in vain.

Experiencing these tragedies at a distance, through the media as is often the case, is far different than experiencing it in your own community. I was to find out later that my nephew Jeremy's mother-in-law, Helen, had a direct connection. Ironically, I learned this by reading the class notes in my college alma mater newsletter: we attended the same college.

Helen is a teacher in Newtown, Connecticut, and when we connected by email she said, "I knew the staff members well, and some of the students had been preschoolers in my building. My counterpart at Sandy Hook was very much present during the event, and she has been deeply affected. I spend a lot of time with her and it breaks my heart to witness her pain. Life in the Newtown Schools has certainly been forever changed."

When I mentioned including a segment on Sandy Hook in this book, she made a point of mentioning that both of her daughters work in the mental health field; Gail as a school psychologist and Miranda as a psychiatric nurse-practitioner working with children and adolescents. She has more than a little "skin in this game."

Through December and well into the New Year, the media was filled with numerous articles, panel discussions, and news briefs on gun legislation and mental illness. *The New York Times* published several Sunday "Invitation to Dialogue" letters from credible and credentialed professionals, seeking input from readers on both sides of gun legislation, mental illness, and Dottie Pacharis' passion – forced treatment.

Invitation to Dialogue: Forcing Treatment
New York Times
January 30, 2013

To the Editor:

Recent tragic events have linked mental illness and violence. Some people — I, for one — consider this link dangerously stigmatizing. People with mental illness are far more likely to be victims of violence than perpetrators. Moreover, psychiatrists have limited capacity to reliably predict violence. Nonetheless, these events increase pressure to identify people who might conceivably commit violent acts, and to mandate treatment with antipsychotic medications.

For a tiny minority of patients who have committed serious crimes, mandated treatment can be effective, particularly as an alternative to incarceration. But for most patients experiencing psychotic states, mandated treatment may create more problems than it solves.

For many medical conditions, better outcomes occur when patients share in treatment design and disease management. Imposed treatments tend to engender resistance and resentment. This is also true for psychiatric conditions.

Patients with psychotic symptoms often feel that their own experience is dismissed as meaningless, like the ravings of an intoxicated or delirious person. Decisions to decline antipsychotic medications are often regarded mainly as a manifestation of illness — an illness the person is too sick to recognize — even though many people might reject antipsychotics because of metabolic and other toxicities.

When a clearly troubled person firmly believes that he or she needs no help, there are no simple answers. These situations are particularly agonizing for families. Safety is paramount — and at times can be elusive. Still, if psychiatrists humbly try to understand the person on his or her own terms, do not dismiss the person's experience as meaningless and truly respect the person's choices about *treatment, sometimes this opens the way to an effective treatment relationship. For some suffering and alienated people — certainly not all — feeling respectfully understood can be a critical step toward recovery.*

Mandated treatment is a blunt instrument that may drive more people away from seeking care than it compels into care.

Christopher Gordon
Framingham, Mass.

The writer is a psychiatrist and an associate clinical professor of psychiatry at Harvard Medical School. [35]

I forwarded Dr. Gordon's letter to Dottie, who was in demand as a speaker now that the topic was a major news story, and she submitted a rebuttal.

Six months after Dr. Gordon's letter ran in the New York Times I spoke with him. More than 150 people responded to his letter, including Dottie.

He asked whether I agreed with him or Dottie and I said, "Dr. Gordon, both sides have merit. What I do know is Dottie and I both have sons who had very different degrees of bipolar disease and yet both ended up in the same place; suicide – death by mental illness. What is important to me is getting these opposing views into the public square, encouraging interactive discussion, seeking common ground and finding constructive solutions. I am encouraged that your letter drew such a high response rate. I am hopeful all stakeholders will be more informed and sensitive to the challenges patients and families are facing, because ultimately society is impacted."

He said, "I have heard from others who faced similar obstacles like Dottie and her family and I can't imagine going through that level of heartache."

Sadly, even a year later, after release of the long-awaited report on the massacre at Sandy Hook, we have few definitive answers on why twenty-year-old Adam Lanza chose to turn his anger outward as well as inward. We know more about the isolated, dark world he inhabited, his obsession with violent computer games, history of disturbing writings as early as fifth grade, mental and behavioral diagnoses and availability of guns: but his motives for choosing Sandy Hook and targeting six adults and twenty children, as well as his mother, are left unanswered.

What is known is the legacy he leaves behind: the trail of fear for all school campuses as well as parents and families of students. Locally, our public school superintendent sent out a community update announcing the safety measures and zero-tolerance for violence policies that have been implemented K-12. Aside from the very real economic costs involved for a school system already facing financial challenges, there is the unquantifiable impact to our community: *"The Fear Factor."*

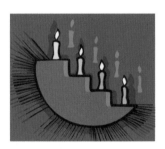

A BRIEF TIME OUT TO HONOR THE CHILDREN AND STAFF LOST AT SANDY HOOK ELEMENTARY

Story will resume shortly

Remembrance

Remembrance is a golden chain death tries to break, but all in vain.
To have, to love, and then to part is the greatest sorrow of one's heart.
The years may wipe out many things but some they wipe out never.
Like memories of those happy times when we were all together.

Author Unknown

Will we remember them? How will we remember them? I struggle with this every time there is yet another senseless shooting and sadly, they do continue to happen. On September 18, 2013, Aaron Alexis, a seriously mentally ill man, drove onto the Washington Navy Yard and went on a shooting rampage, killing twelve people before he was shot. As a nation, we are numbed, and sadly the solution becomes politicized. Can we really identify and lock up every potential schizophrenic who goes off their meds and is intent on mayhem and murder? Do we put them in jails or mental institutions? How do we keep them from easily buying deadly weapons? Gun-rights advocates fear loss of freedom if we make it harder to buy guns. So we end up with all this freedom coupled with all this death and for me, the bottom line message is: a life means nothing. May reasonable people rally together to find common ground: ensuring public safety. Seriously psychotic people should not be allowed to own guns.

HEALING WITH HUMOR AND ART:
THE BEST MEDICINE

"Life does not cease to be funny when people die any more than it ceases to be serious when people laugh."

George Bernard Shaw

There are times when the bowl of life seems to tip so far over, spilling its contents all over the floor, that all we can do is let go and laugh.

One such moment was shortly after Adam and I established the memorial scholarship fund in Kevin's honor at Fenton College. I received an email from my friend Ann.

Date: July 30, 2012 2:52:36 PM EDT
From: Ann T.
To: Deena
Subject: Your son

Dear Deena,

Today I received a letter from Petra Conners, the Director of Development at Fenton College, thanking us for the gift that we made to the College in the name of Elwin R. Treplow III, Class of 1952. Obviously there is an error here because we made the gift in the name of your son. Do you want to make a correction, or should I? If you want me to make the correction, please give me your son's full name and his year of graduation.

And then my Fairy God Mother, Aunt Betty, called me with a similar message, followed by three other friends. How could this be happening? I immediately sent Petra an email alerting her to the fact that there was obviously a major problem with their process and it wasn't making us feel confident about our own contribution. Just when I thought it couldn't get any more screwed up, we received an acknowledgment for a contribution to Kevin's fund that was meant for a different Fenton alumnus. I figured it was Kevin's way of letting me know he was still out there, and doing so in his true-to-form disruptive way: "Hey, Deena and Dad, I'm just messing with you, and I'm okay!"

"Humor is emotional chaos remembered in tranquility."

Frank Thurber

Conundrum
NAMI of Collier County art program artist

Another moment came in the midst of dealing with the U.S. Embassy in Brazil. Computers seem to sense intuitively the perfect time to have a meltdown – in the middle of the night and just when a deadline is nearing. It was close to midnight when I finally got the Apple tech support fellow on the line and together we narrowed it down to a disk problem.

"I need you to type the word 'disk' in your Search browser and tell me what comes up," he said.

I typed it in and read aloud the first item that came up, "Noun: 1) a penis."

Of course, we were on a recorded line "for training purposes." After our mutual hysteria subsided, I saw that I had typed "d-i-c-k."

In the morning I received an email from the Apple support tech letting me know I made their Wall of Fame. This is what happens when you run on empty.

Life Forces by Judi
NAMI of Collier County art program artist

In November, following Hurricane Sandy, I was getting annoyed by the volume of emails flowing to my Inbox with tips for surviving the holidays. Heck, I was just trying to survive getting through the day and thinking of all those people who lost everything they owned, including their homes, and in some cases their life. I didn't have time to read all those emails, and since they often carry viruses, I just delete them. After receiving the same one from six different friends I decided, oh heck, just read it – tips from Dr. Phil. I was annoyed to the point that it inspired me to blast out a rebuttal.

Date: Sun, Nov 18, 2012 at 10:56 PM
From: Deena
To: Dr. Phil
Subject: My 9 Holiday Survival Tips

Dear Dr. Phil – Thanks for sending me your Dr. Phil Thanksgiving Holiday Family Peace Plan. *I received it six different times. I've been trying to apply it to my own life but as you can see I am stuck in a few places. So I figured I would send it to you for some constructive feedback.*

Deena's Road-Kill Rules for a
More Peaceful, Loving, Thanksgiving Holiday

Rule # 1: Remember what it's about.

For me it is a life-long struggle with…well, with just plain keeping my sanity. When the you-know-what hits the fan, I just want to make sure I duck so I don't get hit right between the eyes.

Rule #2: Curb your high expectations.

In my case I would ask Dr. Phil, "On a scale of 1 (disaster) to 10 (perfection), how low can I go and still embrace Rule #1"?

Rule #3: Choose not to fight.

I'm not the one who fights, it's my parents. They believe the holiday dinner is an ideal time to lay out their latest beef with each other and engage the kids, grandkids and invited guests to referee. They each lay out their case, sort of like presenting to the UN General Assembly, sometimes accompanied by visual aids (fancy Power Point slides, flow-charts, photos), in support of their argument. Last year, I diplomatically suggested, "Why don't we table this discussion for another time." Without missing a beat, my mother promptly ripped the drumstick off Mr. Turkey and pounded it on the table, like a gavel, in rhythm to her message, "Table it? I'll show you how we'll table it!" In the future, is it acceptable for me to respond: "Mom, why don't you take a hike?"

Rule # 4: Challenge tradition.

Tradition in my family means Aunt Belle, the not-ready-for-prime-time opera singer, insisting on an after-dinner concert. Last year, our beagle Bugsy started howling so loud that we had to put him outdoors. That didn't work out too well when the police showed up, saying our neighbors had called 911 and lodged a "Disturbing the peace" complaint. Would it be terribly rude to post a big sign on our front door: "Beware - You are entering a No Singing Allowed Zone?"

Rule #5: Delegate.

OK, I tried that. My brother insisted on bringing a big 26-lb turkey, stuffed and fully roasted. Great, except when it arrived, it looked like it had already been eaten on one side. He pretended not to notice but his wife said, "It's all your brother's fault." (Note: when she loves him it's 'My Harry' but when she's mad it's 'your brother'.) Seems Harry loaded the roasting pan with Mr. Turkey in the back of their van and ran inside to gather the rest of the clan…without closing the doors. The kids were upstairs, staring out the window and laughing as they watched the neighbor's black lab drag Mr. Turkey down the street. In horror, Harry realized it was his Big Bird and was soon chasing behind it, wrestling "victory from the jaws of defeat." So I went to Plan B: I sent my son out for three buckets of Kentucky Fried Chicken. This year, I'm not just delegating, I'm outsourcing Thanksgiving altogether and we're going to a restaurant.

Rule #6: Keep your focus.

I really like the idea of the holidays being a time to give thanks from the heart, not from the wallet. But trying to have your family embrace this minimalist spirit when they are constantly bombarded with ads plus all the stuff their friends have makes it tough getting my message heard. Last year, the family coalesced around a common theme, a rare occurrence, and delivered their message to me:

"We took a vote and the unanimous decision is You're Just Being Cheap." Ahhh, a clear case of Lost in Translation. I need help here...

Rule # 7: Grandparents, know your limited role.

Great advice, but in my family I think that means: Wear beige, sit in the back of the church, keep your mouth shut...and your purse open.

Rule # 8: Don't miss the innocent moments.

My question is, "What qualifies as innocent?" My mother's idea of Happy Hour is two valium followed by a double martini. More than once she passed out at the dinner table, her head resting angelically in the middle of her full plate of food. Last year I insisted my sister's teens put away their iPhones and delete the photos, fearing they would be posted on YouTube. If it happens this year, we'll be at a restaurant so is it okay to ask the waitress for an extra-large napkin, gently and lovingly drape it over her head and continue with the meal?

Rule # 9: Don't forget that laughter can be healing.

About rules 1-8, just kidding...sort of.

With the holidays fast approaching, I eagerly await your response.

Kind regards,
Deena

PS: I never did get a response from Dr. Phil.

As 2012 was coming to an end, with some believing that the Mayan calendar's prediction of doomsday was soon approaching on December 21st, I could not believe charlatans were promoting life insurance policies and people were actually buying them in anticipation of that cataclysmic day. Why bother - on the off chance this was true there would be nobody to collect the payout on December 22nd.

Even the last day of 2012 brought yet another test of faith when the neurological surgeon read my MRI and delivered the verdict: advanced arthritis in my upper spine, with four bulging discs at the base of my skull. The good news: no surgery was required. The not-so-good news: I would need eight sessions of physical therapy that would include cervical traction and would also need to have a cervical traction device installed at home.

I wasn't fully present and what was present was pretty tired. Hearing "cervical" my mind immediately went to the Body Parts Compartment and zeroed in on "cervix," but the one I was familiar with was close to my uterus. What did that possibly have to do with my neck and shoulder pain? Besides, I had had a hysterectomy years ago and my cervix was long gone. At least I thought it was gone: I didn't recall it being transplanted to my neck. Thank goodness I had enough presence of mind *not* to share all this information.

Instead, I asked, "What's a cervical traction device?"

"Oh, it's a traction device that they install in a door transom and you suspend from it by your neck. It expands your cervical vertebrae and discs in your neck and it will help manage the nerve pain by easing the tension in your neck. You'll need to do this twice a day," he responded.

"Wait, let me get this straight. I'm going to be hanging from the doorway twice a day? You can't be serious!" I responded, my blood pressure soaring so high I was sure blood would spew from my ears.

"Yes, I'm serious. It will really help."

"Dr. Boyd, our son committed suicide this summer. There is no way in hell my husband can come into the bedroom or my office and find me hanging."

"Well, just lock the door." Really, he said that.

Gallows humor – just what I needed to end the year.

The first thing I did when I got home was to look up the word 'cervix':

> **Noun: (pl. cervices), the narrow neck like passage forming the lower end of the uterus. technical: the neck, a part of other bodily organs resembling a neck.**

Yes, the surgeon *was* serious about needing the device but thankfully it turns out they no longer have you hanging in the doorway twice daily: The device rests on the floor. I called his office to give him the correct information for future patients. And after I had the physical therapy sessions and the home cervical traction device delivered, I cancelled my follow-up appointment – a $325 savings I applied to two counseling sessions with our family psychotherapist to deal with it.

"Life is rather like a tin of sardines - we're all of us looking for the key."

Alan Bennett

WHAT'S LOVE GOT TO DO WITH IT? EVERYTHING!

"In the end, it's not going to matter how many breaths you took, but how many moments took your breath away."

Shing Xiong

Losing a child has impacted me in many of the ways I have shared in this book, and many more that I haven't shared. Truthfully, as I write this, I am confident there will be many more impacts. Given that context, one important survival tool that has gotten me through, is the ability to step back and count my blessings.

At the top of that list is my love for Adam. We have weathered many storms during our 32+ years together. We have had our love tested in ways big and small, like every other marriage. Statistics vary widely but my research revealed that the divorce rate following the death of a child falls in the 16-20 percent range. Combine that with the failure rate of a second marriage (range = 40-67 percent), and that has the potential to be a very real outcome for couples like us. I am grateful that Kevin's suicide happened at a time when our bond was rock-solid. That's not to say that since Kevin's death that bond hasn't been stressed many times, but I always knew we would come through this with our marriage intact. One reason was my willingness to share this concern with Adam shortly after Kevin's death. Another is the trust we have in each other, the shared commitment we have for honoring our marriage's health and longevity, and the acceptance of each other as perfectly imperfect human beings – all priceless gifts that I cherish.

I feel the same way about some of my family who have been there in ways big and small, especially our sons, my nephew Jeremy and my niece Jessica. There have also been friends (veterans and newbies), many whom I have mentioned in this story. I am blessed to have them in my life. I hope I am always there for them in their time of need.

I have also been blessed to have many frenemies and wingnuts who have tested me in ways too numerous to mention in this story. Their presence provided rich material for this book and helped me maintain my humility – and my sense of humor when all else failed.

And then there are my granddaughters Jesslyn and Janelle, who helped me by just being what they are supposed to be – loveable little girls who welcome me into their world in the cherished role of 'Nonie'.

A TOOTH FAIRY BREAK

Story will resume shortly

"The tooth fairy teaches children that they can sell body parts for money."

David Richerby

As I sat at my computer, I received an email from my son Jonathan with a photo of my granddaughter Jesslyn showing the gap where her front tooth fell out – the first one to do so.

I immediately picked up the phone and called them.

"Nonie, Nonie! You're not going to believe what happened!" (She's our little Drama Queen...)

"I think I might know because Daddy just sent me a photo of you and it looks like you have a tooth missing. Did it fall out today?"

"No. I went to sleep last night and it was really loose, Nonie, and it fell out when I was sleeping and guess what, Nonie – it was bleeding and I didn't even choke or swallow my tooth. And I didn't even throwed it up!" (You were forewarned. Pure drama – see what I mean?)

"Did the Tooth Fairy come?"

"Nonie, she's going to come tonight, but I wrote her a letter."

"A letter? What does it say?"

"Dear Tooth Fairy – please leave the money but don't take my tooth." (She may end up being a lawyer someday...)

"I'm sure The Tooth Fairy doesn't get a lot of letters like that! When your daddy lost his baby teeth, I put them in a little box and I still have it in my jewelry box."

She whispers to her sister, "Janelle, Nonie has all Daddy's baby teeth in a little box!" She comes back on the line, "Janelle wants to know if we can see them when we come to Florida."

"Sure you can! Bring yours along and maybe we'll make necklaces out of them. In Africa, the tribal warriors wear animal teeth necklaces to protect them from evil spirits. Maybe we can make some to protect us from the fundamentalists."

"Nonie, are they dangerous?"

"Yes, they come in many different colors and flavors and most of them are dangerous, Sweetheart."

And in December they gave me the most meaningful holiday gift I was to receive.

Date: Monday, December 24, 2012 10:06:53 PM EST
From: Deena
To: Friends & Family
Subject: 'Twas The Morning Before Christmas and …

Maybe you really CAN get something for nothing. Santa came early to me this morning.

(The following tale is inspired by a true story.)

My two granddaughters received the free videos I created for each of them "from Santa Claus" (http://www.portablenorthpole. com). I emailed them to my son and daughter-in-law, who waited to show them to the girls on the drive up to Maine this morning to visit relatives for Christmas.

At 11am my phone rang and it was my granddaughters. Seven-year-old Jesslyn (Little Miss Drama Queen) went first.

"Nonie - Guess what! Santa sent me a video. And you won't believe what he has, Nonie. He has like a million books in this library, maybe even a bazillion books. And he has one just for me, and one for my sister." (I loved the 'my sister' reference, just in case I didn't know she had one…)

Nonie: "Wow, did the book have your name on it?"

Little Miss Drama Queen (LMDQ): "Yes! And guess what, Nonie, he even spelled my name the right way and he said it the right way, too."

Nonie: "Well, he must know you very well!"

LMDQ: "He does! And he even knows that I am 7 years old and that I go to school. And guess what, Nonie - he said I am on his Good Girl List."

Nonie: "And how does he know that?"

LMDQ: "Because he checked with his elves - a girl elf and a boy elf - and they told him I've been good. I sawed it on the video - they were telling him, really. And he even has a picture of me and he knows exactly where I live in Boston and what my house looks like so he can bring my presents."

Nonie: "That's way cool! Do you think he has a book about Grandpa?" (My husband - Grandpa Adam - was on the other extension.)

LMDQ: "Well, I don't think he has books on growed-up people, Nonie. I think they have to be really really good."

Nonie: "I think Grandpa has been good, but maybe not." (At this point, Grandpa isn't too happy with the direction of this discussion and he flicks me the proverbial bird.)

LMDQ: "Actually, Nonie, I don't think he has enough room for growed-up people in his special Santa library because there are so many kids." (She's obviously an authority on this Santa stuff.)

And then I spoke with my other granddaughter Janelle who is 5. She was very laid back and unimpressed about her Santa video and only wanted to talk to us about the hamster she was babysitting for five days. So we had a special chat about how cuddly and furry they are. Meanwhile, LMDQ was in the background making what could only be described as puking sound effects, loud enough to be heard all the way to Florida, about how yucky the hamster was. They are Yin-and-Yang, total opposites and we love them both.

When we got off the phone, Adam knew how much it meant to me to get that phone call. He knows it's been a tough year for us, dealing with health challenges and so much loss. He is a man of few words and he isn't religious but he came into my office shortly after the phone call and said, "Do you want me to go to the Candlelight Service with you tonight?" (This is a big deal for him to go to the Unitarian-Universalist service or any religious service, for that matter. He'd rather have root canal, without an anesthetic.) And in gratitude, I suggested we go to his favorite Chinese restaurant after the service.

Sometimes you REALLY can get something for nothing - the priceless gift of time from those you love.

"As clear as dawn, spreading from the east, and with a glow of hidden fire,

the light comes,

older than the earth, but new every morning.

So in gazing at a child,

Love dawns, older than the sky, but new every morning."[36]

Happy Holidays and may 2013 be filled with good health, happiness and peaceful coexistence.

Love, Deena

"When life gives you a hundred reasons to cry, show life that you have a thousand reasons to smile."

Anonymous

EPILOGUE

"How Can You Mend A Broken Heart?"

The Bee Gees

And how can you mend a broken heart?
How can you stop the rain from falling down?
How can you stop the sun from shining?
What makes the world go round?
Please help me mend my broken heart and let me live again.[37]

Date: Valentine's Day, February 14, 2013
From: Deena
To: The Universe
Subject: My Empty Heart Compartment

I have a compartment in my heart that is empty and hurting tonight. It is the compartment that used to be overflowing with love, care, and concern for our youngest son, my step-son Kevin. His suicide last summer has left a huge hole. I ended a busy day of meetings and client work by unwinding like many other women: doing housework. As I dusted the photos on the shelves around the family room and study, I relived his life from the time he came into my life at age four to his death three decades later. It made me sad that mental illness, when untreated, can have such significant conse-

quences. Part of my way of getting through the pain has been to be more present in the moment and recognize my thoughts and feelings for what they are. So this is how I chose to be "present".

I talked to him, to his spirit, as I looked at the last photo we had of him and I said, "Kevin, I miss the 'you' that came into my life as a little curly-haired boy whose smile lit up his entire being. I miss your stubborn determination that enabled you to take huge risks all your life. I miss the loyalty you had for close relatives and friends when others abandoned them. I miss the dreams you had that were not possible given your life choices. When I am tempted to idolize you, I am faced with the reality of...reality. And that reality forced you to admit – finally – that the sum total of your poor decisions limited your dreams.

"I am so sorry I could not help you, that all the love and guidance couldn't make you whole. I am sorry I failed at helping your own father accept the extent to which mental illness drove so much of your behavior. I regret that society shrouds mental illness in shame and keeps it in the darkness despite its enormous presence and impact. I am so sorry you couldn't accept that your bipolar disorder played a significant role in your life, and that ignoring it and self-medicating had devastating consequences. I do not miss the chaos this created in all of our lives, but your father and I miss the potential of what could have been. I miss your daily emails and frequent phone calls, even though I knew they came mostly when you needed help.

"I am sad that this year we couldn't send you a Valentine's Day card. You left no forwarding address, only memories and an infinite emptiness.

"At the end of life is there pain without a witness? Is it spectacular or a spectacle only if someone sees it? Is it painful only if felt by others? My dreams are haunted by images of your final hours – the unbearable pain that consumed and extinguished your flame of life. Loss is never easy, and it is especially tough when those who are *younger than us enter into eternity. Seems not to be in the natural order of how things should be and yet, maybe eternity needs spirits both young and old.*

"Despite what you and Makyla were going through, I believe there were bonds of love that existed on some level. I will never know for sure, but you did let me know about your ambivalence of being alone. Whatever the circumstances, because I feel no one deserves to come home and find their loved one's lifeless body, I will continue to stay in contact with her. I do this out of compassion, not pity or guilt.

"It makes me sad that I will have no photos of you achieving all your dreams. My "Kevin Compartment" is permanently frozen in time – sometimes the pain of losing you is endless. I hope with all my heart that you are not still suffering, and I just wanted you to know that I miss your presence in my life.

"A friend told me, 'When your son took his life, he didn't want to take yours too.' I don't believe you were thinking clearly enough to make such a determination. I can only hope your passage to eternity was swift and put an end to your suffering. Ours will be endless. Perhaps someday my tears will flow abundantly and freely and help wash away my sadness. In the meantime, I send you this wish: Sweet dreams, my boy, sweet dreams.

"Love,

Deena"

"There is no real ending. It's just the place where you stop the story."

Frank Herbert

POSTSCRIPT

"Reality leaves a lot to the imagination."

John Lennon

Date: July 5, 2013

From: Deena

To: Kevin – wherever you may be

Subject: I definitely know you are out there

Dearest Kevin,

Today marks the one-year anniversary of losing you. I wanted to mark the occasion by honoring your memory quietly, just Dad and me. The plan was to light a twenty-four-hour yahrzeit candle at sundown on July 4th, in the Jewish tradition of sundown-to-sundown memorials, holidays, and other celebrations. Then we would go out for Chinese food at Dad's favorite restaurant, the same one you liked when you visited us. On the way home we would go to the beach and watch the sunset. A simple plan, but the universe has a marvelous sense of humor: We're just playthings and it loves to mess with us, and I am sure you had something to do with this, too.

In reality, as we lit the memorial candle at sunset with your picture next to it, our neighbors chose that moment to start lighting firecrackers and set off fireworks. Yes, it is illegal in Florida to do *this, but I knew you would appreciate that it has never stopped vendors from setting up tents throughout the state, and selling them to any adult who signs a release. Law enforcement just looks the other way since they don't have enough officers to patrol every neighborhood. Somehow the scene that was playing out was fitting considering we were lighting the candle in your honor.*

The candle burned out at 3:30pm, after nineteen hours and five hours short of the tradition. Like most of our products today, the price went up 25 percent, the glass holder remained the same size but the amount of paraffin was reduced. Seems nothing escapes this free-market profit-driven dynamic, not even memorializing our deceased loved ones. Next year I will go to Yankee Candle and buy a twenty-four-hour candle that will most likely burn for thirty-six hours.

On the way to the Chinese restaurant, I had to stop at the Mall to return an item. Storm clouds were forming so Dad left me off at the curb and I rushed into the Mall. You know how impatient Dad can be, and I told him I would just be a minute. When I arrived at the customer service desk, there was a woman ahead of me with her family, yelling at the manager because she wanted to return everything she bought a week ago for her four kids and repurchase it since everything was now 30 percent off for the July 4th holiday sale. Of course, it being a holiday weekend, there was no other sales person who could help me, so I waited...and waited...

Just as I left the mall we had what I call one of our famous Zipper Showers. That's when Zeus, the God of Rain, unzips a huge black cloud and a torrent showers down upon us mere mortals. This time it was directed right at me, sending a sign I'm sure was from you – two thumbs down on my outfit, perhaps?

Then it was on to the Chinese restaurant where our favorite waiter accidentally spilled some soup on me, my steamed veggies were soggy but Dad enjoyed all his hot and sour and spicy favorites, ate some of mine, and suffered from heartburn the rest of the night.

As for "The beach at sunset" idea - fuggedaboutit! No sunset due to the showers. So we went home and watched two movies on Roku that were so bad we stopped watching the first one and kept hoping the second one would get better since Diane Keaton starred in it, as well as many other famous actors and actresses. We were embarrassed such a script would even make it to the funding stage much less be produced and distributed.

So much for my grand plan…

Since we could often count on you to rock The Baxter Family Love Boat with your own agenda, I just knew this was your special way of making your presence known – once again. I truly believe the universe works that way. "Here's your sign," as Jeff Foxworthy would say. Please know that even though our Family Love Boat is re-stabilized, we are missing an important member of the crew – you. But in your honor, we have an empty seat just waiting for your return, if only in spirit.

Love,
Deena

"The difference between fiction and reality? Fiction has to make sense."

Tom Clancy

"I'm sure the universe is full of intelligent life. It's just been too intelligent to come here."

Arthur C. Clarke

"Once you can accept the universe as matter expanding into nothing that is something, wearing stripes with plaid comes easy."

Albert Einstein

NOTES, CREDITS
AND FOOTNOTES

I read, researched, analyzed, and derived information from many sources. The Internet overflows with an abundance of science-based junk and opinions on the topics covered in this book. Finding the "golden nuggets," "keepers," and "take aways" is a tough assignment under the best of circumstances, and this was most certainly not the best of times. The sources of specific quotes and reference materials are cited in footnotes or in this section.

Most clip-art graphics included in this book are licensed from www.iClipart.com and used with permission. iClipArt is a registered trademark, Copyright © 2013 Vital Imagery Ltd.

Sincere appreciation to Mary Suggeret at Universal Uclick, the "angel" who returned my desperate phone call on Sept. 25, 2013 after my eleventh failed attempt to get permission to use the Dear Abby material in this manuscript. Calls like this don't come often and this one was unexpected, given how difficult it is to get through to a human being. This human was very special indeed. Her compassionate confirmation by email included this final note: "I sincerely hope this book becomes a supportive tool for those many people who have been through what you have, and this brings a better understanding of this daunting disease."

I would like to thank Arthur Schwartz, The Food Maven, from Brooklyn, New York, for returning my phone call seeking permission to use his Chinese food jokes. Our discussion was a joy. When I lamented the dearth of good New York bagels or Chinese food down here, he said there aren't any great bagel places in NYC or Brooklyn either, like the ones he grew up with. He and Adam chatted briefly about their common roots growing up in Brooklyn.

Credits & Footnotes:

1. 'Mario Savio', *Wikipedia: The Free Encyclopedia*, at URL: http://en.wikipedia.org/wiki/Mario_Savio, *Speaking on the Steps at Sproul Hall, December 2, 1964. Wikipedia® is a registered trademark of the Wikimedia Foundation, Inc., a non-profit organization. Used with permission.*

2. *John Bradshaw, Healing the Shame that Binds You, 2005 Edition, Health Communications, Inc., Copyright © 2005 John Bradshaw. Used with permission.*

3. *"Monday, Monday", words and music by John Phillips, at URL: http://www.metrolyrics.com/monday-monday-lyrics-the-mamas-the-papas.html.*

4. *As seen in "DEAR ABBY" by Abigail Van Buren a.k.a. Jeanne Phillips and founded by her mother Pauline Phillips. March 30, 2013 and April 19, 2013. Copyright © Universal Uclick. All rights reserved. Reprinted with permission.*

5. *'Chabad', Wikipedia: The Free Encyclopedia, at URL: http://en.wikipedia.org/wiki/Chabad. Used with permission.*

6. *Eckhart Tolle, The Power of Now: A Guide to Spiritual Awakening, New World Library, Copyright © 2013 Eckhart Teachings Inc. Used with permission.*

7. *Footnote: Freddie Wilkinson, "Untamed Antarctica". National Geographic Magazine, September, 2013, p.94. © 2013 National Geographic Society.*

8. *'Twister Game', Wikipedia: The Free Encyclopedia, at http://en.wikipedia.org/wiki/Twister_(game). Wikimedia Foundation, Inc., a non-profit organization. Used with permission.*

9. *Melody Beattie, 52 Weeks of Conscious Contact. Copyright © 2003. Printed in the United States of America by Hazelden. Used with permission.*

10. Arthur Schwartz, *The Daily Gullet* excerpt from *Arthur Schwartz's Jewish Home Cookbook: Yiddish Recipes Revisited*, posted March 14, 2008 at http://forums.egullet.org/topic/113757-why-jews-like-chinese-food, Copyright © 2013 Society for Culinary Arts & Letters. Used with permission.

11. Footnote: Excerpt from full quote by Gilda Radner: "Cancer is probably the most unfunny thing in the world, but I'm a comedienne, and even cancer wasn't going to stop me from seeing the humor in what I was going through. The last thing that I wanted was to be tragic." *Redbook Magazine*, Copyright ©2013 Hearst Communication, Inc.

12. Footnote: Summary based on source document: Sarah Kliff, *The Washington Post*, "Seven facts about America's mental health-care system", December 17, 2012 at URL: http://www.washingtonpost.com/blogs/wonkblog/wp/2012/12/17/seven-facts-about-americas-mental-health-care-system/, Copyright © 2013 The Washington Post.

13. Footnote: Jackie Calmes, Robert Pear, "Rules to Require Equal Coverage for Mental Ills", *New York Times*, November 8, 2013, Copyright © 2013 New York Times Company, at URL: http://www.nytimes.com/2013/11/08/us/politics/rules-to-require-equal-coverage-for-mental-ills.html.

14. This article was created and published by the Center for American Progress Action online. Guest blogger Rachel Howard, Feb. 8, 2013, "Why Addressing Mental Health Issues Means Reforming the U.S. Prison System," at URL: http://thinkprogress.org/health/2013/02/08/1561341/mental-health-prison-reform/, Copyright © 2005-2013 Center for American Progress Action Fund. Used with permission.

15. Quoted in THE WEEK Magazine, October 11, 2013. Original source: www.wsj.com, Gary Fields, Erica E. Phillips, "The New Asylums: Jails Swell With Mentally Ill, America's Jails Face Growing Need to Provide Mental-Health Treatment", Sept. 26, 2013, at URL: http://stream.wsj.com/story/latest-headlines/SS-2-63399/SS-2-338097/, Copyright © 2013 Dow Jones & Company, Inc. Used with permission.

16. Catey Hill, "Ten Things Baby Boomers Won't Tell You," MarketWatch, July 12, 2013, at URL: http://www.marketwatch.com/story/10-things-boomers-wont-tell-you-2013-07-12, Copyright © 2013 MarketWatch, Inc. Used with permission.

17. Footnote: Eric R. Kandel, "The New Science of Mind", New York Times, September 6, 2013, Sunday Review, Copyright © 2013 New York Times Company, at URL: http://www.nytimes.com/2013/09/08/opinion/sunday/the-new-science-of-mind.html?emc=eta1&_r=0.

18. 'Suicide', The Free Dictionary by Farlex, http://legal-dictionary.thefreedictionary.com, Copyright © 2013 Farlex, Inc.; and West's Encyclopedia of American Law, edition 2, Copyright © 2008 The Gale Group, Inc. Used with permission.

19. Footnote: www.fallingwaters.org.

20. 'Len Bias', Wikipedia: The Free Encyclopedia, at URL: http://en.wikipedia.org/wiki/Len_Bias. Used with permission.

21. THE WEEK Magazine, September 20, 2013, "Briefing: Rethinking Mandatory Sentencing," p.11, May, 24, 2013, p.3, Copyright © 2013 The Week Publications, Inc. All rights reserved. Used with permission.

22. 'Baker Act', Wikipedia: The Free Encyclopedia, at URL: http://en.wikipedia.org/wiki/Baker_Act. Used with permission.

23. 'Bipolar Disorder', National Institute of Mental Health at URL: http://www.nimh.nih.gov/health/topics/bipolar-disorder/index.shtml. Used with permission.

24. William Falk, THE WEEK Magazine, May, 24, 2013, p.3, Copyright © 2013 The Week Publications, Inc. All rights reserved. Used with permission.

25. *Benjamin Nugent, "Is Psychiatry Dishonest? And if so, is it a noble lie?," May 3, 2013, at URL: http://www.slate.com/articles/arts/books/2013/05/ book_of_woe_the_dsm_and_the_unmaking_of_psychiatry_by_gary_ greenberg_reviewed.html, Copyright © 2013 The Slate Group, LLC. Used with permission.*

26. *Ethan Watters, "Mad Fashion", Pacific Standard Magazine, July/August 2013, pp. 28-31, Copyright © 2013. Used with permission.*

27. *Brandon A. Gaudiano and Ivan W. Miller, "The Evidence-based Practice of Psychotherapy: Facing the challenges that Lie Ahead." Clinical Psychology Review 22 (2013), p.813 – 814, Copyright © 2013 Elsevier Ltd. Used with permission.*

28. *Brandon A. Gaudiano, "Psychotherapy's Image Problem." New York Times, September 30, 2013, at URL: http://www.nytimes.com/2013/09/30/ opinion/psychotherapys-image-problem.html?_r=0. Used with permission.*

29, 30. *Ethan Watters, ibid. Used with permission.*

31. *Footnote: Barry Meier, "F.D.A. Urging a Tighter Rein on Painkillers," New York Times, October 25, 2013, Copyright © 2013 New York Times Company, at URL: http://www.nytimes.com/2013/10/25/business/fda-seeks-tighter-control-on-prescriptions-for-class-of-painkillers.html.*

32. *Footnote: Linda Logan, "The Problem with How We Treat Bipolar Disorder", New York Times, April 26, 2013, Copyright © 2013 New York Times Company, at URL: http://www.nytimes.com/2013/04/28/magazine/ the-problem-with-how-we-treat-bipolar-disorder.html.*

33. *Footnote: Bill Keller, "How to Legalize Pot", New York Times, May 20, 2013, Copyright © 2013 New York Times Company, at URL: http://www. nytimes.com/2013/05/20/opinion/keller-how-to-legalize-pot. html?pagewanted=all&_r=0.*

34. Footnote: Bob Curley, *"DSM-V: Major Changes to Addictive Disease Classifications"*, February 12, 2010, at URL: *http://www.drugfree.org/join-together/addiction/dsm-v-draft-includes-major*, Copyright © 2013 The Partnership at Drugfree.org.

35. Dr. Christopher Gordon, *"Invitation to a Dialogue,"* New York Times, January 30, 2013 at URL: *http://www.nytimes.com/2013/01/30/opinion/invitation-to-a-dialogue-forcing-treatment.html*. Used with permission.

36. Brian Wren, *"As In A Clear Dawn,"* from Words by Brian Wren, Copyright © 1996 Hope Publishing Company, at *http://www.hopepublishing.com*. Used with permission.

37. Footnote: *"How Can You Mend A Broken Heart?"*, words and music by Barry Gibb and Robin Gibb, Copyright 1971 Gibb Brothers Music, at URL: *http://www.metrolyrics.com/how-can-you-mend-a-broken-heart-lyrics-bee-gees.html*.

ACKNOWLEDGMENTS

To my husband Adam, thanks for your support in honoring my need to write this book. It would never have been your topic of choice. You could have said, "no", but you didn't, and besides you know that wouldn't have dissuaded me. I'm glad we found a middle ground that worked for both of us. That's one of the strengths of our bond and it has grown stronger through this storm.

In grateful appreciation to the National Alliance on Mental Illness (NAMI) of Collier County:

- *Kathryn Leib Hunter, Executive Director, for her compassion and commitment to mental health as well as The Funny Farm Project, and to dedicated staff members Marsha, Becky and Rae. Thank you for making our community stronger, healthier and safer by raising awareness and providing essential and free education, advocacy and support group programs.*
- *In gratitude and heartfelt thanks to the NAMI of Collier County Anything Goes: Art-From-The-Heart project team - Rosemarie Kirk, Susan Joy Smellie, LMHC, ATR, Lisa Blount, and the seven adults, teens and children who participated and contributed their artwork: Alice, Anna, Diegoberto, John C., John, Tim and Yvonne. My vision for the possibilities of this project was exceeded by your enthusiasm and artistic expression.*
- *Thanks, too, to the artwork provided by other NAMI of Collier County art program artists.*

NAMI of Collier County is affiliated with NAMI, the National Alliance on Mental Illness, "the nation's largest grassroots mental health organization dedicated to building better lives for the millions of Americans affected by mental illness. NAMI advocates for access to services, treatment, supports and research and is steadfast in its commitment to raise awareness and build a community for hope for all of those in need."

I would like to thank my "readers" for their time and effort reading the work-in-progress drafts of the manuscript: Kathy A. Feinstein, Kathryn Leib-Hunter, Elizabeth Rudulph Lustenauder, Dottie Pacharis, and David Sendler. Your insights and recommendations were invaluable, and often in conflict. I weighed each one carefully and in the end I did what felt right for me.

A special, "thank you" goes to Dr. Joan Lynch, author and literary educator, who did a "deep dive critique" on the manuscript, asking probing and relevant questions on story structure and reader perspective. Your editorial guidance was invaluable: I valued the process as much as the outcome.

True friends are there through thick and thin, in the good times and the bad. Adam's college friend, Dr. Bob E., flew down from New York for a two-day visit the last week in July. It was right before Adam's birthday and his mother's birthday so it was a priceless gift to us all. Adam and Bob spent time going to some of the local sights – the botanical gardens and parks where they could walk amidst nature and have quiet talks. Bob's wife Jane is a lovely person, too, and she and I were in contact by phone. Their love and outreach during the initial weeks of our journey is something we will cherish forever. In January they came as a couple for a visit, too, and it was yet another gift.

My dearest friend Ressa is full-time caregiver for her ailing husband and although she isn't mobile, I cherished the phone chats we had – and continue to have. My book group friend, Judy J., spends the summer in Wisconsin but that didn't stop us from talking by phone and exchanging emails. Judie G. – thanks for the encouragement, support and cheerleading through all the ups and downs of the Kickstarter project and beyond.

Writing a book is the easy part – getting it published is an arduous process not for the faint-of-heart. Today's world of publishing is a jungle, requiring a machete, endurance training, First-Aid Kit, and survival tools, and even with all that skill and equipment, it doesn't guarantee success. Rather than venturing into the jungle alone, the odds of surviving are greatly enhanced when there is a knowledgeable guide leading the way. I was fortunate to work with Naren Aryal, Founder and CEO of Mascot Books, and his team - especially Laura Vasile, senior project manager. They shared my passion for giving mental illness a voice. The suggested edits, new title, and creative graphic design work added further dimension to the story. Thanks team – for the hard work and the laughs along the way.

www.wackystock.com

THE FUNNY FARM PROJECT
"GIVING MENTAL ILLNESS A VOICE"

The Funny Farm Project is being done in partnership with NAMI of Collier County. The project includes this book and the website www.WriteOnMyMind.com – a blend of writing, art, and technology working in tandem to bring mental illness out of the darkness and into the light – "Giving Mental Illness A Voice." The website was inspired by the NAMI of Collier County Anything Goes: Art-From-The-Heart Project that resulted in the artwork included in this book. Visual art can be a powerful communicator, beyond words. It can send a message if we are open to it, and it can heal. Contact TheFunnyFarm4Me@gmail.com for more information.

THANKS TO MY KICKSTARTER DONORS

I am deeply grateful to Dennis Cox, a talented illustrator who custom designed the blind farmer illustration used for The Funny Farm project. "Blind Farmer," Copyright © 2013 by Dennis Cox, all rights reserved, http://www.wackystock.com. Used with permission.

In grateful appreciation for those whose donor support enabled The Funny Farm Project to become a reality.

The Normal Ones
Adam Baxter
Kevin Brachle
Su Chung
Pat Clancy
Deborah Finn
Judy Jorgensen
Jim Lancaster
Dorothy Ludwig
Michael McClymont
Suzie and John McGowan
Martha & Bill Meyers
Carolyn Musgrave
Mary Schell
Christopher Seavey
Team NAMI-CC
My Anonymous Generous
Kickstarter Donors

The Ones Who Aren't Sure
Summer Abate
Harriet Lancaster
Joan Southwell
Carolynn Tomin
My Anonymous Generous
Kickstarter Donors

The Ones Who are Certain
They Are Anything BUT Normal
Deena Baxter
Kelly Brachle
Gail Damon
Pam Gharabally
Judie Gibbs
Priscilla Gould
Dino Layton
Dr. Myra Mendible
Skip Muller
Jacqueline Pierce
Adria Starkey
Amy Turner
Nazli Wasti
My Anonymous Generous
Kickstarter Donors

ABOUT THE AUTHOR

Deena Baxter is a published author and strategic management consultant with more than thirty years of experience in finance, program management and communications. She earned a B.S. and MBA at Boston University, worked in high-tech for eighteen years and managed an international research project at MIT for nine years. Her business articles and humor columns have been published by *Scripps News Service, Working Woman Magazine, Inc. Magazine* and *èBella*. She co-founded and launched a meditation program in her community in 2013. She lives and works in Southwest Florida.

For more information on her current and upcoming endeavors, contact the author at DeenaBaxter2@gmail.com.